QUEENSHIP AND PO⌐

Series Editors: Carole L

Alter Symmetry, 1999, by Domingo Barreres

ELIZABETH I

THE VOICE OF A MONARCH

Ilona Bell

Cover: Portrait of Elizabeth I, The Hampden Portrait, Anglo-Flemish School, c. 1563, Steven van Herwijck Hampton Palace.

First published in 2010 by
PALGRAVE MACMILLAN®
in the United States—a division of St. Martin's Press LLC,
175 Fifth Avenue, New York, NY 10010.

Where this book is distributed in the UK, Europe and the rest of the world, this is by Palgrave Macmillan, a division of Macmillan Publishers Limited, registered in England, company number 785998, of Houndmills, Basingstoke, Hampshire RG21 6XS.

Palgrave Macmillan is the global academic imprint of the above companies and has companies and representatives throughout the world.

Palgrave® and Macmillan® are registered trademarks in the United States, the United Kingdom, Europe and other countries.

ISBN: 978–0–230–62106–0

Library of Congress Cataloging-in-Publication Data

Bell, Ilona.
    Elizabeth I : the voice of a monarch / by Ilona Bell.
        p. cm. — (Queenship and power series)
    Includes bibliographical references.
    ISBN 978–0–230–62105–3 (hardcover) —
    ISBN 978–0–230–62106–0 (pbk.)
        1. Elizabeth I, Queen of England, 1533–1603—Literary art. 2. Kings' and rulers' writings, English—History and criticism. 3. Great Britain—History—Elizabeth, 1558–1603. 4. Women and literature—England—History—16th century. I. Title.

DA355.B44 2010
942.05′5092—dc22   2009046861

A catalogue record of the book is available from the British Library.

Design by Newgen Imaging Systems (P) Ltd., Chennai, India.

First edition: June 2010

10 9 8 7 6 5 4 3 2 1

Printed in the United States of America.

To my parents nonpareil—
Judith and Irving Isaacson

for in our worke what bring wee but thine owne?
What English is, by many names is thine.
There humble Lawrells in thy shadowes growne
To garland others woold, themselves repine.
Thy brest the Cabinet, thy seat the shrine,
where Muses hang their vowed memories:
where Wit, where Art, where all that is divine
conceived best, and best defended lies.

Mary Herbert, Dedication to
Queen Elizabeth

CONTENTS

IMAGES

Cover Image: Portrait of Elizabeth I: The Hampden Portrait, Steven van Herwijck, c. 1563 (oil on panel, transferred onto canvas), Hampton Palace. Philip Mould Ltd.

Frontispiece: Alter Symmetry, Domingo Barreres, 1999 (mixed media on canvas). By permission of the artist. Photograph by George Vazquez, courtesy of Howard Yezerski Gallery

PREFACE

When I was fair and young, and favor graced me,
Of many was I sought unto, their mistress for to be.
But I did scorn them all, and said to them therefore,
"Go, go, go seek some otherwhere; importune me no more."
.....

But then I felt straightway a change within my breast:
The day unquiet was; the night I could not rest,
But I did sore repent that I had said before,
"Go, go, go seek some otherwhere; importune me no more."

Elizabeth

"She says the most extraordinary things," the Spanish ambassador complained after marriage negotiations between the recently crowned Elizabeth I and the Austrian archduke collapsed. Three years later, when negotiations again reached an impasse, the Holy Roman Emperor reiterated the ambassador's disapproval: "she still abides by her former resolve to marry no one whom she has not previously seen. This is entirely novel and unprecedented, and we cannot approve of it."[1] As these remarks illustrate, the very qualities that make Elizabeth I attractive to us today, daring to speak and act in ways that were "novel and unprecedented," provoked strong disapproval and resistance during her own day.

Elizabeth I: The Voice of a Monarch focuses on the ways in which Elizabeth represented herself in her own words, in speeches, reported conversations, and private poems from the first half of her reign when she was simultaneously establishing her political authority and negotiating marriage at home and abroad.[2] Unlike conventional representations of Elizabeth as the Virgin Queen, the unique portrait of Elizabeth that appears on my cover represents her as a young, marriageable woman. The warm, glowing reds and oranges of her dress are explained by the symbolic fertility of the fruits and flowers by her side, which acquire even greater import from the fact that this was one of the first serious still lifes painted in England. By comparison, the modern face of my frontispiece pops, as if superimposed upon the more conventional pose, costume, and trappings of royalty. As a result, this contemporary American portrait of Elizabeth seems at once recognizably Elizabethan and somehow discomfiting in its novelty. The artist, Domingo Barreres, told me that he wanted to portray Elizabeth's sexuality, a quality that emerges in modern films and television series. I hope that the sense of unease created by the bold new face of Barreres' portrait will remind readers of the uneasy dissonance between Elizabeth's representations of herself and our own impulse to see her in our image, or to see ourselves in her image.

Elizabeth I: The Voice of a Monarch springs from essays and talks about Elizabeth that I wrote while teaching Shakespeare and Elizabethan literature, editing Donne's poems, and writing about Shakespeare, Donne, Elizabethan women, and Elizabethan poetry of courtship.[3] My interpretation of Elizabeth's words is inevitably shaped by my own preferences and premises. I especially admire Elizabeth's writing for being ludic, figurative, enigmatic, multifaceted, and open-ended. Moreover, because I see Elizabethan writing as deeply rhetorical, or persuasive, I believe Elizabethan texts are best analyzed in their entirety, in their original historical situation, as a dialogue with an interlocutor whom the writer or speaker strives to influence cajole, challenge, or answer. Finally, I am struck by the ways in which Elizabeth's words and actions disturbed conceptions of sex and gender and challenged the patriarchal assumptions underlying politics and marriage.

A single monograph cannot provide comprehensive, detailed analyses of Elizabeth's complete works, for her extant corpus is extensive. Instead, this book presents several in-depth case studies of Elizabeth's speech and writing, which explore interconnections between text and world, or between Elizabeth's writing and other Elizabethan texts, to reach a fuller understanding of both. My prefatory epigraph, the first and last stanzas of Elizabeth's poem "When I Was Fair and Young," pithily summarizes Elizabeth's own complexly shifting attitudes towards courtship and marriage. Just as importantly, the refrain articulates and epitomizes the ways in which the same words can acquire very different and even opposing meanings as the context and point of view change.

Our knowledge of the past is always limited to what we can infer from the material objects and written texts that have survived the erasure of time. There is still a great deal we do not know and will never know about Elizabeth the speaker and writer. Above all, we cannot get inside her head or heart to know what she intended her words to mean, or what impact she hoped they would have. But then, we never have unmediated access to anyone's thoughts, feelings, and intentions, even though literature often creates that illusion. The Elizabethans did not open their private feelings to the world as people do so readily today. (Autobiography did not become a popular genre until the seventeenth century.)

Even for her day, Elizabeth was unusually guarded and secretive. Her motto, *video et taceo* (I see yet I remain silent), may have reflected the ideology of the day that equated female honor with chastity and silence. Yet even more importantly, Elizabeth's motto is a sign of how resolutely she defended her private thoughts from public exposure.[4] Nonetheless,

Elizabeth's every word and gesture were intently scrutinized, and her confidential, personal utterances were repeated and disseminated. Consequently, we know more, much more, about her than we do about any other Elizabethan writer. There is a surprising amount of information about her childhood and adolescence. After she became queen, it is possible to reconstruct where she was, whom she was seeing, and what she was doing and concerned about at any given time.

Since we know so much more about Elizabeth than we do about her contemporaries, her speech and writing have a lot to teach us about the Elizabethan writing culture. As we shall see in chapter 2, her writing epitomizes the rhetorical or persuasive nature of private dialogues between speakers and their interlocutors, or writers and their readers, even as it elucidates the transition from speech to manuscript to print. It also plays a uniquely important role in shaping and explaining relations between patrons and writers.

Because Elizabeth's words were implicated in and complicated by the specific historical situations out of which they emerged and that they in turn comprised, their intricacy and significance can be grasped only by an interpretive methodology that is simultaneously literary, historical, and biographical. The goal of this book is not to use Elizabeth's language to illustrate her life, but rather to let both Elizabeth's words and the historical documents speak.[5] I have tried neither to subordinate her language to a predetermined view of the history she lived nor to subordinate the complexity of the historical situation to a predetermined reading of her language. The literary critic's ability to open up a variety of possible interpretations has a lot to offer the historian, even as the historian's access to texts and methods of analysis and narration have much to offer literary critics.[6]

My narrative is shaped by Elizabeth's own speech and writing, especially those moments where she struggled to balance the conflicts between her personal and public life. To represent Elizabeth as a political leader, recent histories analyze her dealings with parliament, Privy Council, and international powers. These larger political, military, and economic considerations were always on Elizabeth's mind, governing the choices she could and could not make. They underlie, propel, and complicate the story this book tells. By representing Elizabeth as the amorous queen and giving weight to her "liking" and "desire," I have risked making her seem less serious or significant a leader and more susceptible to the very gender stereotypes she struggled to surmount. Yet, it is important to remember that when Elizabeth ascended the throne the language of love was almost exclusively a male domain.

Not only were Renaissance love poems written by men but the rhetoric of love was also traditional political discourse, regularly used by male monarchs to win the support of their subjects. Moreover, as political records illustrate, politics and government were themselves less bureaucratic and more personal in Elizabeth's day than in ours. When we put Elizabeth's speech and writing in dialogue with Elizabethan literature and popular culture, political history merges with social history, reminding us that the personal is political and that histories of women, courtship, marriage, and private life are, after all, as important as the histories of war, government, and diplomacy. Finally, I hope that the circumscribed boundaries of the texts and events considered here will prompt other scholars, teachers, students, and readers to look more closely at Elizabeth's words and to formulate their own very different ideas about Elizabeth's language and its connections to Elizabethan politics, culture, and society.

Chapter 1 provides a brief overview of Elizabeth's life story as writer, orphan, unmarried woman, and monarch. Chapter 2 examines Elizabeth's place in the Elizabethan writing culture and connects her art of courtship to the art of Elizabethan poetry. Chapter 3 shows that Elizabeth's characteristic readiness to use the male language of love to fashion her public image was already evident in the spontaneous speeches she gave during her pre-coronation procession. Chapters 4 to 6 look closely at poems, speeches, and diplomatic conversations in which Elizabeth insisted upon her right, first, to marry or not as she desired and, second, to govern the country herself, whether or not she chose to marry. Chapter 7 examines the wider, ongoing cultural conversation that placed Elizabeth's politics and rhetoric of courtship in dialogue with Elizabethan literature and popular culture. Chapter 8, a contextualized reading of her private love lyric "On Monsieur's Departure," teases out the multiple layers of meaning—the ambiguities, ironies, and uncertainties—that emerge when we read Elizabeth's words in their original historical situation.

It seems remarkable, though insufficiently remarked upon, that so many of the greatest love poems in the English language and so many of the feisty, outspoken Shakespearean heroines who maneuver the plot, win our hearts, and steal the show were produced during Elizabeth's reign. *Elizabeth I: The Voice of a Monarch* demonstrates that Elizabeth had an even greater impact on and connection to Elizabethan literature and society as a marriageable queen, determined to conduct her own courtships and to make her own decisions about marriage, than she did as the Virgin Queen who dominates so many modern studies. Finally, this book concludes that although Elizabeth's novel and unprecedented art of courtship garnered considerable resistance and disapproval, by the end of her reign it had sparked or merged with a wider, ongoing social controversy over marital freedom of choice and women's lawful liberty—a phenomenon that helped make the Elizabethan era an extraordinarily fertile and creative period in English literature. Elizabeth's reputation as writer and poet is currently in recovery. Recent studies of Elizabeth focus on what was said and written *about* her during her reign and after. I hope this book will help propel a renaissance of scholarly, curricular, and popular interest in what she said and wrote.[7]

ACKNOWLEDGMENTS

My greatest debt is to all the previous scholars, writers, and editors who have made Elizabeth almost as vital a force today as she was during her lifetime, especially to Carole Levin, for this book would not have been written if she had not invited me to give a keynote address on Elizabeth's poetry at the first annual Queen Elizabeth I Society Conference in March 2003.

Robert Bell read these chapters throughout their many incarnations and helped me transform my previous essays into this book. His critical sensibility and sense of style improved the manuscript immeasurably. His enthusiasm and warmth have helped me appreciate the "mutual liking" Elizabeth was seeking. Kaitlin Bell's pointed queries and sharp editing encouraged me to tell Elizabeth's story not only as a literary critic but also as a historian and reporter. Teresa Cader read the opening chapters with the ear of a poet and the generosity of a dear friend and deftly suggested ways to improve the writing. Margaret A. Waller made shrewd comments on the preface and opening chapter. Amanda Bell gave me excellent advice about the final draft. Marilyn Bethany and Edward Tivnan kindly took it upon themselves to help me come up with the title. My colleagues and friends Stacy Cochran, Darra Goldstein, Suzanne Graver, Carol Ockman, and Deborah Rothschild have been lively and incisive interlocutors and warm supporters.

I am grateful to Williams College for providing a sabbatical grant, research funds, and publication costs. Conversations with my students in the Art of Courtship helped me come to terms with Elizabeth's writing and made me aware of the gaps between Elizabeth's world and our own. Williams students and summer research assistants Amy Elise Nolan and Samantha Barbaro provided invaluable and wonderfully intelligent editorial assistance. The staff of the Williams College Libraries—especially Alison O'Grady in interlibrary loan, Lori DuBois in reference, and Wayne Hammond, Robert Volz, and Elaine Yanow in the Chapin Rare Book Library—could not have been more ready to lend a hand. The Information Technology staff bailed me out more times than I care to recall. Series editors Carole Levin and Charles Beem, Palgrave editor Chris Chappell and his assistant Samantha Hasey, and copy editor Joseph D. P. James, were extremely astute and helpful.

Finally, I want to thank my parents, Judith and Irving Isaacson, to whom this book is dedicated, for instilling in me their passion for reading and their commitment to writing the story of the past.

Permissions

Analyses of Elizabeth's poems from chapters 2, 4, and 6 originally appeared in Special Issue: *Images of Elizabeth I: A Quadricentennial Celebration*, ed. Donald Stump and Carole Levin, *Explorations of Renaissance Culture* 30 (2004) 1–22. Reprinted by permission of the South Central Renaissance Conference.

Sections of chapter 7 originally appeared in "Elizabeth I and the Politics of Courtship," in *Elizabeth I: Always Her Own Free Woman*, ed. Debra Barrett Graves, Jo Eldridge Carney, and Carole Levin (Ashgate Publishing, 2003), 179–91. Reprinted by permission of the publisher.

Analyses of Elizabeth's parliamentary speeches from chapters 4 and 6 appeared in "Elizabeth I—A Woman, and (If That Be Not Enough) an Unmarried Virgin," *Political Rhetoric, Power, and Renaissance Women*, ed. Carole Levin and Patricia A. Sullivan (State University of New York Press, 1995), pp. 57–82. Reprinted by the permission of the publisher.

Figure 1. Elizabeth I as princess, Anglo-Italian School, 16th century

CHAPTER 1

FROM PRINCESS TO PRINCE— A BRIEF LIFE STORY

A Woman, and (if that be not enough) an unmarried Virgin, destitute of all helpe of Parents, Brethren, Husband, beset with divers Nations her mortall enemies; (while the Pope fretted, the Spaniard threatned, and all her Neighbour Princes, as many as had sworne to Popery, raged round about her,) held the most stout and warlike Nation of the English foure and forty yeares and upwards, not onely in awe and duty, but even in Peace also.

William Camden, The historie of the...Princesse Elizabeth[1]

To grasp the intricacy and suppleness of Elizabeth I's speech and writing, we first need to understand the back story—the conflicts, challenges, and objectives that Elizabeth brought with her and faced as she ascended the throne.[2]

Elizabeth Tudor was crowned queen of England on January 15, 1559, having spent most of her twenty-five years living away from court, most recently in isolation, banishment, and imprisonment. Her early life was wild and unpredictable. Born on September 7, 1533, she was not quite three when her mother, Anne Boleyn, Henry VIII's second wife, was executed on trumped up charges of adultery. Elizabeth was declared illegitimate and removed from the succession.[3] Elizabeth was fourteen when her father, the king, died and her ten-year-old brother became Edward VI, King of England. Another act of succession legitimized first Mary and then Elizabeth as Edward's successors.

Henry VIII had renounced Roman Catholicism and established an independent Church of England when the Pope refused to annul Henry's marriage to Catherine of Aragon so that he could marry Elizabeth's mother, Anne Boleyn. During Edward's reign, while the country was under the protectorship of Edward Seymour, the Church of England was fundamentally redefined in accordance with the Protestant reformation. After a futile attempt to marry Elizabeth, the Protector's brother, Thomas Seymour, married Catherine Parr, Henry VIII's widowed sixth wife. Elizabeth was a vulnerable, fourteen-year-old princess living with her stepmother when Thomas Seymour began flirting with her, appearing in her bedroom early in the morning before she was dressed, climbing onto her bed to kiss her, and in one bizarre episode in the garden, shredding Elizabeth's clothes while his wife allegedly held Elizabeth down. When Catherine died in 1548, Seymour tried to lure Elizabeth into marrying him, hoping to position himself as the next king of England. The scheme was discovered, Seymour was beheaded for treason, and Elizabeth was left weighing her every word, desperately trying to defend herself, since it would have been an act of treason, punishable by death, for an heir to the throne to marry without official approval.

Edward died in July 1553, and Elizabeth's older sister, Mary, became queen. She reinstituted the Roman Catholic religion, thus starting a bitter battle between the old and the new faiths that continued to disturb the country throughout Mary's and Elizabeth's reigns. Elizabeth herself was again suspected of treason in January 1554 when Sir Thomas Wyatt led a rebellion to prevent Mary's marriage to King Philip II of Spain and to restore England to Protestantism. Convicted of treason, Wyatt was beheaded, his head and his quartered body displayed to deter future traitors. As a result of Wyatt's rebellion, Elizabeth faced rigorous interrogations for the second time in her short life. Despite choosing her words with the greatest of care to avoid incriminating herself, Elizabeth was imprisoned in the Tower of London and then held under house arrest at Woodstock Castle where she carved a poem on the window with a diamond. Choosing words that were as precise as they were ambiguously noncommittal, Elizabeth developed a verbal style that would stand her in good stead throughout her reign.

On November 17, 1588, upon the death of Mary I, the twenty-five-year-old prisoner who had been declared a bastard and twice evaded death as a traitor became queen. Welcomed by cheering crowds, holding the undercurrents of resistance at bay, Elizabeth made her pre-coronation procession through the streets of London on January 14, 1559, and was crowned queen the following day. Elizabeth began her reign on the defensive, fighting to defend her right to rule the country as God's divine representative, struggling to establish her own fragile authority and to restore English Protestantism.[4] Even before parliament had ratified its traditional allegiance to the new monarch, Protestant and Catholic bishops joined forces, refusing to name Elizabeth Supreme Head of the Church on the grounds that God created women subordinate and inferior to men.

Addressing parliament for the first time, Elizabeth was highly conscious that some members of her government had been instrumental in her recent suffering. She knew their identities, she warned, and would not tolerate any attempts to undermine her authority. When the Austrian ambassador arrived in February bearing a proposal for Elizabeth to marry the son of the Holy Roman Emperor, Elizabeth's recent exile and imprisonment were still very much on her mind and tongue. She "had erstwhile been hidden away in the solitude of forests, and then, though guiltless, had long been held captive in [jail] by her relations," Elizabeth told the ambassador. She wanted to "lay before the world the facts which established her innocence and proved the injustice of the oppressions before which she, sorely aggrieved, had retreated."[5]

Most twentieth-century accounts of Elizabeth, especially those that explore her relationship to Elizabethan language and literature, assume that Elizabeth represented herself from the very outset of her reign as the Virgin Queen married to God and country; however, that is a misapprehension, or an oversimplification, based on a mistaken, retrospective view of history. Susan Doran provides massive historical evidence to refute this assumption, which, as we shall see more fully in chapter 4, arose from a posthumously bowdlerized version of Elizabeth's first parliamentary speech.[6]

At the outset of her reign, Elizabeth repeatedly represented herself *not* as an aloof, inaccessible Petrarchan lady "chanting faint hymns to the cold fruitless moon,"[7] but as a marriageable woman. With a kingdom for a dowry, Elizabeth was probably the most coveted bride in all of Europe: "a beautiful, clever, intelligent, and sweet-tempered woman," the Austrian ambassadors reported, "endowed with so many gifts of body and of mind, that she in no wise falls short of the most famous women of her rank and of her land."[8] Although many of Elizabeth's subjects feared that a female ruler would undermine the gender hierarchy and threaten the social order, most people assumed that she would soon marry and that her husband would rule over her and the country.[9]

In the early months of her reign, Elizabeth faced continual pressure to marry and bear an heir to the throne. "Her Council and her loyal subjects daily and hourly begged and exhorted her to marry whom she would," Elizabeth told one ambassador, "so that they might hope to have heirs for this Royal Crown of England."[10] Early modern kings and queens were expected to accept arranged marriages that were rigorously negotiated to strengthen the country's dynastic, financial, political, and military position. Therefore, Elizabeth strove to make it absolutely clear, as her pointed reference to "whom she would" indicates, that *she* would be the one to meet with the ambassadors and to make the final decision.[11]

Elizabeth conducted her courtships neither like a conventional, subordinate early modern woman nor like a typical king or queen. As we shall see in chapters 5 and 8, she was happy to entertain the many suitors bidding for her hand, but, she told parliament, she would neither be forced to marry against her will nor told whom to marry. Moreover, she intended to govern the country herself whether or not she married and would not accept a marriage arranged for expediency alone, as we shall see in chapters 4 and 6. Indeed, she had no immediate desire to marry, she repeatedly informed everyone from her principal secretary William Cecil, to her Privy Council and parliament, to foreign ambassadors who arrived bearing marriage proposals. She was far too busy figuring out how to rule the country to take on the competing demands of a husband, pregnancy, and childbirth. When it came to the question of marriage, there was no escaping the fact of Elizabeth's female body. If a king married, his wife would bear his future heirs to the throne, but a married queen regnant would have to assume the burden of untold pregnancies and the dangers of childbirth in an era with no reliable birth control and frighteningly high maternal mortality.

Though Elizabeth had no wish to marry immediately, she was astute enough to realize that there were considerable political advantages to being courted by the most powerful foreign princes and dukes as well as the most eligible English peers and lords. Therefore, she said, she was prepared to consider any politically appropriate suitor who might make her "desire what at present she had no wish for."[12] She would marry, she insisted, only if she found a husband who was *both* politically advisable and personally desirable, someone whom *she* found physically, emotionally, and intellectually appealing—an astonishing notion for a monarch at that time.

In the opening months of the reign, Elizabeth seemed "positively greedy for marriage proposals." She was, indeed, "the best marriage in the parish," Francis Walsingham quipped. The parish of potential suitors quickly expanded from London to Spain, Sweden, and the Holy Roman Empire.[13] There were a number of English peers to be considered— Arundel, Norfolk, and Westmoreland, as well as Sir William Pickering, whom some saw as an appealing prospect though not a peer. Yet for one reason or another the leading English candidates soon dropped out of the running. There seemed to be no shortage of foreign suitors, from Erik XIV of Sweden, to the dukes of Ferrara, Holstein, Saxony, Savoy, and Nemours. Many of Elizabeth's advisors and subjects thought she should marry a foreigner in order to forge a much-needed alliance with one of the rival European powers. And then, there was Robert Dudley, whose intimacy with the queen pervaded court politics even as it reverberates through this book.

Robert Dudley, Elizabeth's first master of the horse, rode behind the queen in her pre-coronation procession and was among the first group of courtiers appointed to a position in her government. Elizabeth loved riding and hunting and spent a lot of time galloping through the countryside with Dudley. Far from acting like a proper young virgin vowed to celibacy and forever married to God and country, Elizabeth openly displayed her attraction to Dudley.[14] The two were constantly in each other's company, and their intimacy was widely remarked. Did Elizabeth sleep with him? Probably not. It would have been far too dangerous. Since an early modern woman's honor was equated with chastity, and since there was no reliable birth control, an out-of-wedlock pregnancy would have not only tarnished Elizabeth's reputation but also threatened her sovereignty. Moreover, in 1581 during the marriage negotiations with the French prince François Valois, Dudley himself "asked her whether she was 'a maid or a woman'."[15] Was she physically intimate with Dudley? Probably. Elizabeth moved him to a room next to her own on the second floor of the palace because his first-floor rooms were too damp—or so they claimed. Rumors abounded. "It was said that Her Majesty visits him in his chamber night and day," the Spanish ambassador reported. "[S]ometimes she...speaks like a woman who will only accept a great prince, and then they say she is in love with Lord Robert and will never let him leave her."[16]

Except for one short epigram that we'll examine in chapter 4, there are very few surviving texts written by Elizabeth to Dudley. There are many possible explanations for this. Elizabeth and Dudley spent so much time together that she may not have needed to write to him. Moreover, she may have been wary of committing anything to writing that might be discovered and read by someone else, or she may have feared that Dudley himself would use her words to pressure her to marry him. She may have asked him to destroy her letters after he had read them, or her letters may simply have been lost through the vagaries of time.

Elizabeth used the rhetoric of courtship so deftly that it looks almost like a calculated political strategy. Although she could not ultimately control either her suitors or her subjects, she played an active role in the marriage negotiations. It seems that she *did* want to marry at a few key moments but resisted the idea at others. In the end, she never resolved the conflict between her public responsibilities and her personal desires. If she had found an attractive, charming, intelligent, trustworthy suitor who was acceptable to the Privy Council, parliament, and her subjects, Elizabeth may well have married him, but only if she was assured that his ambitions would not threaten her sovereignty.

For a monarch, and for Elizabeth personally, the choice of a husband involved so many contingencies, so many competing factors, that she never convinced both herself and her subjects that a particular marriage was, indeed, the right decision under the circumstances. But she made the decision herself, on a case-by-case basis, and it continued to be a pressing political concern and the subject of widespread political debate and popular controversy until advancing age ended the possibility of bearing an heir to the throne. At that point, she may well have felt some regrets as the conclusion of her poem "When I Was Fair and Young" implies:

> But I did sore repent that I had said before,
> "Go, go, go seek some otherwhere; importune me no more."[17]

CHAPTER 2

THE ART OF POETRY, THE ART OF COURTSHIP: ELIZABETH I AND THE ELIZABETHAN WRITING CULTURE

Robert liked Sam's money, and Sam liked that Robert liked his money. Were that all that motivated them, they could have easily found it elsewhere. Instead, each possessed something the other wanted, and in that way, complemented the other. Sam secretly yearned to be an artist, but he was not. Robert wanted to be rich and powerful, but he was not. By association, each tasted the other's attributes. They were a package, so to speak. They needed each other. The patron to be magnified by the creation. The artist to create.

Patti Smith, describing Robert Mapplethorpe and Sam Wagstaff[1]

Elizabeth's Speech and Writing

Though not the equal of Shakespeare, Donne, or Spenser, Elizabeth was the period's most prominent writer. Because she was the queen, her words acquired great symbolic, political, and literary weight. During her lifetime and after her death, Elizabeth was celebrated for her rhetorical and linguistic powers, and she was remarkably outspoken for a woman. She used all available opportunities and created new ones to disseminate her words, at court, throughout the kingdom, and abroad.[2] First, as an orator: she wrote and assiduously rewrote her own parliamentary speeches and later in the reign delivered them herself. Second, as a political campaigner: her words circulated in manuscript and were repeatedly reprinted; moreover, she left the court in the summer to go on progress, staying with her subjects at their country estates and stopping to converse with masses of people who gathered along the route.[3] Third, as a bold negotiator, she stood her ground against foreign rulers and their ambassadors and, when necessary, against her own counselors and parliament.[4] Fourth, as a policymaker, she solicited opinions and debated issues with individual members and representatives of the Privy Council; received, summoned, and answered parliamentary delegations; and issued an extraordinary number of proclamations.[5] Fifth, as a patron, she extended support directly to her personal favorites at court and indirectly, via her councilors and courtiers, throughout the realm. Finally, as an author, she was an avid writer from the time she was a young girl, and she continued writing until shortly before her death. Even as a princess, Elizabeth had serious concerns weighing on her. Once she became queen, weightier responsibilities pressed upon her. Yet she continued to read and write despite a busy schedule of audiences and events. By the time of her death in 1603, Elizabeth had produced a substantial corpus of poems, speeches, letters, prayers, and translations, which made her "the most prolific author among English sovereigns since the reign of King Alfred."[6]

Elizabeth's words played a central role in the Elizabethan political and cultural scene, yet by the twentieth century her reputation as a poet and writer had declined precipitously. When Leicester Bradner published an edition of her poems in 1964, he excluded "On Monsieur's Departure" from the canon on the grounds that he did not believe she could have written such a good poem. Logic such as that leads to the nonsensical conclusion that Shakespeare could not have written his plays because he was not a member of the aristocracy. Elizabeth's reputation as a writer is now in recovery. Thanks in large measure to the renaissance of interest in early modern women writers, Elizabeth's writing has become readily available over the last decade.[7]

Recent editions of Elizabeth's writings help sort out but do not completely resolve the textual problems that discouraged earlier scholars from giving her words the close attention they deserve and demand. To begin with, we cannot be certain that everything attributed to Elizabeth was actually written by her—at least not in the form it has come down to us. Because she was the queen, Elizabeth had a large staff whose job it was to compose official correspondence. Consequently, many of the letters signed by Elizabeth were actually written by someone else. Although a number of autograph manuscripts have survived, most of her writing remained unpublished during her lifetime and survives only in copies, many made after her death.[8] As manuscripts of her writing circulated, copyists introduced errors, emendations, and annotations. Some variants reflect Elizabeth's own revisions, some were scribal errors, some were deliberate alterations designed to impose the copyist's own views. Sorting out one form of variant from another is crucial but not always possible.

These textual problems should make us wary, but they are not peculiar to Elizabeth. Rather, they are the inevitable outcome of the Elizabethan writing culture that this chapter explores. The texts of Edmund Spenser's and Ben Jonson's major poems are relatively fixed because their publication was authorized; however, Spenser and Jonson were atypical in this regard. Most of the Elizabethan writers we read and study today did not publish their work. Philip Sidney's and John Donne's poems were published posthumously. Samuel Daniel published his own poems after they were pirated. Early printed editions of Donne's poems and William Shakespeare's plays and poems were based on imperfect manuscripts. None of Shakespeare's sonnets or plays and only one minor verse letter of Donne's survive in the author's own handwriting. Yet, even with all the resulting textual uncertainties, we continue to teach and analyze their writings. *Elizabeth I: The Voice of a Monarch* contends that Elizabeth's words deserve the same painstaking scrutiny, with the same caveats.[9]

Oral Culture, Writing, and Print

From her girlhood until her death, Elizabeth was drawn to reading, writing, and learning, both for their sheer pleasure and for their utility. Along with her brother Edward, who was four years younger, she studied with the distinguished humanist scholars William Grindal, John Cheke, and Roger Ascham among others. She read Greek and Latin classics, the Bible, the Church fathers, Protestant theology, ancient and modern history. Elizabeth's education included a solid training in the classical and humanist discipline of rhetoric, the strategies of persuasion that were seen as the basis of Elizabethan language and the key to the acquisition and exercise of power.[10]

Great emphasis was placed on learning languages. In addition to studying Latin and Greek with her instructors, Elizabeth learned Spanish, French, and Italian. She began translating classical and religious writings when she was a girl, and her scholarly activities and literary interests continued into old age. She translated both ancient and Renaissance texts, including Plutarch, Cicero, and Seneca. For Elizabeth, as for any well-educated Renaissance humanist, poetry was a priority. She read and wrote poetry and encouraged her courtiers to write poetry as well. She translated *De Arte Poetica* by Horace and "The Triumph of Eternity" by Francis Petrarch, the seminal Italian Renaissance poet who gave his name to the Petrarchan literary tradition that pervades discussions of Elizabeth and Elizabethan literature.[11]

Elizabeth's life and learning epitomized the humanist culture that dominated the courts of Europe. After ruling for a quarter century, she told parliament, "I am supposed to have many studies, but most philosophical. I must yield this to be true: that I suppose few (that be no professors) have read more. And I need not tell you that I am so simple that I understand not, nor so forgetful that I remember not."[12] In addition to making her own studies central to her self-representation, Elizabeth was a great advocate and supporter of learning. Speaking in Latin but sounding very much like a modern commencement speaker, she told the dignitaries, faculty, and students assembled at Cambridge University, "No path is more direct, either to gain good fortune or to procure my grace, than diligently, in your studies which you have begun, to stick to your work" (CW 88).

Elizabeth appointed the learned humanist William Cecil, later Baron Burghley, as her principal secretary and most trusted advisor. Following the classical rhetorical principle of *in utramque partem*, which encouraged Renaissance writers, orators, and counselors to consider, articulate, and formulate the pros and cons of a complex intellectual argument or a thorny political decision, Elizabeth directed Burghley, when he was sworn in, to speak his mind, even when he disagreed with her: "that you will be faithful to the state, and without respect of my private will, you will give me that counsel which you think best, and if you shall know anything necessary to be declared to me of secrecy you shall show it to myself only" (CW 51). Until his death in 1598, Cecil was Elizabeth's advocate to the Privy Council, parliament, and the world—her most trusted counselor and, in private, her most suasive opponent. His memoranda weighed the complex advantages and disadvantages of important political decisions, including Elizabeth's marriage proposals. His continual regard for Elizabeth's views and his wise counsel epitomized and anchored the intellectual rigor and dialogic spirit of Elizabeth's reign.[13]

Although printed books were becoming more affordable and more widely available, oral culture still exercised an important hold on Elizabethan social practices. Manuscripts and books were customarily read aloud by writers and readers to family and friends, and silent reading had not yet become the norm even when reading to oneself.[14] Instructional manuals such as George Puttenham's *The Art of English Poesy* emphasized the ear over the eye and encouraged writers and their audiences to cultivate and appreciate the performative power of poetic persuasion. Rhetorical treatises taught the quintessentially Elizabethan skills of "witcraft" and "speechcraft." Thomas Wilson's *The Art of Rhetoric* (1560) offered guidance "which we may follow as well in speech as in writing."[15] Providing careful instruction in elocution, memory, and utterance, Wilson stressed the importance of eliciting laughter and moving the emotions. Since writing often turned into speech, and speech into writing, writing was considered a form of speech, and the speaking voice—with its textured, varying intonations, ranging from teasing intimacy or tender playfulness, to fear and anxiety, to irony or sarcasm, to condemnation and fury—was expected to endow words with meaning.

Elizabeth's poems, like most of the greatest Elizabethan lyric poetry, were originally recited, given, or sent to auditors or interlocutors whose points of view, preferences, and predilections she knew or would soon discover. Elizabeth's speeches and writings can, in most cases, be connected to a particular occasion, audience, and persuasive purpose. When read out of context, Elizabeth's language can seem abstract, generalized, dense, or impenetrable, but so too can Donne's verse, Spenser's epic allegory, Shakespeare's sonnets, or Wroth's lyrics.[16] When we recuperate the historical situation, Elizabeth's words become less elusive and more allusive, more individuated, dramatic, and playful, more emotionally intense and deftly persuasive, more unconventional and daring.

A lot of Elizabeth's speech and writing was occasional, but that does not mean it was unusually limited in significance or circumscribed in scope because a great deal of Elizabethan literature was written for particular readers and particular situations. Rather, what distinguishes Elizabeth from other Elizabethan writers is that we know more about her and, therefore, can reconstruct the original audience and situation for her words more readily than we can for Shakespeare's sonnets or Donne's poems, for example.

The expansive reach of modern technologies so pervades our daily lives that we need to remind ourselves that the circulation of information was very different in Elizabethan England. Most poetry and prose written by Elizabeth and her courtiers circulated, if it circulated at all, in manuscript within a select, private audience.[17] More sensitive Elizabethan manuscripts were retained and carefully guarded or destroyed by the writer. Some made their way, with or without the writer's knowledge or approval, from the inner circle to a more general manuscript or print readership. Some of Elizabeth's writings circulated freely, some remained highly secretive, some no doubt were so private that they did not survive. The epigram engraved on a window at Woodstock Castle was well known during Elizabeth's lifetime. "The Doubt of Future Foes," which was written to warn traitors suspected of plotting to assassinate Elizabeth and put Mary Queen of Scots on the English throne, circulated more widely because Elizabeth left her notebook out where it could be discovered and copied by Lady Willoughby. After being passed around in manuscript, "The Doubt of Future Foes" was published by Puttenham in *The Art of English Poesy* (1589).[18] Elizabeth's poems were not collected and printed until the nineteenth century, yet their impact and importance is greater than their circulation because their attitudes and style informed Elizabeth's other, more public modes of speech and writing.

Although the printing press was invented in the fifteenth century, printed books reached an increasingly wide and growing audience during Elizabeth's reign. Just as the internet disperses information today more speedily and widely than ever before, print made it possible, for the first time, to easily, quickly, produce innumerable copies that disseminated the word far and wide. The rapid spread of information created new opportunities and dangers. The implications for literature, politics, religion, and social action were revolutionary. In a world without television, newspapers, newsmagazines, or breaking news online, print provided unique and unprecedented access to information. At the same time, however, because there was no copyright law, writers had no legal right to prevent the unauthorized publication of their writing. As more and more private manuscripts ended up in print, writers began to favor rhetorical strategies of concealment, both to protect confidential material from public exposure and to avoid censorship.[19]

Elizabeth's was the first English monarchy to use the relatively new technology of print as a political strategy; as a result, her language permeated the culture. When Elizabeth's spontaneous speeches put her own fresh stamp on the carefully scripted pre-coronation procession, she and her government seized the public relations opportunity, as we shall see more fully in the next chapter. The first edition of *The Quene's Majestie's*

Passage through the citie of London to Westminster the daye before her corona-cion appeared in print only nine days after the event; it sold out and was quickly reprinted. Elizabeth's first parliamentary speech was published and widely circulated, reaching far beyond parliament into Elizabethan society at large.[20]

The Elizabethans were hungry for information about their queen, but they were also hungry for knowledge in general. During Elizabeth's reign, ancient Greek and Latin classics and continental humanist treatises were being translated and printed in the vernacular, along with courtesy books and advice manuals addressed to a reading public eager to acquire the learning and social graces that were seen as the ticket to social and professional advancement. Printers sometimes paid a modest fee for manuscripts, but without the protection of copyright law, writers did not own their words. In consequence Elizabethan writers sought financial remuneration by dedicating their works to patrons or potential patrons.[21]

Elizabethan England was a tightly knit, hierarchical society where the queen, her courtiers, and the most powerful members of the government all knew each other intimately, where the court was dominated by well-established, aristocratic families who intermarried and passed their privilege from one generation to the next, but where talented newcomers could also hope to gain admittance, receive recognition, and be rewarded for their knowledge and talent.[22] The Elizabethans produced plays, pageants, masques, and treatises, hoping to influence public policy and to win preferment or financial support either directly from the queen, for she was the ultimate and most substantial source of patronage, or through her courtiers, councilors, and court ladies who dispensed patronage on her behalf, or from the gentry or the city's elite, whose networks of wealth and power operated outside the court.

Elizabethan patronage wasn't only about talent, it was also about networking. Elizabethans often addressed the queen, her councilors, and courtiers in the hope that familial or social connections would get their private manuscripts a hearing, and they often did. Nonetheless, a bid for patronage was more likely to succeed if the writer could make a convincing connection between the work, or at least the dedicatory epistle, and the patron.[23] The goal was to convey the writer's accomplishment and talent in ways that would win the patron's interest and support—or better yet, to select and cultivate a patron capable of appreciating the writer's own distinctive interests, ideas, and literary sensibility. If a patron had literary talent or a discriminating literary sensibility, as Elizabeth assuredly did, then trying to earn her admiration and support could be a provocation to excellence, rather like a talented student hoping to impress a professor with a well-written paper.

Walter Ralegh won the queen's favor and the court's resentment with his poetic persuasion and brilliant conversation. Edmund Spenser received an annual pension from the queen for writing his allegorical epic,

The Faerie Queene, which placed Elizabeth at the center of the Elizabethan literary scene. Thomas Wilson, having established himself as a Protestant humanist during Edward's reign by writing *The Rule of Reason* and *The Art of Rhetoric,* fled England upon Mary's accession. After being denounced by Mary, he was tortured and imprisoned by the Roman Catholic Inquisition. He returned to England when it returned to Protestantism. His learning, humor, and ready laughter helped him win favor with Elizabeth and her courtiers. He became a member of parliament, the queen's envoy to Portugal and the Netherlands, and finally secretary to the Privy Council.[24]

Fewer writers and intellectuals won favor at court or positions in the government than the above list of notable examples might suggest, since Elizabeth was always trying to save money, leaving positions unfilled, expecting her civil servants to do double duty. Nonetheless, success stories such as these gave Elizabethan writers and intellectuals reason to hope that Elizabeth would heed their voices, read their words, and reward their wit and talent. Writers as diverse as Sir Edmund Tilney, Sir Walter Ralegh, Sir John Harington, Lady Mary Sidney, Edmund Spenser, and George Puttenham acknowledged the queen as their most important audience and patron—or potential patron.

Puttenham—Patronage and Dissimulation

Patronage, which has played a dominant role in English Renaissance scholarship for the last quarter century, was an extremely complex system of petitions and rewards that linked politics and literature; court, country, and city; crown and reading public. One of the texts most commonly cited to elucidate the connection between poetry and patronage is George Puttenham's *The Art of English Poesy,* which has been "unanimously considered by scholars the central text of Elizabethan courtly poetics."[25] I want to reexamine *The Art* here because it shows how seemingly compelling but unsubstantiated assumptions about the patronage system can yield fallacious conclusions about Elizabeth's relationship to Elizabethan literature.

The Art was first published in 1589 with a dedicatory epistle, allegedly written by the printer but probably written by the author: "To the Right Honorable Sir William Cecil, Knight, Lord of Burghley, and Lord High Treasurer of England." *The Art* is particularly interesting for our purposes because, as the dedication asserts and the text repeatedly attests, it was "intended to our Sovereign Lady the Queen, and for her recreation and service chiefly devised." Puttenham was also seeking a general courtly audience—"the ear of princely dames, young ladies, gentlewomen, and courtiers."[26] Yet his primary audience was Elizabeth herself. He pauses to address Elizabeth directly at key points in the text and commends her active support of poets and poetry. Moreover, he prints her manuscript poem "The Doubt of Future Foes" and extols her

Figure 2. Elizabeth I, Frontispiece from *The Art of English Poesy* (1589)

as England's greatest living poet: "your self being already, of any that I know in our time, the most excellent poet." This extravagant tribute would have been more believable at the time, before Sidney, Spenser, Donne, and Shakespeare raised English literature from what literary historians call "the drab age." Still, it looks considerably more self-seeking than sincere as Puttenham continues, "Forsooth, by your princely purse, favors, and countenance, making in manner what ye list, the poor man rich, the lewd well learned, the coward courageous, and vile both noble and valiant."[27]

Puttenham's declaration that *The Art* was written to and for Elizabeth helps explain why he repeatedly represents poetry and rhetoric as suitable for both amorous and political courtship, since (as we shall see repeatedly throughout this book) the language of love was Elizabeth's most characteristic linguistic signature and political strategy. If Ben Jonson was right that *The Art* was "done 20 yeers since & Kept Long in wrytte as a secret," Puttenham wrote it for Elizabeth's "recreation and service" when (as we shall see in the coming chapter) she was actively using the language of "love" and "mutual liking" to negotiate her courtships.[28]

The Art praises the genre of love poetry, which it recommends for both political and amorous purposes: "so commendable, yea, honorable a thing as love well meant, were it in princely estate or private, might in all civil commonwealths be uttered in good form and order as other laudable things are." Significantly, most of the poems Puttenham quotes as examples of the various rhetorical figures are courtly love poems, many from unpublished manuscripts. Puttenham's text also provides historical arguments to demonstrate that *The Art* would be useful to the queen: poets "were the first legislators and politicians in the world," and in ancient times "good poets and poesy were much favored highly esteemed and much favored with the greatest princes." When taken together, the focus on love poetry, the apostrophes to Elizabeth, and the links between amorous and political courtship suggest that Puttenham first wrote *The Art* in the hope of securing a place in Elizabeth's "service" by offering her a compendium of rhetorical devices that she could use both to woo her subjects and to conduct her marriage negotiations.[29]

The most characteristic feature of *The Art* and Puttenham's most original contribution to humanist learning is the rhetoric of concealment.[30] By way of comparison, consider Thomas Wilson's *Art of Rhetoric* where the main "end" is clarity: "an orator must labor to tell his tale that the hearers may well know what he meaneth, and understand him wholly, the which he shall with ease do if he utter his mind in plain words."[31] By contrast, Puttenham favors figures of concealment such as enigma, ironia, and, above all "the Figure of False Semblant or Dissimulation," "the courtly figure *allegoria*, which is when we speak one thing and think another, and that our words and our meanings meet not...in earnest as well as in sport; under covert and dark terms, and in learned and apparent speeches...as well when we lie as when we tell truth." Puttenham presents *allegoria* as "the chief ringleader and captain of all other figures either in the poetical or oratory science." By dubbing it "the courtly figure," he specifically associates it with Elizabeth and her court: "inasmuch as not only every common courtier, but also the gravest counselor, yea, and the most noble and wisest prince of them all are many times enforced to use it."[32]

Puttenham returns to the courtly figure *allegoria* in his final chapter, which begins with another apostrophe to Elizabeth, "And now, most excellent Queen." After paying Elizabeth (and himself!) the supreme compliment of assuming that she will read *The Art* through to the very end, Puttenham makes his final plea for a place in her service. While ostensibly describing "the beauty and gallantness" of the poet's "language and style," Puttenham presents a mini-allegory of his own self-fashioning:

> pulling him first from the cart to the school, and thence to the court, and preferred him to your Majesty's service, in that place of great honor and magnificence to give entertainment to princes, ladies of honor, gentlewomen,

and gentlemen…that being now lately become a courtier, he show not himself a craftsman, and merit to be disgraded, and with scorn sent back again to the shop or other place of his first faculty and calling, that so wisely and discreetly he behave himself as he may worthily retain the credit of his place and profession of a very courtier, which is, in plain terms, cunningly to be able to dissemble.

In moving from the cart to the school to the court, Puttenham suggests that his professional advancement was the result of his learning, as demonstrated by *The Art*'s wide-ranging references to ancient classics and contemporary Elizabethan and continental writers.[33] Yet what really qualifies him for "the profession of a very courtier,"[34] Puttenham asserts, is his ability to seem to speak plainly while cunningly dissembling.

Most twentieth-century scholarship about Puttenham began with the assumption that our man was a courtier with direct access to Elizabethan courtly culture, which favored the poetic and rhetorical devices of dissimulation that *The Art* catalogues and elucidates. Critics claimed, moreover, that being a courtier, Puttenham was constrained by the stigma of print to publish *The Art* anonymously.[35] It turns out, however, that Puttenham was not a courtier but a criminal and a fugitive who had been excommunicated four times and imprisoned at least six times for behavior so heinous that the Privy Council was repeatedly called upon to adjudicate his transgressions and to enforce his legal sentences. The many charges against him include attacking a parson in church; high treason (though he seems to have been exonerated of this one); repeatedly abusing his wife, throwing her against a wall and cracking her ribs; tricking her into signing away her children's inheritance so that he could turn a profit on the family estate; repeatedly failing to pay alimony; deceiving, coercing, and entrapping a series of vulnerable, young serving women into having sex with him and then abandoning them when they became pregnant; raping, abducting, and incarcerating his last sex slave.[36] Steven May's revelatory account of recently discovered documentary evidence, based largely on testimony from court trials, sets forth the entire tale of "[s]pouse abuse, sexual slavery, and multiple excommunications from the Church of England." Puttenham published *The Art* anonymously, May concludes, not because he was a courtier inhibited by the so-called stigma of print, but because his honor and reputation were so sullied that anonymity was his only hope of gaining an audience.[37]

By 1569, when, according to Jonson, *The Art* was written, Puttenham's conduct had already created serious legal and financial difficulties, which help explain the rather puzzling account of patronage cited above: "Forsooth, by your princely purse, favors, and countenance, making in manner what ye list, the poor man rich, the lewd well learned, the coward courageous, and vile both noble and valiant." Puttenham was not only so "poor" that he was in desperate need of patronage but he was also widely perceived to be so "vile" and "lewd" (in the sense of *wicked, base, and unprincipled*) that nothing short of a magical metamorphosis could have saved him from utter ruination.[38]

As Puttenham's editors Gladys Doidge Willcock and Alice Walker demonstrated, his original manuscript was revised and expanded before being published in 1589.[39] The last book, including the final chapter we have been examining, was probably added later when he had even stronger reasons to fear that he would be once again "disgraded" and carted off to "that other place," prison (as Whigham and Rebhorn note, a "cart" referred not only to a rustic farm cart but also to the wagon that carted criminals ignominiously through the streets), unless "so wisely and discreetly he behave himself as he may worthily retain the credit of his place and profession of a very courtier, which is, in plain terms, cunningly to be able to dissemble." In the context of Puttenham's life story, "profession" means neither a solemn declaration nor a courtly career, as earlier critics assumed, but the false pretense of being a courtier. Indeed, his transgressions were so "lewd" and "vile" that both his fantasy of Ovidean metamorphosis and his allegory of the learned, courtly poet dissolve under the weight of his own felonious self-seeking.

Puttenham's earlier hope of presenting Elizabeth with a private manuscript was presumably foiled by the dishonor resulting from his criminal activities. Shortly before *The Art* was published, Elizabeth's principal advisor William Cecil, Baron Burghley, rewarded Puttenham for writing *A Justification of Queen Elizabeth in Relation to the Affair of Mary Queen of Scots*. No doubt, 1589 seemed like a propitious time for Puttenham to approach Elizabeth via Burghley with a printed presentation copy of *The Art*. Hence, Puttenham's dedicatory epistle is addressed to Burghley, though it identifies Elizabeth as the "intended" audience. We do not know whether either of them read it, or if they did what they thought of it, although Elizabeth expressed her own scathing view of Robert Dudley's much less grievous dissimulations in the psalter posy that we'll examine in chapter 6.

There is no doubt that Elizabeth and Cecil would have known, as twentieth-century critics did not until May rediscovered Puttenham's "lewd and illicit career," that Puttenham's elaborate "profession of a courtier" consisted of *nothing but* "cunningly to be able to dissemble." The word "dissemble" meant not only *to disguise or to give a false or feigned appearance,* but also *to ignore, to shut one's eyes to the fact.* As he himself implies in the closing chapters, Puttenham hoped to convince Cecil and Elizabeth to shut their eyes to the facts and to pardon his crimes.

Indeed, by the time *The Art* appeared in print, Puttenham's integrity had been so thoroughly "disgraded" and discredited that his only hope was to convince Cecil and the queen that lying and dissimulation could be of service. That may suggest another reason for publishing *The Art* anonymously. A man who could dissemble with such aplomb could perhaps be put to use as a spy. But then again, how could he be trusted not to become a double agent, especially since there had been allegations that Puttenham was involved in secret Roman Catholic practices?[40]

Until Puttenham's criminal record was rediscovered by May and reported by Whigham and Rebhorn in 2007,[41] *The Art* was widely praised as the most important account of Elizabethan courtly poetics. But what are we to make of it now? After reviewing the facts, Whigham and Rebhorn reached a relatively forgiving view, suggesting that *The Art* should be judged apart from the life. Yet, their own close reading of Puttenham's language reveals what mine confirms: that the life and *The Art* cannot be separated because the life underlies, propels, and shapes the rhetorical strategies Puttenham uses throughout *The Art*.

On one hand, *The Art* makes a genuine and original contribution to our understanding. It highlights the use of poetry and poetic language for both political and amorous courtship. It showcases the enigmatic, figurative concealments that Elizabeth and the Elizabethans used to disguise their private persuasive purposes in generalization and abstraction. It offers a case study of how Elizabeth's courtly rhetoric of love made its way into Elizabethan society at large. On the other hand, Puttenham's dissimulations and anxieties about his own ulterior motives are so pressing and pervasive that they repeatedly disrupt, derail, and diminish the larger argument.[42] Perhaps most damaging of all, Puttenham's own desperate need for the figure of false *semblant* reduces the dialectical play of mind to coarse duplicity. Compared to Elizabeth's point-by-point critique of Ralegh's logic and language that we shall examine next, Puttenham's literary interpretation seems flat-footed and unsophisticated. His frequent self-quotations are not much better, as the following verses to Elizabeth illustrate:

> Then if there be
> Any so cankered heart to grutch
> At your glories, my Queen, in vain
> Repining at your fatal reign,
> It is for that they feel too much
> Of your bounty.[43]

Rather than probing the logic and redoubling the interpretive possibilities, Puttenham's duplicities erase the overt, plain meaning in order to substitute a contrary but equally reductive underlying meaning. As we shall see in chapter 5, that is precisely what the Spanish and Austrian ambassadors did when they dismissed Elizabeth's expressly stated conditions for marriage because they could not believe she meant anything so unprecedented. Then, having discounted what she said, they accused her of cunningly being able to dissemble. Elizabeth could not have endorsed Puttenham's view of courtly rhetoric without confirming her opponents' sharpest criticisms, nor would she have wanted to endorse Puttenham's account of her rhetoric, for it would have eliminated the complexities and qualifications that her speech and writing worked so hard to make her interlocutors confront and consider.

Because it replaces one simplistic meaning with another, Puttenham's art of dissimulation can only take us so far in understanding Elizabeth's language and its connection to Elizabethan literature. Going beyond the rhetoric of concealment, Elizabeth relied on the classical rhetorical practice of *in utramque partem*, which encouraged Renaissance writers, orators, and counselors to see both sides of the question—to formulate and articulate the pros and cons governing any complex political or personal choice.[44] In both her speech and writing, Elizabeth scorned simplicity, proposed qualifications, and held opposing viewpoints in suspension. In this regard, her self-correcting, open-ended language is closer to the many-layered ambiguities of Donne's poems or the radical uncertainties of Shakespeare's sonnets and plays than to Puttenham's simplifications and dissimulations.

Petrarchism and New-made Idiom: Elizabeth, Ralegh, Harington, Spenser, and Donne

It is an axiom of English literary history that the Petrarchan language of love became a dominant symbolic system of language in Elizabethan England because it suited Elizabeth's reign as Virgin Queen.[45] Initially, critics argued that Elizabeth herself found it advantageous to adopt the conventionally feminine persona of a Petrarchan lady to mute the threat her power may have posed. That paradigm was replaced by the now dominant view that Elizabeth's male subjects constructed her as a chaste and unexpressive Petrarchan lady in order to circumvent her power, using their authority as writers to "project and symbolically master the condition of their subjection to a female ruler."[46]

Unhappy with the ways in which the theory undercut Elizabeth's agency and authority, feminist scholars countered with revisionist arguments that emphasized Elizabeth's powerful disruption of traditional gender roles. Leah Marcus constructed a more regal, androgynous Elizabeth who claimed the authority of a king by habitually using the male title "prince" and claiming that, although she had the body of a weak woman, she also had the strength and courage of a king's immortal male soul. Mary Crane argued that Elizabeth used the male rhetoric of council to establish her authority. Phillipa Berry emphasized "the potentially subversive representation of Elizabeth as a Petrarchan or Neoplatonic beloved who also had both worldly and spiritual power."[47] *Elizabeth I: The Voice of a Monarch* also offers a revisionist account of the political Petrarchism of the Virgin Queen, both by reaffirming Susan Doran's point that the icon of Elizabeth as Virgin Queen emerged only in the 1580s and by proposing an alternative, multidirectional model of patronage that gives equal weight to the ways in which Elizabeth fashioned herself, defended her authority, and redefined the role of monarch and private woman.

Petrarchan love language eternizes the male poet's unrequited, idealized longing for an inaccessible, distant beloved object. By contrast, Elizabeth's language of love is reciprocal and interactive. In her pre-coronation procession (which we'll examine in chapter 3), Elizabeth began to build her political base by expressing her love for her subjects and thanking them for their answering love, and she continued to invoke this loving exchange between monarch and people throughout her reign. Indeed, in her final "Golden Speech" to parliament, she declared, "this I count the glory of my crown—that I have reigned with your loves" (CW 340). As Harington pithily remarked after her death, "We did all love hir, for she said she loved us, and muche wisdome she shewed in this matter."[48]

The best evidence of how Elizabeth herself would have viewed the Petrarchism of the Virgin Queen is her lyric response to and critique of a conventional Petrarchan love poem addressed to her by her courtier Sir Walter Ralegh. Thanks to his charm, eloquence, and literary brilliance, Ralegh won a prominent position at court, military commissions, a knighthood, valuable licenses and monopolies, extensive lands in Ireland, an appointment as captain of the guard, and more. Ralegh addressed this lyric to Elizabeth when he feared that his fortunes would slip away if he lost the queen's favor:

> Fortune hath taken thee away, my love,
> My life's joy and my soul's heaven above;
> Fortune hath taken thee away my princess,
> My world's delight and my true fancy's mistress.

Ralegh presents himself as a noble knight errant—the allegorical figure of sorrow, searching the heavens and earth armed with sighs and tears to rescue his "love," his "princess," his "true fancy's mistress," from "Fortune's hands."[49] Ralegh's lyric is so carefully veiled in allegorical abstractions that it is impossible to know, on the basis of the poem alone, what caused Ralegh to write this traditional Petrarchan complaint, though Steven May argues convincingly that it was written in the first half of 1587 when Ralegh's position as court favorite was challenged by the rise of the Earl of Essex.[50]

As the lyric dialogue between Ralegh and Elizabeth demonstrates, even now-canonical poets such as Ralegh used abstract, universal language to conceal a more intensely persuasive, private subtext. Elizabeth's response, a companion poem that matched Ralegh's stanza for stanza, rhyme for rhyme, mocks his conventional abstractions, dismisses his attempt to curtail her power, and advises him that he would be more likely to win her favor with a more colloquial, playful lyric voice.

Since Ralegh has traditionally occupied a more important place in English literary history than Elizabeth, it is not surprising that until recently his poem received more critical attention and praise. Stephen Greenblatt finds "something vast and heroic in [Ralegh's] sorrow" but doesn't look closely enough at Elizabeth's poem to appreciate her pointed satire. "From heroic love and despair," Greenblatt writes, "we descend to [Elizabeth's] reassuring but demeaning pleasantries."[51] Demeaning pleasantries? Elizabeth's deflationary rhetoric comprises a withering critique of Ralegh's conventional poetic persona, disingenuous rhetoric, and contradictory logic.

To some extent, Ralegh's poetic persuasion had the desired effect, for Elizabeth's lyric response gave him the attention he craved:

> Ah silly pug, wert thou so sore afraid?
> Mourn not, my Wat, nor be thou so dismayed;
> It passeth fickle Fortune's power and skill
> To force my heart to think thee any ill.

The opening adjective "silly"—meaning, *deserving of pity; defenseless; weak, sick; lacking in judgment; weak or deficient in intellect; foolish; poor; of humble rank*—encapsulates Elizabeth's mixture of sympathetic warmth and disparaging irony.[52] The opening question invites an answering response, while the teasing banter, the reference to "my heart," and the terms of endearment—"pug" was applied both to persons and to pets, and "Wat" was Elizabeth's pet name for Walt—instantly dissolve the distance Ralegh bemoans. Indeed the poem sounds like colloquial speech, suggesting that Elizabeth read or recited it to her woebegone poet/lover in front of a private courtly audience, which would have been jealous of his meteoric rise and amused to see him outwitted.[53]

The very fact that Elizabeth took the trouble to match Ralegh's poem, thought for thought, quatrain for quatrain, was a tribute not only to his place in her imagination and regard but also to the seriousness she accorded his lapses in logic and his lack of lyric innovation.[54] Not only did Elizabeth reuse many of Ralegh's rhymes in order to interrogate and parody his conventional tropes, but her initial rhyme words "afraid" and "dismayed," which do not appear in Ralegh's poem, disclose what Ralegh sought to conceal—that his poetic complaint was motivated neither by the elevated Petrarchan sentiments proclaimed by his opening couplet ("My life's joy and my soul's heaven above") nor by the heroic suffering Greenblatt admires in the following stanzas ("Dead to all joys, I only live to woe") but by the much less noble or impressive emotions of fear and dismay.

Alluding to Elizabeth's earlier epigram on Fortune, Ralegh attributed his loss of favor not to himself, for he was too proud to admit his own failing, nor to Elizabeth herself, since that would have been counterproductive, but to Fortune, that blind goddess whose arbitrary acts neither recognize nor reward "virtue right." In her response Elizabeth reminds Ralegh that *her* epigram (which we'll examine in chapter 4) resisted fortune's power, praying to God to punish the guilty and free the innocent:

> No Fortune base, thou sayest, shall alter thee;
> And may so blind a wretch then conquer me?
> No, no, my pug, though Fortune were not blind
> Assure thyself she could not rule my mind.

The blunt, straightforward diction, softened by the endearing reassurances ("my pug," "assure thyself"), asserts Elizabeth's powerful independence of mind, reiterating that Ralegh's rise at court was due not to Fortune but to Elizabeth's regard for his intelligence and literary merit. Elizabeth's critique makes it very clear that her thoughts and actions were no more controlled by "fickle Fortune's power" than her reactions and favors were controlled by Ralegh's words.

Ralegh's lyric epitomizes the modern critical paradigm of political Petrarchism, which argues that Elizabeth's male subjects used their literary power to resist their subjection to Elizabeth's female authority. Elizabeth's critical response shows that she distrusted the strained logic and disingenuous dissimulations that stance produced. Since the goal was to win her favor, her opinion mattered. By wallowing in self-love and self-pity ("And only love the sorrow due to me") and pledging allegiance to sorrow ("Sorrow, henceforth that shall my princess be"), Ralegh undermined his own initial protestations of love and loyalty ("my Love," "my princess"). Worse yet, after describing Elizabeth as "my life's joy," Ralegh's lyric takes a perverse pleasure in subjecting Elizabeth to Fortune: "And only joy that Fortune conquers kings, / Fortune that rules on earth and earthly things." From Elizabeth's point of view, this was not merely disingenuous, it was insulting and "silly," or foolish.

Ralegh concludes by grandly proclaiming, "No Fortune base shall ever alter me." Yet, as Elizabeth's reply indicates, his reliance on Fortune had already altered him, turning his characteristically clever poetry and incisive intelligence into self-pitying fear and irrational despair. By refusing to take responsibility for his own behavior, Ralegh was implicitly attacking Elizabeth's wisdom and judgment. "With wisdom's eyes had but blind Fortune seen," Ralegh wrote, "Then had my love my love for ever been." That was not only presumptuous, it was downright offensive. As Elizabeth's acerbic representation of herself as "Thy love, thy joy" points out, Ralegh was free to represent her as "My love, / My life's joy" if he liked, but his repeated reference to her as "my princess" was going too far. As a courtier poet, Ralegh could declare his love for her in poetry, if he wished; however, it behooved him to remember that poetry of courtship depended for its success upon eliciting her favorable response.

Having begun with a series of questions, Elizabeth's lyric ends with a series of imperatives that exhort Ralegh to show some spirit: "Pluck up thy heart, suppress thy brackish teares." Elizabeth's directive speech produces its own answers, culminating in a performative speech act: "The less afraid the better shalt thou speed." By satirizing Ralegh's self-aggrandizing, self-indulgent sorrow, Elizabeth's lyric comprises an astute literary critique of his conventional Petrarchizing: "But must thou needs sour sorrow's servant be, / If that to try thy mistress jest with thee."[55] Elizabeth's impatience with his "sour sorrow" and her desire instead to "jest with thee" suggest that Ralegh could make his courtship more efficacious and his poetry more creative if he replaced his weary, woebegone abstractions with some fresh imagery and sprightly diction.

By appropriating the politics and poetry of love, which were both traditional masculine preserves, and calling attention to the fact that she was not only the object of male desire or the subject of male discourse but also the agent or speaker, Elizabeth's lyric disrupts ordinary gender categories. Although designed to resolve a private disagreement, her historically situated lyric dialogue comprises a larger literary and cultural critique, demonstrating that she could be as impatient with shop-worn Petrarchizing and as attuned to anti-Petrarchan innovation as were later Elizabethan poets such as Sidney, Spenser, Shakespeare, and Donne.

The dialogue between Elizabeth and her male suitors was, at times, tense and fraught, but it could also be loving and ludic. Like Ralegh, Elizabeth's godson, Sir John Harington, sought to win her favor by writing love poetry, but he used Petrarch in the fresh, innovative way Elizabeth recommended to Ralegh—to "jest with thee." Harington's diary offers a particularly revealing commentary on the courtly writing culture because it combines a godson's devotion to a queen he knew from boyhood with a savvy courtier's sophisticated esthetic distance: "The Queene stoode up, and bade me reache forthe my arme to rest her thereon. Oh, what swete burden to my nexte songe! Petrarcke shall eke out good matter for this businesse."[56] The mixture of hyperbole and self-irony is precisely what Ralegh's poetic persuasion lacked. A few days later, after being advised to "lay goode holde on her Majesties bountie, and aske freely," Harington wrote in his diary: "I will attende to-morrowe, and leave this little poesie behinde her cushion at my departinge from her presence":

TO THE QUEENS MAJESTIE.

For ever dear, for ever dreaded Prince,
You read a verse of mine a little since,
And so pronounc'st each word, and every letter,
Your gracious reading grac'st my verse the better:
Sith then your Highnesse doth, by gift exceeding
Make what you read the better for your reading;
Let my poor muse your pains thus farre impórtune,
Like as you read my verse, so—*read my Fortune.*

From your Highnesse saucy Godson.[57]

By implying that Elizabeth read his previous poem aloud, Harington calls attention to the oral nature of courtly lyric dialogues. Whereas Ralegh's lyric was disingenuous, self-serving, and finally unpersuasive because it failed to acknowledge Elizabeth's critical intelligence and active involvement in the lyric exchange, Harington's impish impudence suggests that writing for Elizabeth and imagining her reading his poem inspired him to write wittier, more sophisticated poetry. Mingling the respectful language of subjection, "for ever dreaded Prince," with the cheeky license of "your Highnesse saucy Godson," Harington asks Elizabeth to treat both him and his poem generously: "Like as you read my verse, so—*read my Fortune.*" Cognizant that courtship was a rhetorical act that depended for its success on an answering response, Harington's dialogic model of the conversation between prince and courtier, patron and suitor, writer and reader, acknowledges that Elizabeth used her dramatic ability and critical powers to give "each word, and every letter" her own interpretation.

Unfortunately, there is no record of Elizabeth's response. When she died, however, Harington recorded his gratitude to her, not only for showing affection to his mother and bettering his father's fortunes, but also for actively encouraging his learning and literary pursuits: "her watchings over my youthe, her likinge to my free speech, and admiration of my little learninge and poesy, which I did so muche cultivate on her commande, have rooted such love, suche dutyfull remembrance of her princelie virtues."[58]

Much has been written about the ways in which Spenser praises and idealizes Elizabeth as the Virgin Queen in both *The Shepheard's Calendar* and *The Faerie Queene.* Much less has been said about the fact that Spenser stopped writing his epic in order to woo his future wife in the *Amoretti.* After producing over seventy sonnets extolling her beauty, wit, and power, Spenser finally convinced his beloved Elizabeth Boyle to marry him.[59] Significantly, it is at this key turning point in the sonnet sequence that *Amoretti* 74 appears, celebrating the "three Elizabeths" who shaped his life: his fiancé, his mother, and his queen, whose favor he was now eager to regain by associating her with that other Elizabeth who took all his heart for love. After completing the *Amoretti,* Spenser addressed Queen Elizabeth as Cinthia in the "Epithalamion," asking her indulgence since she had been a lover too: "O fairest goddesse, do thou not envy / My love with me to spy: / For thou likewise didst love, though now unthought" (376–79).

With his marriage secured and his love poems in print, Spenser resumed his epic labors, seeking to make amends by addressing Queen Elizabeth directly in the Proem or preface to Book 4, where he added an important new emphasis to his epic bid for her patronage. Appealing directly to that distinctly un-Petrarchan queen whose amorous language propels this book, Spenser transformed Elizabeth into "The Queene of love." He even asked her to defend his love poems against the "grave," "frosen hearts" of "Such ones who ill judge of love, that cannot love."[60] By inserting Elizabeth's private love story into his public allegory, Spenser placed his impassioned "looser rimes" in dialogue with Elizabeth's own love language.

John Donne, our last lyric poet, wrote his love poems at the end of Elizabeth's reign while serving as the secretary to Sir Thomas Egerton, Lord Keeper of the Privy Seal. Donne was not a courtier, but he had business and connections at court. He made a bid for patronage in "Satire V," which addresses Egerton as well as Elizabeth, "thou greatest and fairest Empress." Donne was certainly familiar with Elizabeth's self-representations and probably knew her more widely circulated poems, though he would not have had access to her private love lyrics. Moreover, it is unlikely that Elizabeth knew Donne's love poems, which were published for the first time in 1633 and which began to circulate in manuscript only after Elizabeth's death.

In the love poems Donne wrote at the end of Elizabeth's reign, as in the rhetoric of courtship Elizabeth pioneered in the first half of her reign, the political is eroticized and the erotic is politicized, calling conventional notions of "the he and she" into question. Like the poems Elizabeth wrote to Ralegh, Dudley, and Monsieur, Donne's colloquial, witty, dialogic language mocks the stale tropes of Petrarchism, even as it anticipates, invites, responds to, and seeks to shape an answering response. Although at times Donne's male bravado and satiric scorn include the familiar antifeminist stereotypes that made it so difficult for Elizabeth to establish and exercise her power, his poems of reciprocal love express the kind of "mutual liking" Elizabeth actively sought in her marriage negotiations. Like Elizabeth's insistence upon conducting her own courtships, Donne's "Valediction of the Book" urges his beloved to write her version of their love affair, based on an epistolary dialogue of love in which her words have equal weight:

> Study our manuscripts, those myriads
> Of letters, which have past twixt thee and me,
> Thence write our annals.

Her love story, "In cipher writ, or new-made idiom," recalls Elizabeth's enigmatic, novel, and unprecedented language of love. Elizabeth's difficult, qualified, self-correcting, figurative language, which left her options open and her meaning open to interpretation, finds its counterpart in Donne's love poems, which combine "abstract spiritual love" with "Something which they may see and use."

John Donne did not write love poems for publication any more than Elizabeth did. Rather, he wrote private lyric dialogues that could be read differently by different members of his audience, like Elizabeth's Woodstock epigrams or "On Monsieur's Departure." In the poems of mutual love such as "The Anniversary," Donne's clandestine lovers, "Who prince enough in one another be," create a brave new world, a unique private world where they share power and passion equally: "Here upon earth, we'are kings, and none but we / Can be such kings, nor of such subjects be." Donne's male and female lovers are both kings and subjects, both rulers and ruled. Indeed, their monarchy of love is all the more extraordinary because it was, as "The Anniversary" proudly declares, unparalleled on earth and unprecedented in English poetry.

Outwitting the Wittiest: Shakespearean
Courtship and the Queen

The simultaneously political and amorous discourse of courtship was introduced at the start of the Elizabethan era in Elizabeth's own speeches and marriage negotiations. After being taken up by the popular controversy over women and marriage, which we shall examine in chapter 7, it culminates in Shakespeare's comedies of love. Any one of his Elizabethan comedies would illustrate the point, but *Much Ado about Nothing* provides a particularly useful case study because Beatrice, rather than adopting a male disguise, uses her female wit to defend women's liberty.[61] When a false rumor suggests that Don Pedro is planning to propose to Beatrice's cousin Hero, Leonato says, "Daughter, remember what I told you. If the Prince do solicit you in that kind, you know your answer" (2.1.66–68). While recognizing that it is Hero's duty to do as her father commands, Beatrice nonetheless objects, urging Hero to assert her own will: "Yes, faith, it is my cousin's duty to make cur'sy and say, 'Father, as it please you.' But yet for all that, cousin, let him be a handsome fellow, or else make another cur'sy and say, 'Father, as it please me'" (2.1.66–68). Hero seems like a conventional, chaste, silent, and obedient young woman. Indeed, she barely says anything in the opening scenes of the play. Yet, when Don Pedro asks her to dance at the masked ball, Hero defies her father's command and insists on her right to "walk away" unless or until she decides that "I like your favor." When pressed by Pedro, Hero responds, "I may say so when I please," echoing Beatrice's exhortation to say, "as it please me" (2.1.88–95). This sounds remarkably like what Elizabeth said in response to parliament's marriage petitions, "As for me, I shall do no otherwise than pleases me," or what she said when the Spanish ambassador was pressuring her to agree to a marriage with Archduke Charles sight unseen: "nothing would suffice to make her think of marrying, or even treating of marriage; but the person she was to marry pleasing her so much as to cause her to desire what at present has no wish for."[62]

Beatrice scoffs at conventional gender roles in which all women were "to be understood either married, or to be married, and their desires are subject to their husbands."[63] Like Elizabeth, Beatrice refuses to be "fitted with a husband" (2.1.57–8) or "overmaster'd" (2.1.61) by a man. Instead, she uses her wit to assert her will and to defend the liberty she so evidently enjoys. She even fancies herself enjoying a place in heaven "where the bachelors sit, and there live we as merry as the day is long" (2.1.48–9), which makes heaven sound remarkably like Elizabeth's court. Yet, when Hero and Claudio seal their betrothal with a kiss, Beatrice experiences a pang of regret—"Good Lord, for alliance! Thus goes every one to the world but I, and I am sunburnt. I may sit in a corner and cry 'Heigh-ho for a husband!'" (2.1.318–20)—which sounds a lot like the conclusion to Elizabeth's lyric:

> But I did sore repent that I had said before,
> "Go, go, go seek some otherwhere; importune me no more."
> (CW 304)

Beatrice's sprightly banter prompts Don Pedro to propose marriage, which enables her to counter her uncle's claim that she is "too curst" (2.1.25), or too shrewish, to get a husband. Beatrice gives Pedro a tactful but evasive excuse like those Elizabeth gives her suitors, but the real reason she rejects Pedro (as he immediately realizes) is Benedick: "Indeed, my lord, he lent [his heart to] me awhile, and I gave him use for it, a double heart for his single one. Marry, once before he won it of me with false dice, therefore your Grace may well say I have lost it" (2.1.278–82). Like Elizabeth's enigmatic allusions to Dudley during the marriage negotiations, Beatrice's "double" speak enables her to deny what her words imply: that she has already given her heart to Benedick, as the sexual vibes of their "merry war" attest.

Like Elizabeth, Beatrice enjoys being single. Yet she also boldly articulates the marital freedom of choice, the right to say "if it please me," that Elizabeth fought so actively to defend. Shakespeare may have hoped to win patronage for his acting company by pleasing Elizabeth with clever, independent female characters such as Beatrice, Rosalind, and Viola, much as the mechanicals in *A Midsummer's Night's Dream* hope to be rewarded for performing their play at the duke's wedding: "If our sport had gone forward, we had all been made men" (4.2.17–18). Yet, whether or not Shakespeare was consciously alluding to Elizabeth's love language as Spenser clearly was, *Much Ado about Nothing*—and any one of Shakespeare's comedies would provide an equally apt example—nonetheless demonstrates that Elizabeth's resolve to say "if it please me" had become part of Elizabethan popular culture by the end of the reign.

What English Is

The political Petrarchism of the Virgin Queen cannot adequately describe the Elizabethan literature of love because the female figures who inhabit the great Elizabethan love poems and Shakespeare's great comedies of love are neither conventional Petrarchan ladies nor destined to remain virgins for long. They do sound a lot like the witty, amorous queen whose speech and writing are the subject of this book. Of course, courtship was a very different matter for a prince than for a private woman, as Elizabeth herself recognized. Yet it is precisely because Elizabeth's politics of courtship was "entirely novel and unprecedented" both for a monarch and for a woman that her marriage negotiations exercised such a profound impact on the Elizabethan imaginary. Her amorous words disturbed the sex/gender system, infusing the political unconscious with a gender unconscious. Placed in the role of monarch and hero when the culture's myths cast women in the role of the savior's mother, the hero's beloved, or the patriarch's wife, Elizabeth generated political, ideological, and representational contradiction.[64]

Simultaneously subject to and powerful enough to transgress cultural constraints on women, provoking and dashing antifeminist stereotypes, Elizabeth gave the traditional male discourses of politics and love a female body and a female voice, turning her "liking" into a female counter-text that was radically difficult to read because it could not be interpreted or overmastered with the culture's assumptions about monarchs or women. Elizabeth's marriage negotiations gave relations between the sexes an unprecedented public visibility and import, "displacing aesthetic hierarchies and generic categories," merging with a broader social and political debate about courtship and marriage that vitalized Shakespearean drama and Elizabethan love poetry, yielding "a new aesthetic, a rewriting of culture."[65] Throughout her reign, Elizabeth continued to write poetry, or to invoke the artistry of poetic rhetoric, whenever the situation demanded blunt assertion, deft persuasion, and complex analysis. Her poems, like her speeches, expose and conceal, deride and cajole, edify and critique. They not only reflect the circumstances that comprise the poem's historic and (quasi) fictionalized dramatic situation but also define a characteristic Elizabethan style that Elizabeth uses in her other forms of speech and writing and that she shares with later, more renowned Elizabethan writers: colloquial speech and the direct expression of personal feeling; epigrammatic wit and ironic judgment; veiled allegorical inference and face-saving deniability; principled moral judgment and hermeneutical self-reflexiveness. In her prose and poetry Elizabeth deftly turned conventional language inherited from her predecessors to surprising new uses.

Elizabeth's amorous speech and writing preceded by over two decades the great Elizabethan writers who continue to exercise such a powerful hold over our imaginations, which makes it tempting to venture an old-fashioned claim that Elizabeth's language "influenced" later Elizabethan writers, and to some extent, no doubt it did. Yet the aim of this book is not to prove what Virginia Woolf witheringly called "the influence of somebody on something." Whether or not Spenser's, Donne's, and Shakespeare's female characters were consciously modeled on or alluding to Elizabeth's art of courtship, their distinctly un-Petrarchan obsession with the language of reciprocal love and marital freedom of choice demonstrates that the conditions Elizabeth asserted and the kind of language she deployed in the first half of the reign became a central part of Elizabethan culture.

By the end of her reign Elizabeth's voice had acquired formidable force. To the French ambassador de Maisse who visited England in 1597 she was the very image of "a very great princess who knows everything."[66] Even after she was no longer alive to receive or reward their accolades, seventeenth-century writers continued to laud her as a scholar, linguist, orator, poet, and supporter of art and learning.[67] Elizabeth was *the* icon of the Elizabethan era, and she remains an icon today. Because she was so ready to use speech, manuscript, and print to construct her voice and to shape her reign, her words acquired enormous force, reverberating throughout Elizabethan England and merging with a vital literary and social debate about language, gender, power, and marital freedom of choice. In dedicating her and her brother Philip Sidney's translation of the psalms to Queen Elizabeth, Mary Sidney Herbert posed a question that still resonates: "for in our worke what bring wee but thine owne?" By the end of Elizabeth's reign the answer was self-evident: "What English is, by many names is thine."[68] Elizabethan English was the Queen's English, as divine as it was amorous.

Figure 3. Queen Elizabeth I in Coronation Robes, English School, c. 1559–1600

CHAPTER 3

THE PRE-CORONATION PROCESSION: SO PRINCE-LIKE A VOICE

She made me a great discourse of the friendship that her people bore her, telling me that it was unbelievable, and how she loved them no less than they her, and she would die rather than see any diminution on the one part or the other. I replied that I was well informed on that score.

Monsieur de Maisse, Ambassador in England[1]

Pageants and Procession

On January 14, 1559, the day before her coronation, Elizabeth I made her royal entry into the city of London: "The Queenes Maiestie at 2 of the clock in the after-noone roade from the Tower throughe the Cittie of London to her pallace at Westminster, the Londoners havinge then made sumptuouse provision of pageantes and otherwise, as hath bene accustomed."[2] On the following day, a Sunday as custom dictated, Elizabeth would be crowned monarch. Only nine days later, on "the. xxiii. day of January," there appeared in print a pamphlet entitled *The passage of our most drad Soveraigne Lady Quene Elizabeth through the citie of London to westminster the daye before her coronacion.*[3] Written by Richard Mulcaster for the city fathers and sent directly to the queen for her express approval, this pamphlet provides a remarkably detailed public account of the pre-coronation procession—an account that is cited throughout this chapter, although its persuasive purpose is explicitly analyzed only towards the end.

The coronation was a sacred ceremony where Elizabeth began to distance herself from the Roman Catholic mass and the Marian bishops. By comparison, the pre-coronation procession was an ancient, secular rite of passage, designed to introduce the monarch to the city, to symbolize her union with the people, and to give the city elite an opportunity to offer support and counsel. Elizabeth was a skilled horsewoman, perfectly capable of riding from the Tower of London to Westminster, as her father, brother, and previous male monarchs had done. But gender trumped sovereignty. Elizabeth was carried in a litter, like all previous queens, whether they were queens regnant like her older sister, the recently departed Queen Mary, or queens consort like her mother, Anne Boleyn, Henry VIII's second wife. Wearing her long hair down to symbolize her maidenly chastity, Elizabeth wore Mary's gown of gold tissue, "furred with powdered ermine about the skirts," which had been altered to fit the new queen's slim figure.[4] Following her on horseback was a procession of leading elites from the aristocracy, parliament, and church, all dressed in sumptuous costumes betokening their high status, in the order established by rank and precedent. The parade route from Fenchurch to Eastcheap was lined by guildsmen wearing their livery hoods, rich furs, and red silk ordered by the queen herself. The streets were thronged with shouting, jostling, cheering crowds, the carnivalesque spirit of festivity and rejoicing fueled by wine flowing freely from the city's water fountains.[5] Platforms erected along the route presented historical and biblical scenes containing lessons for the new queen and her subjects. Signs identifying the figures and "tables" (epigrammatic explanations) covered every "void" space behind the tableaux. Poems, posted in both English and Latin, explained the meaning of the tableaux to the queen, the members of the procession, and the commonality. These constituent elements of the royal entry, recreated with great ceremony, artistry, and expense for the coronation of each new king and queen, having evolved since the Middle Ages, took shape in the fifteenth century.

Figure 4. Drawing of Queen Elizabeth in her Coronation Procession from College of Arms manuscript

Preparations for Elizabeth's royal entry and coronation began on November 18, 1558, the day after her sister passed away, when William Cecil wrote a memorandum of tasks that required immediate action, including number "VIII. To appoint commissioners for the coronation; and the day."[6] The two months between Mary's death and Elizabeth's coronation offered barely enough time for the aldermen and guilds to organize a spectacle worthy of the occasion.[7] While artists designed the tableaux, writers generated poems, labels, and speeches explaining the pageants' allegorical significance. The city was decked in fresh paint and festooned with banners. Artisans built elaborate arches and multi-tiered stages in the five traditional places: the conduits, or watering cisterns, where London's narrow winding streets opened into city squares large enough to hold masses of spectators. Child actors were selected to recite poems and speeches to the queen. Elizabeth offered her personal support for the pageant in a letter, written and signed in her own hand, directing the master of the queen's revels to provide "such and so much of the said apparel as they shall require for the setting forth of those pageants which be appointed to stand for the show of our City at the time we are to pass through the same towards our coronation."[8]

Although the constituent elements of the royal entry were bound by tradition, the content of each pageant represented the historical moment, especially the challenges facing the young queen and her new government. With a battered economy and depleted government coffers, the country was reeling from the violent upheavals of Mary's Roman Catholic reign. The widespread excitement about the restoration of a reformed Church of England couldn't entirely conceal the sobering fact that many were still committed to the old faith. Ireland, Scotland, and France posed immediate military concerns. Catholic powers in Spain, the Holy Roman Empire, and the Papal See presented an ongoing threat of war. Lingering questions about Elizabeth's legitimacy only exacerbated the anxiety that many felt about the prospect of another female monarch, especially one as young and inexperienced as Elizabeth.[9]

These social, political, and economic pressures could be evaded but not completely suppressed by the spirit of festivity, optimism, and rejoicing that the pre-coronation procession was designed to promote.[10] The first tableau showed the new queen emerging triumphantly from an embattled past. A "gorgeous and sumptuous arch" extended from one side of the street to the other, containing various battlements and "three several stages in degrees." On the lowest stage Henry VII and "Elizabeth his wife" were represented holding the red and white roses of the houses of Lancaster and York, "royally crowned and decently apparelled as appertaineth to princes, with scepters in their hands."[11] The two rose branches joined and led to the second stage where Henry VIII appeared with Anne Boleyn. Anne's own pre-coronation procession through the streets of London had celebrated her as the mother of England's next king: "*when* thou shalt bear a new son of the King's blood, there shall be a golden world unto thy people!"[12] But Anne failed to fulfill her sole obligation as queen—to produce a male heir; she was accused of adultery and executed for treason so that Henry could try again. Elizabeth, who made her own initial entry into London in her mother's visibly pregnant belly, was declared illegitimate and barred from the succession, only to be reinstated by a subsequent act of parliament. This recent history hung thick in the air as Elizabeth made her royal entry into London.

To quell doubts about Elizabeth's legitimacy, the first tableau restored Anne to her position as "wife to the said king Henry the eighth and mother to our most sovereign Lady Queen Elizabeth that now is." Seated next to Henry VIII, Anne was represented, like all the other royal figures, "with sceptres and diadems and other furniture due to the estate of a king and queen." On the uppermost level of the tableau there was "set one representing the Queen's most excellent Majesty Elizabeth now our most dread sovereign Lady."[13] Elizabeth's "dread" (meaning, *revered or held in awe*) position atop this monarchical pyramid proclaimed—and defended—her right to the throne.

In the introduction to her invaluable edition *The Queen's Majesty's Passage & Related Documents*, Germaine Warkentin presents Elizabeth in her familiar role as the Virgin Queen and contends that Elizabeth must have intervened to prevent the pageant-makers from mentioning her marriage, but this is implausible on three counts. First, Elizabeth had not abjured marriage when she ascended the throne. Second, Elizabeth could not have been actively involved in planning the pageants because as her chariot approached each successive stage, she asked to be told what the next pageant represented. She clearly had no idea what to expect, for she did not even know that the presentation of the Bible was part of the plan.[14] Third, the implicit but overarching subject of the first tableau was indeed Elizabeth's marriage.

The three-stage construction—with the solitary figure of the new queen placed visibly alone on top of the two fruitful, married couples— depicted by a symbolic absence Elizabeth's eagerly awaited marriage, which would perpetuate the Tudor dynasty and provide an heir. The tableau sought to quell fears of political unrest—fears that the lack of a clear succession might encourage Catholic powers abroad and Catholic sympathizers at home to plot against the queen. The explanatory poem, displayed in English and Latin for the assembled multitude and recited to the queen to "open the meaning of the pageant," emphasized the marriage rings displayed prominently on the hands of "Henry VII and Queen Elizabeth his mate, / By ring of marriage as man and wife unite." To make the symbolic significance even clearer, the printed text notes that "these personages were so set that the one of them joined hands with the other, with the ring of matrimony perceived on the finger."[15] The choice of the word "perceived" declares that the symbolic significance of the marriage ring was carefully planned by the pageant's creators and reiterated by the printed text so that it would be noted by the populace.

This first historical tableau "was grounded upon the Queen's Majesty's name." By blazoning the connection between the two Elizabeths, the tableau implied that *this* Elizabeth should emulate her queenly predecessor and namesake by making a marriage and producing an heir who would once again bring unity and peace to a country torn by civil strife. Much as the previous Elizabeth's matrimonial union established the Tudor dynasty, ending the Wars of the Roses between the houses of York and Lancaster, Elizabeth's own eagerly anticipated marriage would, it was hoped, preserve the Tudor dynasty and end the long painful conflict between England's Catholics and Protestants: "So now that jar shall stint, and quietness increase, / We trust, O noble Queen, thou wilt be cause alone."[16] The lines allude to the recently deceased Queen Mary who is not mentioned by the pageant and who had been buried without a monument in what John King describes as "an act of dynastic erasure."[17] Mary's Roman Catholic faith and childless marriage to the Catholic King Philip II of Spain had created civil discord as frightful to many Londoners in 1559 as the War of the Roses had been to the English in days past.

The printed text glorifies Elizabeth's popularity, preempting any other reaction: "on either side there was nothing but gladness, nothing but prayer, nothing but comfort." The theme of "unity" signified the country's unified support for its new queen and denied that any of the rowdy onlookers could have felt anything but complete love and devotion to their new queen: "the whole people gave a great shout, wishing with one assent as the child had said."[18] Yet another meaning of "unity" was matrimonial union, which transformed two separate souls into one. The first tableau implies that the new queen's eagerly anticipated matrimonial union will bring peace and stability to a commonwealth torn apart by religious and political dissension. Thus the pre-coronation procession sets the stage for the discussion of the queen's marriage that would dominate the first half of the reign.

Elizabeth Speaks Out

The pageant's idealizing, allegorical view of the world hearkens back to the medieval origins of the royal entry, where morality plays presented religious allegories on wagons that moved through the city. In Elizabeth's pre-coronation procession the signs, sayings, poems, and speeches purport to open the meaning of the tableau—a meaning simple enough for the "child, which at the Queen's Majesty's coming declared unto her the whole meaning of the said pageant."[19] Although the pageant-makers sought to enforce a one-to-one correspondence between representation and meaning, an astute observer would surely have noticed what Elizabeth herself could not help but observe: that the repeated protestations of "unity" could not displace the disparate, contradictory forces, the fears of civil unrest, and the threat of Elizabeth's enemies—all factors that continued to disturb the calm surface.

"The noise [was so] great by reason of the press of people" that Elizabeth "could scarce hear the child which did interpret the said pageant."[20] After silencing the rowdy crowd, Elizabeth listened carefully to the explanation provided and then, once she "had understood the meaning thereof, she thanked the city, praised the fairness of the work, and promised that she would do her whole endeavour for the continual preservation of concord, as the pageant did import."[21] In this, her first public speech as queen, Elizabeth graciously thanked the city for its great expenditure of funds and labor and praised the artists and artisans who designed and constructed the pageant. Then she proceeded to offer her own more complicated counter-explanation of the story the tableau told: she knew all too well that the protestations of "unity" were as fleeting as the tableaux themselves, which would be dismantled a few days later. The pageant-makers imagined "unity" as "the end whereat the whole device shot," but Elizabeth knew she would have to "do her whole endeavour for the continual preservation of concord." Whereas "unity" suggests a harmonious oneness of mind, feeling, and purpose, "concord" suggests a state of peace and amity established between *contending* parties or nations. It was all well and good to proclaim that dissension shall cease now that Elizabeth had become queen: "now that jar shall stint." Yet Elizabeth knew it was not that simple, and she thought it was important for her subjects to understand that keeping dissension in check was going to be a "continual" labor that would require her "whole endeavour."

Not content with merely approving and applauding, Elizabeth began to construct her own voice as sovereign. By intervening in the prepared script, she not only demonstrated her readiness to speak in public, despite the ideological pressure on women to remain silent, but also acknowledged that it would require her "whole endeavour" to direct the drama in which she had been given the role of leading lady. The ideological and epistemological move from "the fairness" of the visual display to the *réal politique* of ruling a country torn by religious strife—from idealizing, eternizing language that yielded the "unity" of "full meaning" to "continual" "endeavor" that yielded interpretive dissonance—characterized Elizabeth's speeches and writing from the outset and throughout her reign, much as it informed the enigmatic, multifaceted poetry and drama written by Elizabethans later in the reign. Elizabeth's subjects continued to try to influence her with idealizing allegories and laudatory verse. Yet, as we have already learned from Elizabeth's lyric dialogue with Ralegh, disingenuous, simplistic abstractions were likely to provoke Elizabeth's own, more fraught sense of conflict and complication.[22] About her all-important marital plans, Elizabeth remained strategically silent. She could not even begin to explain the complexities *that* would entail.

In addition to responding to the pageants' formal recitations, Elizabeth paused again and again to engage in personal conversations with individual bystanders:

> For in all her passage she did not only show her most gracious love toward the people in general, but also privately. If the baser personages had either offered her Grace any flowers or such like as a signification of their good will, or moved to her any suit, she most gently, to the common rejoicing of

all the lookers on, and private comfort of the party, stayed her chariot and heard their requests.[23]

Elizabeth's interactions with the crowd displayed her readiness to listen and respond to her people's needs and desires. Even though she could not frequent the taverns of Eastcheap, drinking with every tinker in his own language like Shakespeare's Prince Hal, she went out of her way to demonstrate that she could talk to the common people in their language.

Like a modern political candidate, Elizabeth worked the crowd, listening attentively to the folks who approached to express their support and to seek favors. Like a commanding stage actress, Elizabeth used body language to signal even more than her few brief words could convey:

> Here was noted in the Quene's Majesty's countenance, during the time that the child spoke, besides a perpetual attentiveness in her face, a marvelous change in look, as the child's words touched either her person or the people's tongues and hearts. So that she with rejoicing visage did evidently declare that the words took no less place in her mind than they were most heartily pronounced by the child, as from all the hearts of her most hearty citizens.[24]

The pamphlet's overly "hearty" reassurances—"heartily pronounced by the child, as from all the hearts of her most hearty citizens"—betray what they simultaneously strive to suppress: the possibility that visual display might be a mere semblance, as Hamlet scathingly points out: "Seems, madam? nay, it is, I know not 'seems' /.../ For they are actions that a man might play / But I have that within which passes show" (1.2.76–85).[25] The pre-coronation procession posits a much simpler hermeneutic universe: Elizabeth's "rejoicing visage" is presented as direct evidence of what was taking "place in her mind." The syntax dissolves boundaries between pageant and audience, queen and people, equating Elizabeth's "person" with "the people's tongues and hearts," interpreting words "most heartily pronounced by the child, as from all the hearts of her most hearty citizens," creating a seamless unity of "tongues and hearts," inward feelings, outer appearances, and spoken words. If there were any Iagos in the crowd, secretly thinking, "not I for love and duty, / But seeming so, for my peculiar end... I am not what I am" (*Othello* 1.1.59–60, 65), the pageant writers did not acknowledge them.

The reciprocal expression of love between monarch and subjects was a conventional aspect of royal entries.[26] Yet, the printed text suggests that Elizabeth's use of the conventional male rhetoric of love was somehow wondrous or extraordinary: "The people again were wonderfully ravished with the loving answers and gestures of their princess... This her Grace's loving behaviour, preconceived in the people's heads upon these considerations, was then thoroughly confirmed, and implanted a wonderful hope in them touching her worthy government in the rest of her reign."[27] Queen Mary, Elizabeth's sister and predecessor, avoided the conventional rhetoric of love, since Renaissance women were not supposed to express desire in public. By contrast, Elizabeth boldly broke with the gender ideology of the day when she "ravished" her subjects with her "loving answers and gestures." Whereas the pageant cast Elizabeth as the conventional female, beloved and adored with "blessing tongues" and "true hearts, which love thee from their root,"[28] Elizabeth's own authoritative bearing and powerfully pithy speech represented herself as an open-hearted, solicitous lover of her people, not an adored Petrarchan lady hiding behind a veil, but a precursor of Shakespeare's vocal, impassioned heroines—Rosalind "in a more coming-on disposition" (*As You Like It* 4.1.112–13).

Elizabeth chose to give her most important speech at the upper end of Cheapside, the great square that housed the city's central market. The city fathers who were not already in the procession had gathered there to watch as the Recorder presented her with one thousand gold marks, symbolizing the city's support of their new queen and reminding her that her impoverished government coffers would need the city's wealth, even as the city merchants would need the crown's licenses and monopolies to sell their merchandise abroad. After listening to the Recorder's brief remarks, Elizabeth responded

> marvellously pithily, and so pithily that the standers by, as they embraced entirely her gracious answer, so they marvelled at the couching thereof, which was in words truly reported these: 'I thank my lord mayor, his brethren, and you all. And whereas your request is that I should continue your good lady and Queen, be ye ensured that I will be as good unto you as ever Queen was to her people. No will in me can lack, neither do I trust shall there lack any power. And persuade yourselves that for the safety and quietness of you all, I will not spare, if need be, to spend my blood. God thank you all.[29]

Elizabeth began by graciously thanking the mayor and his brethren. She proceeded to acknowledge the Recorder's words: "your request is that I should continue your good lady and Queen."[30] So be it. If the city wished her to play the good lady, she would be their lady, both a woman who was the object of chivalrous attention, a mistress, a lady-love, and a woman to whom homage and subservience were due. At the same time, however, Elizabeth seized the moment to offer a pointed critique and pithy corrective to the subtle innuendo, repeated a number of times in the course of the procession, that she would be able to rise above her female sex and protect her country from its enemies only if she received extraordinary aid from God.

Before setting out on the pre-coronation procession, Elizabeth had kneeled in prayer to thank God for protecting her from her enemies, a scene that the printed account saves for its triumphant finale. Similarly, in her first parliamentary speech Elizabeth would invoke divine guidance as a way of silencing and disarming her opponents. But here, at the moment when the most important, powerful men from the aristocracy, the church, the parliament, the military, and the city had gathered together to hear her response to the city's gift, she spoke on her own authority, expressing her courageous spirit without invoking God's support.

Elizabeth's responses to the pageant were clearly shaped by economic, political, and ideological forces that defined her as a "good lady and Queen." At the same time, however, her brave words redefined what society could expect of her. Much as the prospect of marriage highlighted the vulnerabilities caused by her female sex, so too did her monarchical responsibility to protect the country from its enemies and to serve as England's supreme military commander. (Even today, women are not accorded an equal right to lead America's fighting forces.) Renaissance women did not receive training in martial arts or military strategy.[31] Thus, in *Twelfth Night* the cross-dressed Viola impresses Olivia with her bold bearing and verbal prowess only to dissolve at the prospect of a duel with the weak-kneed, pathetic Andrew Aguecheek. Similarly, in *Much Ado about Nothing* the independent, fiery Beatrice cannot challenge Claudio to a duel for defaming and belying her cousin. Because she is a woman, she is forced to enlist Benedick to serve as her proxy. "O that I were a man," she complains, "I cannot be a man with wishing" (4.1. 317, 322–23). Like Viola and Beatrice, when it came to war and fighting Elizabeth was at a distinct disadvantage. Knowing this, Elizabeth used the pre-coronation procession to make it very clear that she would be not only as gracious a "lady" and "as good unto you as ever Queen was to her people," but also as courageous as any male monarch, "if need be, to spend my blood."

The pre-coronation procession was Elizabeth's first public performance as monarch, and by all accounts she performed brilliantly. Apparently, acting came naturally to her, though she seemed and probably was genuinely moved by the spontaneous outpouring of love and support. Perhaps, she had decided in advance what she wanted to say and how she would present herself; nevertheless, she created the impression of spontaneity by deftly responding to particular details of the pageant and seizing the moment to intervene. By interrupting the prepared script to express her spontaneous love and addressing the assembled dignitaries in "so prince-like a voice," Elizabeth demonstrated that she would be "so worthy a sovereign"—the very embodiment of power and authority traditionally reserved for men.

Elizabeth played a much more active role in the pre-coronation procession than either her Tudor predecessors or her Stuart successors. Edward was a mere child, captivated by the jugglers but uninterested in the allegorical significance of the tableaux. Mary kept her distance from the crowd[32] and avoided conventional monarchical expressions of love.[33] Elizabeth's successor, James I, showed little interest in the pageantry or the populace and could barely be induced to listen to the official speeches.[34] By contrast, Elizabeth's active engagement with the procession demonstrated a love of spectacle that made her reign the highpoint of English pageantry, while her continual questions about what to expect from each successive tableau and her concerted efforts to hush the crowd so that she could hear and respond to the recitations also demonstrated her eagerness to understand and shape the pageant's meaning. Her gracious praise for "the fineness" of the tableaux expressed her appreciation for the writers, artists, and artisans who created the magnificent spectacle. Her acknowledgment of the city's generosity showed her desire to establish good relations with the city's wealthy merchants. Her silence about the tableau representing "Deborah with her estates, consulting for the good government of Israel"[35]—where the pageant-makers' didactic purposes were most evident—demonstrated that although she would listen to the counsel offered her, she would also keep her own counsel.[36] Above all, her tactful but pointed critique of the role the pageant assigned her shows that she would exercise her regal authority as she saw fit. If her subjects hoped to counsel and sway her through the masques, pageants, and didactic verses they constructed for her and about her, they could expect her to respond with a skeptical critique that raised complications and objections they may have preferred not to acknowledge.

The Power of Print

The pre-coronation procession used the power of theater to sway the hearts and minds of a live audience, though, unlike the dramas mounted at Elizabethan playhouses, it was performed only once.[37] Three days after the procession, the Court of Aldermen ordered the stages and tableaux to be "taken down with speed," and the materials stored to be used "at another time."[38] Pageants were by their very nature as fleeting as English sunshine. Royal entries had been celebrated for centuries, but Elizabeth's was the first to be reprised at length, in detail, in print.

The immediate and persistent popularity of the printed text, *The Quene's Majestie's Passage,* provided a prototype for Elizabethan public relations. Elizabeth's was the first English monarchy to recognize that the relatively new technology of print offered a powerful means of publicity. In a world without television, newspapers, newsmagazines, or breaking news online, printed pamphlets provided information that was not otherwise available. Many Elizabethans could not attend the pre-coronation procession because they were far away, or old, or sick, or working. Even the vast numbers of people who turned out for the festivities could observe only a small part of the spectacle. The "commonality" jamming the streets and city squares and the guildsmen lining the route from Fenchurch to Eastcheap would have had at most an obstructed view of one tableau and a glimpse of the queen. The elite who merited a place in the procession would have seen only part of the tableaux as they rode by; they could not have observed the queen's countenance or overheard her comments, unless they had one of the few highly coveted positions next to Elizabeth. *The Quene's Majestie's Passage* enabled Elizabethans who were literate, or who knew someone who was, to join the queen as she moved from station to station—to see what they had not seen and to overhear what they had not heard.

The narrative was written by Richard Mulcaster, a schoolmaster and supporter of the reformed church, who would soon become a member of the first Elizabethan parliament. Mulcaster was paid by the Court of Aldermen, which oversaw and financed public festivals mounted by the city. The court record from March 4, 1559, includes the following: "Item, it was ordered and agreed by the Court here this day that the Chamberlain shall give unto Richard Mulcaster for his reward for making of the book containing and declaring the histories set forth in and by the City's pageants at the time of the Queen's highness coming through the City to her coronation forty shillings, which book was given unto the Queen's grace."[39] *The Quene's Majestie's Passage* is often described as propaganda, but was it propaganda for the city of London or the crown?[40] Mulcaster was paid by the city, but there are no documents telling us whether the publication of his "history" was initiated or reviewed by Elizabeth or her advisors. Relations between the city and the court pervade and complicate the text. Mulcaster's account not only advertises the great effort and expenses the city made in mounting the pageants and decking the route but also offers a laudatory account of the queen.

The Quene's Majestie's Passage provides a case study in the complex network of forces that underlies bids for patronage, preferment, and political influence in Elizabethan England. First of all, Mulcaster needed to please the city elite who hired him to memorialize the event through the lavish display they funded and the extraordinary efforts they orchestrated on Elizabeth's and their own behalf. Indeed, most of the narrative does exactly what Mulcaster was commissioned and paid to do: "for making of the book containing and declaring the histories set forth in and by the City's pageants at the time of the Queen's highness coming through the City to her coronation."[41] The mayor, aldermen, and leaders of the guilds wanted the new queen to acknowledge her debt to them, and to realize that she would continue to depend on their financial support. In return, they expected her to seek their counsel and to enhance their profits by granting monopolies and licenses to sell their goods. Many, though not all of them, also wanted Mulcaster to advance their Protestant agenda, as the gift of the Bible, the tableau representing Deborah receiving "counsel," and the religious thrust of the conclusion indicate.[42] As one of the three people responsible for creating the pageantry, Mulcaster was perfectly positioned to "open the meaning" of the tableaux.[43] The didactic verses he wrote for the tableaux explicate the visual symbolism. The narrative history he wrote for publication provides a more extensive prose commentary designed to explain at greater length what his original verses stated more tersely and symbolically.

At the same time, however, Mulcaster also needed to please the queen herself, for she was undoubtedly his most important audience. Indeed, his "reward for making the book" was paid only after the "book was given unto the Queen's grace," that is, after Elizabeth had received and approved or at least not rejected his account of her words and actions. A "book" could refer to any written document, so Elizabeth may have been given a manuscript to read before the final draft went to the press, although, given the rush to print only nine days after the procession, that would have been possible only if she gave it a high priority. Yet, even if Elizabeth was presented with the book only after it appeared in print, Mulcaster surely wrote it with her reaction in mind.

One of Mulcaster's primary goals was "to influence public opinion" and "to convince Englishmen that Elizabeth was a worthy successor of her father"; however, the prose narrative was also Mulcaster's bid for patronage and professional advancement.[44] Consequently, it not only blazoned the city's pageants and extolled the queen's speech and bearing but also memorialized and explicated the poems Mulcaster himself wrote for the pageant.[45] Mulcaster had a powerful incentive to provide an idealized account of what transpired, but he would have undermined his credibility and his prospects if he glaringly misrepresented either "the histories set forth in and by the City's pageants"[46] or the queen's speeches. As he was himself all too aware, there were countless eyewitnesses ready to affirm or discredit his account. By constantly pointing out Elizabeth's eagerness to understand the meaning of the tableaux and praising her oratorical skills, Mulcaster portrayed her as an effective leader and intellectual. If his account pleased the queen, and if his skill as poet, pageant writer, and reporter/historian impressed his readers, then aspiring Elizabethans who were themselves seeking to please the queen and hoping to win preferment at court or a position in the government, might hire him to write speeches, pageants, and encomiastic verses for them. To be sure, Mulcaster's name does not appear on the title page, but his authorship was a matter of public record, and anyone prominent enough to seek his services could easily have learned his identity. Indeed, thanks largely to the success of *The Quene's Majestie's Passage*, "Mulcaster enjoyed a primacy among the pageant-makers in the Elizabethan age."[47] In 1561 and 1568, the Merchant Taylor's Company hired him to write the Lord Mayor's pageants, and in 1575 Elizabeth's favorite courtier, Robert Dudley, hired Mulcaster to help write the Kenilworth pageants.

Mulcaster knew all about the pageants and texts that had been constructed and written in advance; however, he had extremely limited first-hand information about what Elizabeth herself said and did since a mere schoolmaster would not have merited a position alongside her in the procession. To establish his credibility, Mulcaster repeatedly mentions that his account was based on eyewitness testimony. Like any good reporter, he seems to have spoken to a number of people. Yet he probably received most of his information from someone such as William Cecil who was close enough to observe Elizabeth's responses and politically astute enough to realize that a published account of her brave speech and princely bearing could fortify her image and establish her authority. Mulcaster probably positioned himself at upper Cheapside where the city elite gathered to present Elizabeth with their gift of a thousand gold marks, for he provides the most direct and detailed quotation of the speech Elizabeth gave there, "which was in words truly reported these."[48]

Even though Mulcaster himself could have observed Elizabeth at only one place along the route, he made a point of describing her majesty's bearing, words, and actions at each station along the way. Lavishing attention on her interactions with the common people, his narrative declared that her remarkable readiness to intervene transformed the elaborately staged pageants and formal verse into an intimate, spontaneous dialogue between a loving monarch and her loving people. He also reported and explicated her most important speeches, highlighting the places where her words corrected or complicated the explications provided by the pageant itself.[49] Thus Mulcaster made every effort to show Elizabeth that he grasped and appreciated the image that she was trying to construct of herself as queen. To compensate for devoting so much space to the tableaux, Mulcaster framed his narrative with an introduction that highlighted Elizabeth's words and actions: "So that if a man should well say, he could not better term the city of London at that time than a stage wherein was showed the wonderful spectacle of a noble hearted princess toward her most loving people, and the people's exceeding comfort in beholding so worthy a sovereign and hearing so princelike a voice."[50] His conclusion also reiterated the powerful impact of her words: "The answer which her Grace made unto Master Recorder of London, as the hearers know it to be true, and with melting hearts heard the same, so may the reader thereof conceive what kind of stomach and courage pronounced the same."[51]

Because so much of the text describes the tableaux and prepared texts, recent scholars have concluded that Elizabeth played a minor and passive role in a drama that was scripted for her. Yet her performance left her contemporaries with a very different impression. After her death, when James ascended the throne, the text was reprinted with a new title page that eternized the powerful impact of Elizabeth's own speeches: *The Royall Passage of her Majesty from the Tower of London to her Pallace of White-hall, with all the Speaches and Devices, both of the Pageants and otherwise, together with Her Majesties severall Answers, and most pleasing Speaches to them all.*[52] So loving a queen, and so princelike a voice!

Figure 5. Portrait of Elizabeth I, The Clopton Portrait c. 1558

CHAPTER 4

EARLY DAYS: PARLIAMENTARY SPEECH (1559) AND THE WOODSTOCK EPIGRAMS

She made me a great discourse of the friendship that her people bore her, telling me that it was unbelievable, and how she loved them no less than they her, and she would die rather than see any diminution on the one part or the other. I replied that I was well informed on that score.[1]

The Husband This Woman May Take

When Elizabeth was crowned in 1559, there were serious doubts about whether, as a woman, she had the capability to rule the country herself. Her status as an unmarried woman had dominated discourse from court gossip and diplomatic dispatches to parliamentary debate. "The more I think over this business, the more certain I am that everything depends upon the husband this woman may take," the Spanish ambassador reported. Everyone assumed that a suitable match would soon be arranged—everyone, that is, except Elizabeth herself.[2]

Elizabeth convened parliament only three times during the first decade of her reign, in 1559, 1563, and 1566, and each time the principal state business was the queen's marriage. The first parliament was required to authorize the new government. Elizabeth convened the 1563 and 1566 parliaments because she needed them to authorize much needed subsidies, or financial backing. Parliament seized all three occasions to petition the queen to marry forthwith. In so doing, Elizabeth's government was trying to fulfill its fundamental patriarchal responsibility—to preserve the social order by securing a husband for the queen and an heir to the crown. Elizabeth had strong incentives to acquiesce, not only to get parliament to grant a subsidy but also to produce a strategic foreign alliance and to settle the succession for the present and future stability of the country. But instead of bowing to parliamentary pressure, Elizabeth bristled and hedged and then proceeded to write some of the most politically consequential speeches of the reign. They show her refining and developing her rhetorical skills to establish her political power.[3] Her goals were threefold: first, to decide for herself whether or not she would marry; second, to choose the man she would marry, if she decided to marry; third, to rule the country herself, whether or not she chose to marry. It is difficult to imagine and impossible to overstate just how radical those demands were because monarchical marriages were the primary means of consolidating international alliances and because the reigning patriarchal ideology subordinated women to men. Elizabeth was expected to marry for the good of the country and, as Philip II of Spain put it, to "relieve her of those labours which are only fit for men."[4]

Supreme Head

The first major confrontation between the queen and parliament concerned the sensitive and highly symbolic question of her title. Should she be named the "Supreme Head of the Church"? The title was claimed by Elizabeth's father, Henry VIII, when he broke from Rome to marry her mother, Anne Boleyn. The issue had not arisen during Mary's reign because the Pope once again became the supreme head of the English church. Protestant members of parliament joined forces with the bishops and refused to make Elizabeth the head, lest, that make them the feet. Archbishop Heath gave a detailed account of why Elizabeth as a woman could not stand in Christ's stead, could not preach, could not administer sacraments, and thus could not be named Supreme Head of the Church.[5] According to the traditional patriarchal analogy, Christ ruled over the church as the monarch ruled over his people and as the husband ruled over his wife. Indeed, as John Knox explains, the biblical metaphor of the head and feet was a synecdoche for the entire patriarchal system of government:

> for the man is heade to the woman, and Christ is heade to the congregation, and he is the saviour of the bodie: but the congregation is subject to Christ, even so oght women to be to their husbandes in all thinges. He procedeth further saying: women are commanded to be subject to men by the lawe of nature...as Christ is the head of the churche, so is man of the woman....all woman is commanded, to serve, to be in humilitie and subjection....the head shuld not folowe the feet.[6]

To those Elizabethans who agreed with Knox, Mary's disturbing reign provided proof that a woman should never be given power over men. Yet, Elizabeth was Henry's only remaining child, and she was England's best hope for preserving the social order and restoring the reformed church. The bishops and parliament had no choice but to accept Elizabeth's reign, but they refused to concede her power over the church.

After protracted discussion a compromise was reached: Elizabeth was named governor, which was neither as provocative to her opponents as "head" nor as demeaning to Elizabeth herself as the previous proposal, "governess."[7] Elizabeth concurred, the Spanish ambassador reported, and "only left open for consideration the clause where she is to take the title of head of the Church and for the present only assumes the style of 'Governor.' This is said to have been done on the ground that she may marry and her husband might then take the title."[8] If parliament hoped that Elizabeth would soon marry and resolve the issue along with the other problems posed by her female reign, Elizabeth hoped to reclaim the title. "It is only a question of words as 'governor' and 'head' after all mean the same thing," the Spanish ambassador concluded quite sensibly but a bit naively, since the distinction struck at the heart of Elizabeth's power to rule.[9] To assuage their discomfiting subordination to a woman, parliament used the symbolic and ideological power of words. That discursive battleground suited the new queen perfectly.

To officially open parliament on January 25, Lord Keeper Nicholas Bacon gave the two traditional speeches on the monarch's behalf. Elizabeth seized this opportunity to assert her authority: "Now her Majestie having this authoritie in her as head of the pollitique bodye of this realme..."[10] The lord keeper's speeches are filled with the requisite, tradition-bound formalities, but they nonetheless reveal a great deal about the complexities created by Elizabeth's position as female monarch. It was the lord keeper's responsibility to speak for the new monarch; therefore, Elizabeth's concerns and expectations are still visible beneath his formal rhetoric. Significantly, his first speech began by asserting her royal prerogative and declaring that the issues facing the government could not be "reformed without Parliamente."

The conventional format and elaborate, official rhetoric masked an important underlying, unresolved question. Was parliament's power an inherent right claimed by virtue of its historic inheritance, or was it a conditional right granted by the monarch as long as parliament acted as the monarch saw fit? This question was heatedly debated throughout Elizabeth's reign and beyond and is still actively disputed by modern studies of parliamentary history.

Much as Elizabeth used her words to insert her views into the traditional pre-coronation procession, here too she used the lord keeper's traditional speeches to assert her right to grant the members of parliament the power they sought—as long as they behaved as she saw fit. Thus, the lord keeper went on to explain, Elizabeth had brought them together because she "meaneth not at this time to make any resolucion in any matter of weight before it shalbe by you sufficiently and fully debated, examined and considered." Thus Elizabeth promised the members of parliament that she would consult them when important decisions needed to be made; however, the qualifier "at this tyme" contains a pointed warning that she would continue to bring important matters to parliament only if they fully and readily acknowledged her authority now.

By observing that he himself did not know what was the best course of action, the lord keeper pointedly reminded the more aggressive members of parliament that they too did not necessarily know the best course for Elizabeth or her newly formed government to follow. Elizabeth asked each member of parliament to put aside his "private affection" and to embrace the common good. In exchange, she promised that she would do only what was "just and acceptable in Gode's sight." Thus, the lord keeper reminded parliament that Elizabeth's imperial monarchy rested upon the divine right of kings. Her power was an extension of God's will, and it was God who chose to make her, though a woman, his divine representative on earth: "God of his devine power and ordynance hath brought the imperiall crowne of this realme to a princesse." Therefore, she trusted that there was nothing that she could ask of them, "her loving subjects," that they would not willingly grant of their own freewill:

> so greate is the trust and confidence that she reposeth in them and the love and affection that her Highnes beareth towardes them, nothing at all doubting but that they will soe lovingly, carefully and prudentlie wey and consider this great and weightie matter that such provision shall out of hande be taken therein as her Highnes shalbe preserved in all honor and royall dignitie, and you and the rest of her loving subjectes in common quiette and suertie.[11]

Through the lord keeper's traditional opening speech Elizabeth extended to parliament the amorous dialogue she introduced so dramatically and effectively during the coronation procession. Her father had also used the rhetoric of reciprocal love, but Elizabeth's expression of love for parliament and her expectation of their answering love were more fraught than her father's had been, not only because the language of love was traditional male discourse but also because the preceding debate over her title made it impossible to forget that she was "a princesse" cast in the traditional male role of monarch.

As a woman, her authority would be questioned at every turn. Therefore, parliament needed to be all the more "careful"—and the word is repeated a number of times—to ensure and preserve her "honor and royall dignitie." Although the official rhetoric sounds *pro forma*, there was actually a "great and weightie matter" at stake, as the lord keeper's gendered epithets make clear: "our soveraigne Ladye and Mistris" could become "so princely a patronesse" only if her male subjects ratified and fully supported her female power. The concerns were real. A failure to respect her "honor and royall dignitie" would be disastrous, not only for Elizabeth and individual members of parliament but for the country as a whole.[12]

Eschewing the Danger

The second major topic of parliamentary debate was the queen's marriage, which once again brought her female sex to the fore. The traditional patriarchal view of government and society rested on the analogy between the household and the state. The monarch derived his power from the father's authority over his family, as passed down from Adam to the biblical patriarchs. Robert Filmer's *Patriarcha* is the classic exposition of the theory:

> To confirm this Natural Right of *Regal* Power, we find in the *Decalogue*, That the Law which enjoyns Obedience to Kings, is delivered in the terms of *Honour thy Father*, as if all power were originally in the Father.... If we

compare the Natural Rights of a Father with those of a King, we find them all one, without any difference at all, but only in the Latitude or Extent of them: as the Father over one Family, so the King as Father over many Families extends his care to preserve, feed, cloth, instruct and defend the whole Commonwealth. His War, his Peace, his Courts of Justice, and all his Acts of Sovereignty tend only to preserve and distribute to every subordinate and inferiour Father, and to their Children, their Rights and Privileges; so that all the Duties of a King are summed up in an Universal Fatherly Care of his People.[13]

Not surprisingly, Filmer's treatise was published after Elizabeth's death, when the restoration of male monarchy gave the ancient analogy a renewed sense of inevitability. A female monarch threw the whole system into disarray. If the king ruled over his subjects as a man ruled over his wife and children, how could a woman rule over her male subjects? And what would happen if the monarch became a married woman? On one hand, if her husband ruled over her in marriage, how could she rule over her male subjects? On the other hand, if she ruled over her husband, what then? As John Knox put it, the "empire of women is the subversion of good ordre equitie and justice."

Elizabeth's debut speech was delivered by the speaker on February 10, 1559. She was twenty-five years old. She had been exiled from court and incarcerated for much of her sister Mary's reign. Perhaps Elizabeth felt unprepared to address that venerable body, or perhaps her advisors discouraged her from speaking in deference to the reigning ideology that God commanded women not to speak in public. God subjected woman to one man, Knox explained, and God "will never permit her to reigne over manie. Seing he hath commanded her to heare, and obey one, he will not suffre that she speake, and with usurped authoritie command realmes and nations."[14] Even though Elizabeth did not rise to address parliament in her own voice, she wrote the speech herself, and her words reverberated through the chambers of government, asserting her right to "command realmes and nations."

Since Elizabeth's speech was a reply to the House of Commons' marriage petition, to some extent she was on the defensive, responding to a situation she did not create and did not relish. At moments, she sounded young and hesitant; at other times, she sounded imperial and authoritative. Her words strove to establish her prerogative, even as she strained to avow what could not be said as forcefully or openly as she might have liked. The result was a remarkable combination of unshakable determination and profound uncertainty. Rather than trying to suppress the challenges facing her, Elizabeth chose to confront the gap between her youthful inexperience and the regal authority she needed to establish: "my youth and words may seem to some hardly to agree together."[15] By acknowledging that "some" members of parliament doubted her authority, Elizabeth invited those who *were* ready to recognize her will, despite her age and sex, to step forward and declare their support. When she then paused to address the lord treasurer directly, she introduced a method of governance that would characterize her reign: direct personal communication with advisors chosen by her for their loyalty to her.[16]

The members of parliament knew her history, but she nonetheless took the opportunity to recount the dangers she had passed in order to demonstrate her courage and eloquence, much as Othello does when he tells the Senate his story "of hair-breadth scapes i' th' imminent deadly breach, / Of being taken by the insolent foe / And sold to slavery, of my redemption thence / And portance in my travel's history" (1.3.136–39).[17] Elizabeth began by reminding parliament that she had already successfully evaded a number of previous marriages that had been proposed out of political expediency. Elizabeth represented the earlier attempts to force her into marriage as one of the greatest dangers confronting her when she was a beleaguered princess:

> [I]f either ambition of high estate offered to me in marriage by the pleasure and appointment of my prince (whereof I have some records in this presence, as you our lord treasurer well know); or if the eschewing of the danger of mine enemies; or the avoiding of the peril of death, whose messenger or rather continual watchman, the prince's indignation, was not little time daily before mine eyes, by whose means although I know or justly may suspect, yet will not now utter. (CW 56–57)

The epigrammatic brevity gives the account a weight that exceeds its length. Elizabeth invites parliament to empathize with her suffering and to share her point of view. By equating arranged marriage with "the danger of mine enemies," "the prince's indignation," and "the peril of death," Elizabeth highlighted the depth of her aversion, not to marriage itself, but to any attempt to subordinate her will through marriage. Having evaded so many perils when she was a powerless princess through her discriminating choice of words, Elizabeth was not about to be forced into marriage by remaining silent now that she was the queen.

Elizabeth does not detail her grievances against her sister Mary since she thought the dead should be allowed to rest in peace. Nonetheless, her cryptic reference to "the prince's indignation" reminded parliament of her own imprisonment in the Tower of London and her ensuing house arrest. At the same time, by referring to Mary as "the prince" rather than the princess, Elizabeth alluded to the statute passed during Mary's reign that granted all monarchs, whether male or female, the right to rule in "the name of King": "the kingly or regal office of the realm, and all dignities, prerogative royal, power, preeminences, privileges, authorities, and jurisdictions thereunto annexed, united, or belonging, being invested either in male or female, are and be and ought to be as fully, wholly, absolutely, and entirely deemed, judged, accepted, invested, and taken in the one as in the other."[18]

While asserting her independence from parliament's control, Elizabeth was also posing another related question: were those who were now trying to force her into marriage the same men who had incited her sister's anger against her? Elizabeth wanted her opponents to know that she knew or at least suspected who they were ("by whose means although I know or justly may suspect, yet will not now utter"), and that she would take steps to prevent them from stirring up further trouble should that prove necessary. At the same time, she did not want to provoke their hostility by attacking them directly. The evasive diction and ambiguous syntax were the residue of her immediate past when anything she said could have been used against her.

Much Suspected by Me

Elizabeth had learned the value of enigmatic, elusive language during her perilously insecure younger years, when she was placed under house arrest at Woodstock Castle after being accused of supporting Wyatt's plot to prevent Mary's marriage. Confined to a decrepit, drafty old castle and restricted to a small private garden, Elizabeth was refused permission to wander in the park, or to study with her tutor, or to see anyone other than her guard, Sir Bedingfield, without special permission. It was under these conditions that Elizabeth wrote the epigram that she carved with a diamond on a window at Woodstock:

> Much suspected by me,
> Nothing proved can be.
> *Quod* Elizabeth the prisoner
> (CW 46)

This couplet, with a total of eight words and twelve syllables, is about as concise as an epigram can be. The brevity and concision embody the circumscribed role assigned her, the role of prisoner and suspected traitor. The epigram demonstrates how little—and how much—could be made out of a few, carefully chosen words. The terse poetic diction epitomizes what the poem asserts: Elizabeth's enemies were waiting to use her words against her, but they could elicit only what she chose to speak. The epigram asserts Elizabeth's control over her own speech and writing, even as the verbal ambiguity acknowledges that she could not control the meaning that others would place on her words. This fundamental hermeneutical assumption—a foundational principle of modern critical theory—was a central guiding principle of Elizabeth's rhetoric and reign.

The oppressive constraints of Elizabeth's incarceration and the ominous, unresolved charges against her pervade and propel the poem. The passive construction ("Nothing proved can be") captures Elizabeth's situation: as prisoner, she was reduced to an unwelcome yet undeniable position of passivity; her response, her only recourse, was constant vigilance and continued resistance. The first words of the two lines, "Much" and "Nothing," announce that there had been "much" ado about "nothing," and that (although the outcome was not hers to decide) she would continue to do everything she could to ensure that nothing would come of nothing.

The epigram provides only the barest facts because Elizabeth was wary of saying anything that might jeopardize her legal standing. If "by" is taken in the Elizabethan sense of *concerning*, the couplet declared that although much was suspected *about* or *concerning* her, nothing could be proven against her. The poem did not say Elizabeth had *done* nothing, since her opponents would contest that regardless of what she said. Instead, it only said that nothing could be proven—a point she made again and again, both when she was being interrogated and when she wrote to her sister demanding justice and seeking love and compassion. Mary responded coldly to Elizabeth's first letter, and Bedingfield refused to forward her pleas to the Council. Complaining that this made her position worse than that of a common prisoner at Newgate Prison, Elizabeth continued to lobby for permission to write to the queen and the Privy Council because she believed (or at least hoped) that her rhetorical skill would convince them of her innocence.

Elizabeth was well aware that she might be condemned and executed without due cause, but, the poem argued, that would be an injustice, for she was innocent until proven guilty. The epigram acknowledges Elizabeth's vulnerability and powerlessness while demonstrating her courage and strength. That tension gives her words a second, deeper meaning. If "by me" is taken not only as a prepositional phrase, meaning, much is suspected about me, but also as the implied subject of the passive verb "suspected," then the words transform Elizabeth from a passive victim into an agent, telling her accusers that much is also suspected about them "by me." They may have their suspicions about her, but Elizabeth also had her suspicions about them. The two assertions coexist, shifting the position of subject and object, balancing her enemies' interpretation of events against her own quite different interpretation of the situation.

But why engrave the poem on a window? First of all, Elizabeth's access to writing materials was carefully controlled; the Privy Council warned her jailer to prevent her from sending tokens, letters, or messages to her friends and supporters. The window and diamond were there, ready to be used, and Elizabeth was clever enough to take advantage of them. By engraving the poem on the glass, which could easily shatter under pressure but did not, Elizabeth could see herself reflected in the somewhat murky surface of a sixteenth-century window, both a mirror of her innocence and an image of the distortions forced upon her.[19] By using her own diamond ring, one of the few remaining vestiges of her privileged status, as her instrument, Elizabeth could use its strength to combat her vulnerability. The diamond's hard core and sharp edges were far more important in her current situation than its beauty or net worth.

The multifaceted form of the diamond offers an analogy to the interpretive challenge the poem represents, reminding both its author and its potential readers that words have different facets when refracted in different lights or seen from different points of view. The window and diamond were the medium, but they were also the message. Writing the poem enabled Elizabeth to imagine Mary reading the poem and speaking the words quoted above. The materiality of the poem invites Mary and her proxies to adopt Elizabeth's perspective. If the men sent by Mary to interrogate Elizabeth relayed the poem, and if Mary read the poem herself, then she (or they) might be induced to admit, "Nothing proved can be."

The indefinite pronouns, cryptic diction, and ambiguous syntax could be most readily comprehended by viewing the poem and the situation from within, from Elizabeth's vantage point. Viewed from outside, the letters were reversed, so the meaning was less accessible, though not entirely impenetrable, since the text was short enough to be deciphered and remembered by anyone who cared enough to do so. The epigram would have had different meanings to different readers. First of all, it consoled and exhorted Elizabeth herself, reminding her that she needed to use all her wit and vigilance to avoid incriminating herself. Second, it was a message to Mary and her agents, warning them not to confuse their suspicions with legally verifiable proof. Third, it assured Elizabeth's supporters that she was well and reminded them to remain vigilant and circumspect. If they said nothing to incriminate her, the situation (like the writing on the window) could be reversed.

Elizabeth was not allowed to communicate directly with her allies, either in writing or in person. Yet Elizabeth's old friend, Thomas Parry, had taken lodgings at a local inn. From there, he managed Elizabeth's finances, gathered provisions to be delivered to the castle, and received visits from scores of Elizabeth's supporters. Parry was permitted to bring funds for the kitchen staff and to send servants bearing provisions. Elizabeth was lodged in the gatehouse rather than the castle, so her window would have been visible to Parry and his staff as they walked past.[20] The epigram was an ingenious way of assuring her allies that she was safe, and of informing them that her foes had no evidence against her. Most important of all, it warned them to be exceedingly careful since anything they said or did could potentially be used against her and them.

Ultimately, the epigram addressed posterity. If Elizabeth had been executed, it would have survived, eternizing her innocent martyrdom. After she became queen, Woodstock Castle became a famous tourist destination, and the epigram, a widely admired emblem of her ability to triumph against adversity.[21] By choosing language that was as artfully evasive as it was bluntly assertive, Elizabeth outmaneuvered her interrogators, thwarted her enemies, heartened and warned her supporters, and thus gained a small measure of control over a situation that threatened to render her not only powerless but defunct—to turn her into the "nothing" that the poem's very creation sought to hold at bay.

The final line, "*Quod* Elizabeth the prisoner," could have been added when the poem was later copied onto the wall where it was admired and transcribed by foreign visitors to England in the 1590s, but I think it was written by Elizabeth herself to frame the epigram—to transform her life into art and to turn her personal suffering into history. By writing the epigram, Elizabeth reconstructed the situation, giving it her own form and meaning. Just as the artful doubleness of "Much suspected by me" enabled

Elizabeth to transform herself from the object of others' designs to the critic and judge of their actions, the narrative frame transformed her from a helpless victim into the leading actor in a drama, or the main character in a narrative that she both constructed and enacted.

When Elizabeth ascended the throne, her experience at Woodstock still weighed on her mind. The painfully acquired knowledge that anything she wrote and said could be misconstrued and used against her colored her first parliamentary speech as it had propelled the Woodstock epigram. Indeed, her parliamentary speech characterized her situation so obliquely ("this kind of life in which I yet live," "this estate wherein you see me," "which trade of life I am so thoroughly acquainted") (CW 57) that one can still sense the danger Elizabeth felt as she began to rally her supporters and suppress her enemies. By turning her private experience into a public story, Elizabeth's parliamentary speech continued the narrative purpose that motivated the epigram—the verbal challenge of transforming herself from a vulnerable victim to a stalwart survivor and powerful prince, resourcefully using language to outwit her foes.

The dense, ambiguous language of Elizabeth's parliamentary speeches recycles many of the defensive strategies developed in the Woodstock epigrams, as the passage from the first parliamentary speech that we examined above illustrates: "the eschewing the danger of mine enemies; or the avoiding of the peril of death, whose messenger or rather continual watchman, the prince's indignation, was not little time daily before mine eyes" (CW 56–57). In personifying "the *prince's* indignation" and giving it a metaphorical embodiment as death's "watchman," Elizabeth was once again carefully choosing her words to exercise control over a problematic situation. At the same time, the murky causality demonstrates just how fraught with danger and difficulty the situation still seemed to her. The clotted syntax inserts "the prince's indignation" as an appositional phrase: "the avoiding of the peril of death, whose messenger or rather continual watchman, the prince's indignation, was not little time daily before mine eyes, by whose means although I know or justly may suspect..." Because it is not clear how "the princes indignation" relates to the surrounding participial phrases and the central passive verb, the members of parliament would have to work their way through the constituent parts of the sentence to figure out the causal links Elizabeth was herself piecing together. The strained diction and syntax were the residue of her immediate past when language was at once her only means of self-defense and a constant danger of self-incrimination. Could the enigmatic, ambiguous language that saved her from being "proven" a traitor protect her against the latest threat to her liberty—parliament's marriage petition?[22]

Much as the epigram gave her earlier plight a formal structure and future voice, Elizabeth's first parliamentary speech presented her recent history as a narrative of triumph over oppression. Like the epigram, the speech invited her listeners to sympathize with her suffering, to applaud her courage, and to recognize her ability to outwit her detractors. At the same time, it warned any former opponents who were still members of parliament that the situation was now reversed, just as she hoped it would be when she engraved her epigram on the window at Woodstock.

Newly empowered but still cognizant of the dangers she had passed, Elizabeth put her listeners on notice: "some" of them were still "much suspected" by her: "by whose means although I know, or justly may suspect, yet will not now utter" (CW 57). The word "suspect," so prominent in the epigram, reappears in the speech, linking this retrospective account to her earlier epigrammatic intervention. The clipped definitiveness of the words, with the repeated "*t*" sounds, "yet will not utter," recapitulates the concision and force of "Nothing proved can be." Once again, Elizabeth deliberately chose to say "nothing" in order not to give her adversaries any verbal ammunition to use against her. Yet, here as in the epigram, saying that she was saying nothing was itself a way of doing something. By announcing that she would "not utter" their names because she had no wish to reignite their hostility, Elizabeth claimed the upper hand. Although she was not planning to take any action against them at present, she would be monitoring their activities, and she would not hesitate to act, should they try to curtail her freedom or her ability to rule by pressuring her to marry against her will.

Distrust was so deeply ingrained in Elizabeth's history and psyche that she was prepared to confront it and fight it wherever it surfaced, both in herself and in her opponents. The verbal equivocations of the Woodstock epigram challenged her opponents' suspicions of her while simultaneously voicing and hedging her suspicions of them ("Much suspected by me"). Now that their positions had been reversed, Elizabeth could more openly express her own thoughts about those "by whose means although I know, or justly may suspect." At the same time, she had reason to think her opponents were harboring their own suspicions of her:

> [I]f any of you be in suspect that, whensoever it may please God to incline my heart to another kind of life, [my determination] is not to do or determine anything with which the realm may or shall have just cause to be discontented. (CW 57)

The repetition of the word "suspect" again connects the speech to the epigram, allying those who incited her sister's "indignation" with those who are now trying to force her into marriage. At stake was not only Elizabeth's own dearly prized and recently acquired liberty but also the stability of the country. Elizabeth insisted that she would only marry "whensoever it may please God to incline my heart to another kind of life." By declaring that she would follow God's will and not parliament's petition, Elizabeth asserted the newly acquired power of her imperial monarchy. At the same time, she declared that she would marry only when and if "it may please God to incline my heart" (CW 57).

In *Arcana microcosmi: Or, The Hid Secrets of Man's Body Discovered*, Alexander Ross explained that the heart was understood to be "the fountain of heat" and "the seat of Passions."[23] Elizabeth's few carefully chosen words deftly introduce the attitude toward marriage that would govern her decisions for the next two decades. On one hand, she would not let parliament force her into marriage for pragmatic reasons alone, whether political, dynastic, diplomatic, economic, or military. She would marry only if her heart made her desire to marry. On the other hand, she would not allow herself to be so carried away by passion or emotion that the country had "just cause to be discontented" with her choice of a husband.

Thus, the first parliamentary speech, like the Woodstock epigram, demonstrated Elizabeth's determination to outmaneuver her opponents even as it assured her supporters that she was equal to the challenges and dangers facing her. In isolating her foes, Elizabeth was building a political base, reminding her allies that she was still under attack and that she needed their backing now more than ever. In asserting her authority, she defined the terms that would govern any future marriage negotiations. Finally, and remarkably given her youth and vulnerability, Elizabeth was addressing posterity, meticulously and cannily constructing a personal narrative of triumph over adversity to fortify the image of a formidable yet loving monarch.

Fraught with Cares

To buttress her imperial power, Elizabeth invoked the divine right of kings, reminding parliament that God, having saved her from her enemies, would now provide the requisite guidance: "With which trade of life I am so thoroughly acquainted that I trust God, who hath hitherto therein preserved and led me by the hand, will not now of His goodness suffer me to go alone." In attributing her victory and vindication to God, Elizabeth deployed a rhetorical strategy that she had worked out in another, somewhat longer epigram that she also wrote while imprisoned at Woodstock:

> O Fortune, thy wresting, wavering state
> Hath fraught with cares my troubled wit,
> Whose witness this present prison late
> Could bear, where once was joy flown quite.
> Thou causedst the guilty to be loosed
> From lands where innocents were enclosed,
> And caused the guiltless to be reserved,
> And freed those that death had well deserved.
> But all herein can be naught wrought,
> So God grant to my foes as they have thought.
> *Finis.* Elisabetha a prisoner, 1555 (CW 46)[24]

Like the brief tale of adversity that introduces the parliamentary speech, this poem begins with a terse but surprisingly powerful expression of personal distress: "Hath fraught with cares my troubled wit." By providing only a glimpse rather than a full-fledged narrative, the epigram, like the speech, avoids self-pity, asserts righteousness, and claims justice in the hope of garnering support.

The poem focuses less on physical suffering than on intellectual and emotional constraint. Here too Elizabeth seeks support from history, specifically her place in the history of Woodstock Castle, which witnessed a long line of injustices. Elizabeth traced her own sorrow back to an original moment: "where *once* was joy flown quite" (my emphasis). Woodstock Castle was the legendary home of Henry II and his mistress, Rosamund Clifford. The medieval castle had been destroyed by Elizabeth's day, but Rosamund's story was well known. It was widely believed that Rosamund was poisoned by Henry's wife Eleanor of Acquitaine when she discovered the secret passage leading to the apartment where Henry and Rosamund enjoyed their illicit love. The vagueness of the reference ("where once was joy flown quite") protects Elizabeth from any direct association with Rosamund's sexual dishonor while expressing sympathy for the loss of her joie de vivre.

The final couplet—"But all herein can be naught wrought, / So God grant to my foes as they have thought"—imagines that Woodstock's history of releasing the guilty and restraining the innocent "can be" reversed, when or if fortune's random acts are overturned by God's justice. The final rhymes, "wrought" and "thought," strengthened by the internal rhyme, "naught wrought" and "fraught," echo and envisage a release from the constraint that "Hath fraught with cares my troubled wit." The conclusion, "So God grant," posits a much-anticipated answer to the prayer the poem comprises. The liberation the final couplet foresees could take a number of different forms, depending on how one interprets the phrase "all herein can be naught wrought."

To begin with, all those who remain imprisoned "herein," that is, "here in" Woodstock Castle, "can be" made "naught" if God grants Elizabeth's foes what they wanted, the opportunity to convict and execute her. Death would make her "naught," but it would also bring a welcome liberation from the "cares" of this world, giving the previous line—"And freed those that death had well deserved"—a positive spin. Yet the line "all herein can be naught wrought" could also mean that all Elizabeth has said "here in" the poem will be turned to "naught" if God fulfills what her foes "thought." Not only would their schemes be negated and nullified (for there's a pun on naught/not), but they would also be shown to be "naught" in the sense of evil, wicked, or wrong.

If God did to Elizabeth's foes what they thought about doing to her, if Elizabeth was released from prison, they would be "naught" as would the poem's previous claims, for it would no longer be true that the guilty are "freed" while the "guiltless" are "reserved" in prison. By warning her enemies that God would punish them for treating her unjustly, Elizabeth exercised some limited measure of control over her fate, a measure of control that she would later reprise and fortify in warning the first Elizabethan parliament that they could not force her to marry because her decision would be guided by God alone, "who hath hitherto therein preserved and led me by the hand" (CW 57).

A final, even more veiled meaning gives the poem's final epigrammatic turn yet another interpretation. If God should grant what her foes have thought—if the treason plots she has been accused of should come to pass—then Mary would be killed, her foes would be rendered "naught," Elizabeth would be crowned queen, and everything they "wrought" by imprisoning her would be undone. Of course, Elizabeth could not ally herself with the rebellion against Mary's government without incriminating herself and bringing about her own execution. Elizabeth could prophesy her foes' defeat only by concealing it, as an amphibologous subtext, beneath the poem's more obvious image of her own destruction.

As the poem draws to a close, it makes a self-reflexive move, meditating on its own enigmatic form: since her foes "caused the guiltless to be reserved" (in the sense of close-mouthed), Elizabeth would remain tersely self-protective, using the epigram's oblique twists and turns both to protest her bondage and to declare her innocence. They imprisoned her, but perhaps even worse, they took away her freedom of speech, forcing her to be "reserved" in the sense of *oblique* and *evasive*. Curt and cautious, the epigram's twists and turns protest Elizabeth's bondage and declare her innocence. If Mary and her representatives chose to identify with the "guilty," let that knowledge weigh on their consciences. If challenged, Elizabeth could always cite the penultimate line, claiming that she was merely praying for their will to be done. Having acknowledged that words are always subject to reinterpretation based on the reader's own goals and presuppositions, the ending takes a final epigrammatic turn that mirrors the other Woodstock epigram. If "naught" can be made of "all" that is written "herein," then "Nothing proved can be."

To Be Queen of This Realm

Elizabeth conceived her first parliamentary speech much as she imagined the Woodstock epigrams: as a way to evade danger and transcend constraint. Tactics developed in the epigrams recur in the speech as she summons her verbal skills and political acumen to protect her newly acquired liberty, assert her power, and defend her character and reputation. Even as monarch, she knew, her power would be challenged and could be severely circumscribed if she was not vigilant. Thus, Elizabeth told parliament, God would guide and protect her now as He had in the past, for God could still do to them what they once thought about doing to her.

At this key moment, as Elizabeth turns to address the question of her marriage, her diction and syntax become even more deeply evasive:

> With which trade of life I am so thoroughly acquainted that I trust God, who hath hitherto therein preserved and led me by the hand, will not now of His goodness suffer me to go alone. (CW 57)

This convoluted sentence seems to mean that a single life was thoroughly acceptable to Elizabeth because God, who had protected her from previous attempts to subordinate her through marriage, was still present, providing solace and guidance as she continued her current state "alone" without a husband. But the sentence can also mean that Elizabeth might not remain single for long because God, always her guide and savior, "will not now of His goodness suffer me to go alone." The cryptic diction makes it impossible to know whether or not she would marry. As so often with Elizabeth's rhetoric, the enigma is itself the point. It was no more possible to know whether she would be freed from house arrest at Woodstock than it was possible to know now, at the outset of her reign, whether Providence would provide a husband she would want to marry. Parliament's marriage petitions were moot because she would decide for herself, guided only by God and not by them, whether or not any given suitor was both desirable to her and advantageous for the country.

In both the poem and the speech Elizabeth balanced her feelings of anxiety and constraint which "hath fraught with cares my troubled wit" with her determination to assert her own judgment and will. Thus after warning parliament not to interfere, she proceeded to praise them for endorsing her right to marry whomever she desired, whether an Englishman or a foreigner: "the manner of your petition I do well like of and take in good part, because that it is simple and containeth no limitation of place or person" (CW 57). Then, recognizing the very real danger that her female "will" and "liking" could easily be subjected by those domineering men who were all too willing to rule for her until they could find a man to rule over her, Elizabeth continued:

> If it had been otherwise, I must needs have misliked it very much and thought it in you a very great presumption, being unfitting and altogether unmeet for you to require them that may command, or those to appoint whose parts are to desire, or such to bind and limit whose duties are to obey, or to take upon you to draw my love to your liking or frame my will to your fantasies. (CW 57)

While leaving her underlying motives and ultimate intentions inscrutable, Elizabeth made it absolutely clear that she would not countenance any attempt to limit her marital freedom of choice. Still, the force of the statement is tempered by the syntax, which is descriptive rather than declarative. Sternly forbidding and yet tentative, Elizabeth told parliament what she would have thought " [i]f it had been otherwise." Then she proceeded to declare, in no uncertain terms, how she would have felt had they tried to limit her freedom of choice: "I must needs have misliked it."

Here, as in the second Woodstock epigram, Elizabeth uses the first person singular "I" to express her own strong feelings. Yet, much as the epigram's signature distanced and framed her words for a potential, future audience, the 1559 speech mutes the immediacy and intensity of her personal experience, first by having the speaker read the speech aloud and then by moving from the first person singular to the third person plural: "them that may command, or those to appoint whose parts are to desire" (CW 57). This impersonal third person pronoun associates Elizabeth with all those powerful monarchs whose will was their subjects' command. At the same time, the ambiguous pronouns that lack a clear antecedent abstract and veil the queen's private "desire," much as the epigram allegorized and distanced Rosamund Clifford's sexual pleasure ("Where once was joy flown quite"). Finally, the complexity of the syntax and the ambiguity of the pronouns pose the question at the heart of the debate between Elizabeth and parliament: who "may command" and who may "desire"?

Yet, despite the syntactical slippage and the resulting interpretive uncertainties, the bottom line is clear. Elizabeth left no doubt that she would act according to her own "liking" rather than parliament's "fantasies." At this key moment, Elizabeth sounds rather like Hermia when, at the opening of *A Midsummer Night's Dream,* she is informed that she must marry Demetrius, her father's choice, rather than Lysander, the object of her love and desire. Hermia quips, "I would my father look'd but with my eyes" (1.1.56). Like Hermia, Elizabeth declared that she would marry *only* if she found someone who pleased *her* eyes, *her* heart, and *her* mind.

In asking parliament to recognize *her* "will"—meaning not only *determination to act, wishes,* and *inclination,* but also *carnal desire*—Elizabeth was raising a matter so delicate and potentially dangerous to her female honor that it could not be spoken in public, not even by a monarch whose speech was being read for her, except in carefully guarded fragments of displaced poetic language: "love," "desire," "liking," "will," and "fantasies." To allude to her "desire" for sexual pleasure was to risk arousing the most potent and potentially damaging misogynist stereotypes of the time: the deeply ingrained and widespread belief that women were vain, irrational, inconstant, and completely unsuited for governance because they were driven by uncontrollable passion and lust. John Knox put the case for women's "naturall weaknes, and inordinat appetites" pithily: "[they] haue burned with such inordinat lust, that for the quenching of the same, they haue betrayed to strangiers their countrie."

Along with these antifeminist stereotypes, Elizabeth was bucking historical precedent, which dictated that monarchical marriage should be arranged for political, dynastic, financial, and military reasons. Misogynists might immediately assume she was nothing but a weak, self-indulgent, lustful, irrational woman, but that was far from the case. By warning parliament not to try to bend her "will" to their "fantasies," Elizabeth was being pragmatic and surprisingly mature for someone who had been held in isolation for so long, because, as she was all too aware, her marriage would produce the all-important heir to the throne only if her husband aroused her "will" and "liking." She was not about to repeat the mistake her father made when he married Anne of Cleves, who looked appealing enough in her formal portrait but proved so undesirable in person that Henry could not wait to be rid of her. Elizabeth also had a scientific reason to insist that any future husband must satisfy her "will" and "desire" because it was widely believed that female orgasm was necessary to conception.²⁵ If parliament forced her to marry a man who repulsed her or infuriated her, there would be no heir to the throne.

Defending her conjugal freedom of choice was Elizabeth's most pressing concern, but the debate also had much larger political ramifications, which set the terms for her future relationship to parliament. After the opening sermons and the debate over her title, Elizabeth had reason to fear that her opponents in parliament would try to use her female sex to subordinate her to their will. She, therefore, took the opportunity of this first parliamentary speech to declare, first, that she planned to govern the country herself whether or not she married, and, second, that it would be "unmeet" and "unfitting" for them who thought they could command to try to exert their power over her because it was she, not they, who had the divinely given authority to "command."

Drawing upon the original meaning of the word "unmeet," Elizabeth suggested that any attempt to impose parliament's will over and against hers would be *immoderate* or *excessive*. The second meaning of "unmeet"—*unequal, unevenly matched*—asserted what the rest of the speech demonstrated: the parliamentary debate over her marriage was the occasion for a much larger power struggle, and Elizabeth wanted to make it very clear that parliament was the unequal or weaker party.²⁶ Finally, therefore, Elizabeth used the word "unmeet" in a third sense, meaning that it was *not fitting* or *not proper* for parliament to try to subordinate her will to theirs. The latter meaning is reinforced by her second adjective, "unfitting," which also means, *not fitting or suitable; unbecoming, improper,* though interestingly, the first usage cited by the Oxford English Dictionary is from 1590, three decades after Elizabeth's speech. Perhaps "unfitting" was a recent coinage, just beginning to be used by the Elizabethans when Elizabeth wrote her speech in 1559. More likely, it was a neologism, coined by Elizabeth to emphasize the inappropriateness of parliament's attempt to force her into marriage.

Whether Elizabeth coined a new word or used a newly created, colloquialism, the word's very newness suggests that rather than resorting to conventional political discourse, Elizabeth was seeking "new-made idiom" (to borrow a term from Donne) to re-conceive and redefine the relation between monarch and parliament. The reiteration stands in sharp contrast to the preceding obliquity, reminding her audience that she could make her meaning absolutely clear when it was advantageous for her to do so.

To drive this key point home, Elizabeth's language suddenly becomes as blunt as it is commanding: "put that clean out of your heads" (CW 57). Even if she could not control her opponents' thoughts, Elizabeth's regal tone and imperial imperative, strengthened by the simple colloquial diction and straightforward syntax, counters their apprehensions and misapprehensions, rather like Prince Hal's chilling reply to Henry IV's accusations: "Do not think so, you shall not find it so" (3.2.129). Turning once again to those skeptics who "suspected" her judgment, Elizabeth answered their doubts and accusations, lucidly and definitively: "I will never in that matter conclude anything that shall be prejudicial to the realm" (CW 57). At this crucial juncture, there could be no mistaking her meaning: parliament need not interfere because she would not marry for passion alone any more than for expediency alone.

Elizabeth's Speech vs. Camden's

Modern scholars have neglected Elizabeth's defense of her right to decide for herself whether to marry and whom to marry for two reasons. First, neither historians nor literary critics have given Elizabeth's language sufficiently close analysis. Second, the right or need to choose her future husband herself was nullified by the prevailing and mistaken view that Elizabeth never considered the possibility of marriage. This erroneous premise stems from William Camden's posthumous history of her reign. In fact, Camden rewrote Elizabeth's first parliamentary speech to make it seem as if she was committed from day one to living and dying a holy virgin.[27] Camden's myth of the Virgin Queen, married to God and country, underlies so much of what has been written about Elizabeth over the last half century that it shapes our assumptions and misshapes our reading of the documentary evidence in ways that we do not even realize. It is, therefore, crucial to salvage Elizabeth's words from Camden's distortions.

Ironically, one of the most frequently quoted remarks from all of Elizabeth's parliamentary speeches is a passage from the first parliamentary speech that Camden apparently fabricated, since it does not appear in Elizabethan versions of the speech: "I have already joyned my selfe in marriage to an husband, namely, the Kingdome of *England*. And behold (said she, which I marvaile ye have forgotten,) the pledge of this my wedlocke and marriage with my Kingdome, (and therewith, she drew the Ring from her finger and shewed it ...."[28] Camden celebrated Elizabeth as a type of the Virgin Mary at the very moment when the Protestant reformation was discrediting the cult of the Virgin, closing the nunneries, smashing beloved images of holy mother and child, and sanctioning marriage for the clergy, thereby ending the medieval exaltation of chastity over marriage. To enforce the iconic image of the Virgin Queen, Camden ignored key differences between Elizabeth and Mary, namely that Elizabeth did not give birth to the son and savior her government so desperately desired. Nor, as we shall see in the following chapters, did she speak or act like a saint, sublimely free from carnal desires and worldly considerations.

Elizabeth's symbolic marriage to her country, with its implicit rejection of any *other* marriage, is conspicuously absent from Elizabethan versions of the speech, which explicitly declare that Elizabeth *will* consider the possibility of marriage "whensoever it may please God to incline my heart to another kind of life" (CW 57). Unlike Camden's interpolations, Elizabeth's own language suggests that the decision to marry was not merely a matter of submitting to parliament's petitions. It was also a question of a "heart" and "will" "inclined" to "love" and "liking."

Camden's creative revisions make the young queen seem like a nun, seeking spiritual fulfillment through pure devotion to God and country: "Hereupon have I chosen that kinde of life, which is most free from the troublesome cares of this world, that I might attend the service of God alone." Camden's Elizabeth disdains the very idea of marriage as utter folly: "now that the publike care of governing the Kingdome is laid upon me, to drawe upon me also the cares of marriage, may seeme a point of inconsiderate folly."[29] This pointed rejection of marriage is repeatedly cited or presumed by modern scholars, but it does not appear in Elizabethan texts. To Elizabeth, who was rapidly discovering the unique political power of courtship, it was not marriage but a categorical commitment to virginity that would have been "a point of inconsiderate folly."

The disparity between Elizabeth's original speech and Camden's mythic reconfiguration culminates in the two different conclusions:

And in the end this shall be for me sufficient: that a marble stone shall declare that a queen, having reigned such a time, lived and died a virgin. (CW 58)

And to me it shall be a full satisfaction both for the memoriall of my name, and for my glory also, if when I shall let my last breath, it be ingraven upon my Marble Tombe, *Here lieth* Elizabeth, *which Raigned a Virgin, and died a Virgin*. (Camden 27)

Whereas Camden gave priority to Elizabeth's virginity—he repeated the word to give it added importance—Elizabeth gave priority to her sovereignty, asserting first and above all that she wanted to be remembered as "a Queen" who "reigned such a time," and mentioning only secondarily that she would be satisfied in the end if she lived and died a virgin. Camden's "And to me it shall be a *full satisfaction*" (my emphasis) created an inalienable, absolute commitment to virginity. By contrast, Elizabeth's choice of words, "this shall be for me *sufficient*" (my emphasis), made the ultimate determination dependent on a measured balance and as yet unresolved tension between long-range personal and professional priorities. Elizabeth concluded her speech by declaring that she might never marry because she wanted parliament to understand that its petitions could not force her to do what she did not desire.

As a newly crowned queen whose qualifications were being judged by all and attacked by many, Elizabeth had every reason to fear that she would be remembered for a prompt, dutiful marriage rather than a long, successful reign. Camden's interpolations and revisions confirmed his overarching vision of Elizabeth as the Virgin Queen wedded to God and country. Elizabeth's original speech made it impossible to know whether she would marry or not, though her words made it absolutely clear that she would marry only if she herself desired and chose to do so.

Figure 6. Elizabeth I Receiving Ambassadors, unknown Artist, 16th century

CHAPTER 5

DIPLOMACY AND CORRESPONDENCY: ELIZABETH'S REPORTED SPEECH

Lost, is it, buried? One more missing piece?
But nothing's lost. Or else: all is translation
And every bit of us is lost in it
(Or found...)

James Merrill, "Lost in Translation"

No Desire to Marry

Shortly after being crowned queen of England in January 1559, Elizabeth began discussing her first serious marriage prospect, King Philip II of Spain, her sister Mary's widowed husband. Elizabeth discussed the possibility with Philip's trusted advisor and close friend Don Gomez Suarex de Figueroa, Count de Feria.[1] Feria had accompanied King Philip to England for his marriage to Elizabeth's sister, Queen Mary, in 1554, and made England his home when he married one of Mary's maids of honor. Feria was, therefore, on location when Mary died in November 1558, and he stayed on to serve as the Spanish ambassador to the new regime.

For the first four months of Elizabeth's reign, Feria and Philip exchanged frequent letters discussing the pros and cons of marriage to the new English queen, but the courtship floundered almost as soon as it began for a number of reasons. First of all, Elizabeth was caught up in her new responsibilities and reluctant to consider marriage until she had a chance to establish her authority as queen regnant. Second, Philip pursued the possibility only half-heartedly out of a sense of religious duty, thinking it might deter the Protestant reformers who were gathering their forces to reinstitute the Edwardian, reformed Church of England. Third, Feria's close ties to Mary and Philip and to Roman Catholicism, combined with his irascible temper and barely disguised scorn for the new English regime, made it difficult for him to carry out his ambassadorial duties, "for truly they run away from me as if I were the devil."[2]

The negotiations with Philip came to an end in May when Elizabeth told Feria, who related the conversation in a letter to Philip, that the marriage was impossible because of "the impediment she discovered in the fact of your Majesty having married her sister, and after that she denied point-blank the Pope's power."[3] Henry VIII's first marriage to Catherine of Aragon was annulled by the newly created English Protestant church on the grounds that Catherine was his brother Arthur's widow. Consequently, Elizabeth could not marry her own deceased sister's widower without rejecting the legal grounds for her parents' marriage and thereby undermining her own legitimacy and right to the throne.

Surely, that would have been explanation enough for terminating the courtship, but Elizabeth proceeded to present a number of additional reasons, religious, political, and personal. Philip had said he would marry Elizabeth only if she converted to Roman Catholicism, so Elizabeth told Feria "she could not marry your Majesty as she was a heretic." Moreover, she explained, her "people did not wish her to marry a foreigner." In addition, "several persons had told her that your Majesty would come here and then go off to Spain directly," which meant that he could not offer the conjugal intimacy that might induce Elizabeth to give up her unmarried state. Under the circumstances, Elizabeth said she "had no desire to marry, as she had intimated from the first day."[4]

Most scholars have taken Elizabeth's declaration that "she had no desire to marry" to mean that she had already "from the first day" defined herself as the Virgin Queen, but that is not what her remarks to Feria (and subsequent ambassadors) implied any more than it is what her first parliamentary speech declared. In context, Elizabeth's words suggested that she had changed her mind because Philip's lackluster courtship had failed to make *her* "desire to marry" *him*, which is virtually the same formulation Elizabeth used when she told parliament that she would only marry a suitor who aroused her "love" and "liking." When speaking publicly to parliament, Elizabeth was extremely discrete, lest by speaking too openly or emphatically about her own personal "desire" she mar her reputation as an unmarried woman and undermine her authority as monarch. When speaking privately to the Spanish ambassador, Elizabeth was again careful to demonstrate her political judgment and protect her maidenly reputation. Feria discerned her meaning nonetheless, for he reported she was not at all pleased that Philip had failed to woo her with the fervor she might have wished.

Although she could not marry him, Elizabeth was eager to maintain Philip's friendship in order to deter a Spanish attack on England—an attack that materialized in the 1588 Spanish Armada. Furthermore, Philip's protection might ward off military threats from France and Scotland. Philip was also in a position to help broker a politically desirable (though religiously problematic) marriage with one of his Hapsburg cousins, the archdukes Ferdinand and Charles, sons of the Holy Roman Emperor Ferdinand I. For these reasons, it was important for Elizabeth both to provide Philip with a face-saving excuse for the failure of his courtship and to clarify her own thoughts about marriage in general.

Consequently, Elizabeth told Feria and Philip what she had already told parliament. She had no immediate desire to marry, but she might nonetheless be swayed by a suitor who wooed her more seriously and convincingly than Philip had. Thus, she told Feria, as he reported to Philip, "your Majesty could not have been so much in love with her as I had said, as you had not had patience to wait four months for her; and many things of the same sort."[5] Despite his scornful dismissal of Elizabeth's remarks, Feria's acknowledgment that she said "many things of the same sort" reveals just how eager Elizabeth was for Philip to know that his courtship had failed not only because there were political and religious impediments but also because she could not love and marry a man who neither loved nor wanted to marry her. As Donne writes in "Love's Deity": "Correspondency / Only his subject was; it cannot be / Love, till I love her that loves me."

Clearly, Feria disapproved. Like most of his contemporaries, he believed that personal considerations should not influence marriages between heads of state. Still, he was not exactly surprised for he had already written to Philip, "[t]he most discreet people fear she will marry for caprice."[6] To Feria, the notion that sexual attraction might affect political decisions was mere frivolity and vanity. Feria, therefore, concluded that Elizabeth was "a very strange sort of woman"[7]—certainly not the "sort of woman" he was used to dealing with. Alienated by Elizabeth's increasingly Protestant regime, unable to overcome his detrimental connection to Mary's court, and dismayed by Elizabeth's blatantly unconventional words and actions, Feria asked to be relieved of his ambassadorial duties and permitted to return to Spain. Before leaving, he warned the Austrian envoy that "the English are cunning, and when of the mind can dupe others very easily."[8]

The Monarch and the Orator

Despite Elizabeth's oft-repeated declarations that she was not ready to take a husband so soon after ascending the throne, talk of her marriage continued to dominate international relations and domestic politics. During the early months of the reign, the major powers of Europe were vying for Elizabeth's hand, and the English court was alive with balls and festivities. Once his own suit ended, Philip began to actively promote a marriage between Elizabeth and the Austrian archduke. Philip wanted to maintain his sphere of influence in England, to prevent further reformation of the English church, and to strengthen Spain's ties with the Holy Roman Empire. Feria tried but failed to convince the Austrian emperor to see the proposed marriage between his son and Philip's sister-in-law, the queen of England, as Philip's "gift."[9]

Philip chose Feria's successor, Don Alvaro de la Quadra, Bishop de Aquila, in the hopes that his diplomatic skills and social graces would enable him to win Elizabeth's trust and to promote the Austrian match. On May 24, 1559, shortly after arriving in England, de Quadra wrote, she "received me graciously, and promised to hear willingly whatever I had to say on your Majesty's behalf, and I will take care, as your Majesty orders me, to advise you fully of all that happens here."[10] Feria had sailed for Spain a week earlier. De Quadra assumed his responsibilities as ambassador, which entailed writing regular, detailed reports about his meetings with the queen and others who were in a position to provide valuable information. The Austrian ambassador, Caspar Breuner, Baron von Rabenstein, arrived the following week, and he too began writing detailed letters to his master, the Holy Roman Emperor, Ferdinand I. From May 24 until the following March, the Spanish and Austrian ambassadors deployed their diplomatic skills to press for a marriage between Queen Elizabeth and Archduke Charles.

At the beginning of her reign, when Elizabeth was a new queen with virtually no political or diplomatic experience, it was not clear who would make the decision about her marriage—the Privy Council, parliament, or the queen herself. Elizabeth fought hard for the right to make the decision herself, but even after the Lords and Commons conceded that she could choose her own husband, they continued to pressure her to marry. For that reason among others, Elizabeth convened parliament only when absolutely necessary: in 1559 she needed parliament to ratify her reign; in 1563 and 1566 financial exigencies forced her to seek subsidies from parliament. On these three occasions, Elizabeth planned her words with great care. She wrote out her speeches in advance for the speaker to deliver in her stead. The autograph draft of the 1563 speech, with numerous interlinear corrections in Elizabeth's own handwriting, shows how rigorously she thought through her position and how meticulously she selected and revised her words. It was not until 1566, six years after ascending the throne, that Elizabeth would rise to address parliament in her own voice.

Elizabeth's parliamentary speeches were formal, highly wrought, premeditated performances. Her diplomatic speech was closer to the give and take of spontaneous conversation. Although by no means artless or unplanned, Elizabeth's diplomatic conversations were more ad hoc, more confidential, more colloquial, and more dialogic, unfolding in real time, adapting to what the ambassadors said and shifting course to correct their misprisions or to accommodate their objections. The first Austrian ambassador to Elizabeth's court, George, Count von Helfenstein, Baron von Gundlfingen, arrived in England on February 12, 1559. Elizabeth offered him the choice of a public or private meeting. When he graciously left the decision up to her, Elizabeth greeted him amidst her court and then "retired, very kindly giving me a sign to follow her, leaving behind all the nobles of the Court and the Councillors, in order that I might at my ease talk with Her Royal Highness secretly and confidentially about anything that I might have to discuss." Greatly impressed with her verbal skills, the Count reported that Elizabeth "replied to my embassage, speaking extempore and with many brilliant, choice, and felicitous phrases."[11]

Elizabeth allotted a remarkable amount of time to private conversations with the Spanish and Austrians ambassadors and no doubt gave a great deal of thought to how she could best represent herself and her position on the marriage negotiations. Clearly, she knew her words were being reported and carefully scrutinized, but it was nonetheless to her advantage, as it was to the ambassadors' advantage, to maintain the illusion that they were talking openly and frankly. Both sides were trying to build alliances and establish trust while cognizant that the religious divide between the ancient, Roman Catholic churches of Spain and Austria and the Church of England, which was being reformed even as these conversations were unfolding, could at any moment turn their countries into bloody enemies.

Unfortunately, Elizabeth did not record her own account of what was said during discussions with the ambassadors or her advisors, for she would have provided a very different view. Her principal advisor, William Cecil, prepared detailed position papers, describing the pros and cons of her various marriage options, but he did not record either her view or his own view of these diplomatic conversations. Thus the ambassadors' "minutely" written reports provide our only access to these discussions, and they are as close as we can now get to a transcript of Elizabeth's speech. They, therefore, deserve careful scrutiny, even though they are reported from the ambassadors' subjective points of view.

Since there were no audio-recording devices, the ambassadors had to rely on their memories, for it would have been both bad form and bad politics to sit there, like a modern reporter, taking notes while the queen talked. Nonetheless, their memories were trained as ours are not. The classical discipline of rhetoric taught orators and auditors to associate each stage of the argument with a successive room of the house, and then to proceed through the various rooms of the house to recall the various parts of the speech. Ministers delivered their sermons from memory, and students were regularly expected to reproduce entire sermons, which could last an hour or two, from memory.

The ambassadors reported Elizabeth's words more consistently and in more detail than any other extant source. After one particularly thorny conversation with the queen, for example, the Austrian ambassador "wrote down everything as above, recapitulated everything to the [Spanish Ambassador] and gave him a memorandum of all those points that I considered most important and essential, so that he might treat with Her Majesty in the name of his King. He did so three days later...and from his letter Your Imperial Majesty will learn what he said and what she answered."[12] Because they took their reporting so seriously, the ambassadorial dispatches contain some of the most reliably detailed accounts of what was happening at the English court week-by-week.[13] Their intricate, murky, fascinating accounts range from high-level, confidential diplomatic discussions with the queen and her principal advisors, to breaking military, political, and economic news, to shocking rumors about Elizabeth's love for Robert Dudley and their alleged conspiracy to murder his wife so that they would be free to marry each other.

In a world without newspapers, telephones, airplanes, or the World Wide Web, the flow of information was slow and patchy. England was an island, and travel by sea was slow and perilous. The letters exchanged between ambassadors to England and foreign heads of state helped bridge physical, political, and cultural distances. Ambassadorial dispatches provided information that would not have otherwise been available outside

England, and they are still among the most frequently cited Elizabethan sources because they contain information that is not available elsewhere.

The ambassador's responsibilities were multiple:

1. To fulfill specific instructions given or sent by their monarch.
2. To deliver letters to the queen from the emperor or the king, and to send reports back, describing how these letters were received.
3. To advance their country's political and religious agenda.
4. To provide the king or emperor with full and accurate reports of what was happening in England.
5. To gather information, assess the situation, size up the queen, predict her future behavior, and humbly recommend a course of action.
6. To recognize that the king or emperor had other sources of information and other imperatives that might undercut their reports and override their recommendations.

Philip had been in frequent contact with Feria during the weeks following Mary's death when a marriage between Philip and Elizabeth was being discussed. Once his own courtship ended and Feria returned to Spain, Philip was less actively involved in English affairs. De Quadra wrote to Philip on May 24, May 29, June 19, June 27, and July 1, but it was not until July 9 that he received a reply from Philip, saying, "All your letters to 28th ultimo and 1st instant received. I thank you for informing me so minutely of all that occurs, and desire you to continue to do so."[14] Sometimes several days or weeks passed between one letter from de Quadra and the next. When negotiations reached a climax, however, he wrote several days in a row, and even more than once a day. Philip's side of the correspondence was sporadic. In the best of circumstances de Quadra might receive a response within a week or ten days, but more often several weeks or even months passed. Because Philip so rarely sent letters or instructions, de Quadra felt freer to improvise and intervene as he saw fit.

Whereas de Quadra heard from King Philip only sporadically, Breuner and Emperor Ferdinand were in regular contact. As Holy Roman Emperor, Ferdinand was used to issuing commands. Moreover, he had decided opinions about how the negotiations were to proceed. He was deeply invested in his "beloved" son's marriage and took an active and controlling role in the negotiations. Ferdinand generally began his letters by expressing approval or disapproval of Breuner's last report. He made it absolutely clear that he expected Breuner to do as he was told and didn't hesitate to chastise the ambassador when he departed from instructions.

Overseas travel was slow, and even the most assiduous diplomatic correspondence left an unbridgeable gap between the time a message was sent and the time an answer was received. When Elizabeth's conversation took an unforeseen or undesirable turn, Breuner had to improvise, not knowing exactly how the emperor would want him to proceed, but also knowing that he would be reprimanded if he departed from his prescribed role.

Although authorized to speak on the emperor's behalf, Breuner was constrained by his ultimate lack of authority—rather like Agrippa in *Antony and Cleopatra*. When Agrippa proposes a marriage between Antony and Caesar's sister Octavia, Antony responds, "What power is in Agrippa, / If I would say, 'Agrippa, be it so,' / To make this good?" (2.2.140–42). As Antony well knew, Agrippa was merely the intermediary, not the prime actor. He broached the possibility of a marriage so that Caesar would not lose face should Antony shoot down the proposal. Just as it was Caesar, not Agrippa, who had the power to decide whom Octavia would marry, it was Emperor Ferdinand, not his imperial ambassador and certainly not the Spanish ambassador, who had the power to decide whether and on what conditions Charles would or would not be permitted to marry Elizabeth, should she prove willing. If Charles had objected to the match as vehemently as his older brother Ferdinand did, there might have been no courtship. Yet, for the most part the ambassadors assumed and led Elizabeth to believe that Charles' father would arrange the marriage on his behalf, just as many assumed at the outset of the reign that Elizabeth's Privy Council and parliament would arrange a marriage on her behalf.

Elizabeth's command of foreign languages was impressive. She had received a strong classical education in Latin and Greek and was fluent in French and Italian. Nonetheless, she could not be expected to speak *every* European language. Ambassadors to Elizabeth's court were noblemen, chosen because they were "honourable, adroit, and polite and versed in matters of this kind,"[15] but they also needed to have command of the English language, since their primary responsibility was to converse with the queen and her councilors and to curry favor with and gather information from as many other English informants as possible. The Austrian ambassadors addressed the emperor variously in Latin and German; the emperor almost always wrote to Breuner in Latin. Elizabeth wrote two letters to the emperor in Latin, and she greeted Breuner's predecessors in Latin, apologizing that her command of the language was rusty, because, as she made a point of explaining, she had been exiled from court for many years and had only recently been released from prison, where, despite repeated pleas, she was denied access to books and tutors.[16] The Spanish ambassadors corresponded with Philip in Spanish. Elizabeth knew some Spanish and no doubt understood more than she could speak based on her knowledge of Italian and French cognates, but she did not claim to be fluent in Latin, German, or Spanish. Consequently, Elizabeth almost certainly spoke with de Quadra and Breuner in English. Thus, their reports of what she said, written variously in Latin, German, and Spanish, were translations of her original English speech.[17]

Since we are dealing with translations, this chapter focuses less on syntactical ambiguities and verbal nuances than on broader political goals and rhetorical strategies. The goal is threefold: first, to provide a more probing reading of these all-too-familiar documents: second, to encourage other scholars to give more credence to Elizabeth's side of the conversation, for just as scholars have given far less attention to Elizabeth's own writing than to what Elizabethan authors wrote about her, so too they have paid far less attention to what Elizabeth said to the ambassadors than to what the ambassadors said about her; third, to devise a method of analyzing this deeply rhetorical material—a method that students and scholars can use in their own reading of these documents.

Even putting the question of translation aside, the diplomatic letters that comprise the subject of this chapter are not pure, unadulterated historical data (if there is such a thing), but texts with distinct, subjective points of view. What each ambassador chose to report was determined partially by his political assignment and rhetorical objectives and partially by his own views of the queen, which were inevitably inflected by his own personality, presumptions, and values. Even though each ambassador had his own characteristic style and point of view, there is, nonetheless, a remarkable consistency in the stories they tell. The Spanish and Austrian ambassadors collaborated closely and, at particularly difficult or decisive moments, synchronized their letters to the emperor. The Spanish ambassadors were at liberty to tell a very different story to Philip II and their colleagues. Their more unguarded reports, including a few decidedly undiplomatic letters to each other, thicken the plot. Nonetheless, the remarkable degree of overlapping information and the absence of any substantial discrepancies confirm the basic reliability of their reporting. Significantly, the ambassadors did not censor Elizabeth even when they thought she was talking "nonsense," nor did they rewrite her words to suit their own purposes, for what they reported she said was often at odds with what they thought she should have said or what they assumed she meant.

The ambassadorial dispatches are so voluminous that it is impossible to discuss them without being selective, and, of course, the ambassadors were themselves being selective in what they chose to report. The diplomatic dispatches are generally treated as databases to be mined for fragmentary quotations in support of one argument or another. While recognizing that my own process of selection is itself an act of interpretation, I have nonetheless tried to let the ambassadors' reports constitute their own argument. This chapter keeps the process of interpreting the ambassadors' reports and their own process of interpreting their conversations with Elizabeth at the forefront of our inquiry, treating their letters not only as storehouses of information but also as sophisticated pieces of rhetoric that need to be carefully studied in the aggregate in order to understand how the particular information they convey is inflected by and revelatory of the writers' and the speakers' own persuasive purposes.

Like all early modern political discourse, diplomatic discourse was profoundly dialogic and deeply rhetorical. Both the queen and the ambassadors were trying to anticipate, accommodate, and, above all, influence each other. The ambassadors needed to impress the king of Spain and the Holy Roman Emperor with the accuracy of their reports even as they needed to sway the emperor, the king, and Elizabeth with their arguments. Meanwhile, Elizabeth needed to impress the ambassadors and their superiors with the merits of her position. Furthermore, they were all trying to persuade each other to change their view of the situation, even as they were adapting their words in response to what the other side said, or what they thought the other side had said or might say, or what they assumed the other side meant but would not or could not say.

The Renaissance conception of diplomacy was closely allied to the classical notion of rhetoric. In fact, the Austrian ambassador was called "the orator." The Latin word "orator," meaning not only *orator* or *speaker* but also *spokesman, envoy,* was the standard Renaissance term for ambassador. Renaissance education was based on principles of rhetoric that shaped speech and writing alike, and the ambassadors were well schooled in the rhetoric of diplomacy. Elizabeth had been well educated in rhetoric, the classics, religion, and political history, but she had spent most of her adolescence and early adulthood in exile from the court, most recently in prison. While the ambassadors were fulfilling their responsibility—implementing their instructions, recounting and trying to manipulate Elizabeth's response, explaining or defending their actions to the emperor and the king—Elizabeth was working out her modus operandi as monarch and marriageable woman.

Like Philip II and Ferdinand I, Elizabeth was a head of state, but at the time these diplomatic conversations took place she had little experience of diplomacy or international relations. Her first parliamentary speech declared that she would decide whether or not to marry and whom to marry, and that she intended to govern the country herself regardless of whether she married. Yet, Ferdinand had been mistakenly led to believe, via a reported conversation with an English lord, that Elizabeth was seeking a husband to assume the responsibility of governing England. Indeed, Ferdinand's initial instructions to Breuner were based on this crucial piece of misinformation: "She proposed when the time was ripe to do as they desired, but would only wed a man who was not only King in name, but would also govern her Royal self and the whole Kingdom, and who should be agreeable to the Estates." Operating on this assumption, which was the opposite of the true state of affairs, as we saw in the last chapter, Ferdinand instructed Breuner to inform Elizabeth's councilors that Charles "has already attained that age which brings with it the capacity to conduct affairs and to judge the expediency of matters, and besides has always been found most able...having attended many Councils on very important matters."[18] The clear implication was that Elizabeth's own lack of experience had not prepared her to govern the country. Although that was, in fact, true, the converse, that she was not prepared to govern the country because she had not "attended many Councils on very important matters," proved not to be the case.

Frankly and Sincerely

In a world where royal marriages were arranged for political, economic, and military reasons, and where many believed that women were unfit to rule, Elizabeth fought hard for the right to conduct her own courtships, to make her own decision about marriage, and to govern the country in her own way, whether or not she married. No matter how unusual these demands may have seemed, the very fact that she negotiated with the ambassadors herself proved her point.

De Quadra was both the Spanish ambassador and a Roman Catholic bishop; therefore, he felt honor-bound to promote the marriage for political expediency—to strengthen relations between Spain and Austria and to forge an alliance between Spain and England—and for religious imperatives—to defend Roman Catholicism against the threat of a reformed English Church. Yet because he was the Spanish ambassador and not the Austrian ambassador, de Quadra had no direct authority to negotiate marriage on behalf of the emperor and archduke. Nonetheless, he used his considerable diplomatic expertise to facilitate the match, as he was instructed to do by Philip at the outset of the negotiations and subsequently invited to do by the emperor as well.

De Quadra had been in England long enough to have established relationships with the queen and the major political players when Breuner arrived at the end of May. Breuner had been commissioned to determine whether it was advisable for Austria to pursue a marriage between Elizabeth and Archduke Charles, and if so, to ascertain whether Elizabeth and her councilors were prepared to receive envoys to negotiate a marriage contract between Elizabeth and Charles rather than his elder brother Ferdinand, who had been proposed first. Breuner was instructed "to work cautiously and prudently in all matters that concern religion," and to keep the emperor updated on the reformation of the English Church and England's military difficulties abroad. Finally, he was instructed to "zealously inquire how the Queen comports herself towards her other suitors."[19]

The Spanish embassy offered Breuner lodgings in Feria's house in London. Once the Austrian was settled, de Quadra took him to meet the queen. After urging Elizabeth to keep an open mind, de Quadra withdrew so that Breuner could speak privately. Elizabeth's attendants were present, but they also receded into the background, leaving Elizabeth to converse with the ambassador in what seemed like an intimate private space. Ever the diplomat, de Quadra took advantage of the opportunity to grill Cecil about the chances for a match between Elizabeth and Archduke Charles: "I understood from him, although not by his words, that the Queen would refuse the match."[20] Clearly, de Quadra thought it was his duty as ambassador to draw inferences that went beyond, or even superseded, the spoken word. De Quadra doesn't explain how he knew what (he thought) Cecil meant "although not by his words." Perhaps he was sizing up Cecil's body language and facial expressions. More likely, de Quadra was drawing inferences from what he took to be Cecil's use of rhetorical figures such as irony or allegory to say one thing and mean another. Although de Quadra's attempt to offer a more sophisticated interpretation is commendable, there is also something simplistic or reductive about his belief that Cecil's "intentions" were plain to behold, both straightforward in themselves and readily ascertainable to others.

Breuner emerged from his initial tête-à-tête with Elizabeth "quite despairing of the business," so de Quadra approached the queen himself.²¹ As a Roman Catholic bishop who had taken a vow of celibacy, de Quadra believed that service to God and country should trump personal desire. Consequently, he "begged" Elizabeth "to consider that in a matter of this gravity touching the welfare and tranquility of their kingdoms and those of their neighbours kings and queens could not always follow their own desires to the prejudice of those of their subjects without doing great wrong and grievous sin, and therefore she should not consult her own inclination about her marriage but should look at the ruin that would come to her country by her doing so."²² De Quadra believed that diplomatic discourse was never really candid or forthright, but he nonetheless tried to convince the inexperienced young queen to adopt a naïve, straightforward view: "I said that when she had resolved how to act in this case she should treat of her intention frankly and sincerely with the Emperor." Having failed to cajole Cecil into speaking plainly, de Quadra thought Elizabeth might be easier to manipulate: "She knew, I said, how honestly and kindly the worthy Germans negotiated."²³ Right! Even though she was new to the job, Elizabeth was not about to accept such a simplistic view of diplomatic discourse. Before concluding his letter, which goes on to describe events that transpired over the course of a fortnight, de Quadra was forced to admit that he had met his match: "I am not sure about her for I do not understand her."²⁴

Thus, the official discussions of a marriage between Queen Elizabeth and Archduke Charles began. Perhaps because de Quadra was already familiar with her speech and demeanor, or perhaps because he was simply a more wily character than Breuner, or perhaps because he piqued Elizabeth's interest by informing her that it was not Ferdinand, whose known commitment to Roman Catholicism had seemed a deterrent, but Charles whom the Austrians were proposing, de Quadra emerged from his interview with sufficient assurances to convince Breuner, and to report to Philip, that Elizabeth would not reject the Austrian suit out of hand as Breuner feared. Although de Quadra had failed to convince Elizabeth to speak as frankly and plainly as he wished she would, he had nonetheless manipulated the occasion to insert himself at the center of the diplomatic conversation. More importantly, he had demonstrated how essential he could be in keeping the negotiations moving forward. Although there were definite limits to his psychological acuity and analytic capabilities, de Quadra nonetheless worked hard to protect and expand his sphere of influence, using his rhetorical skills to make himself indispensable to Breuner, the emperor, and to Elizabeth herself, or so he hoped.

I'd Rather Be a Nun

Breuner had been instructed by the emperor to present his proposal to the Privy Council, so he dutifully requested and received Elizabeth's permission to meet with some of her councilors. Three days after meeting the queen, the Austrian and Spanish ambassadors were summoned by Pembroke, Bedford, Parry, Bacon, and Cecil, who listened attentively as Breuner presented his suit. De Quadra reported that they "answered that they would refer and discuss the matter with the Queen, showing pleasure at the proposal."[25] As the negotiations progressed, however, Breuner wrote that Elizabeth "apprised us that we should credit only her and no one else in this matter."[26] Breuner acceded, despite misgivings, because he was afraid to impede his suit by disregarding the queen's express command. When the negotiations fell apart, it was this decision that he had the most difficulty justifying to the emperor.

The original proposal for Elizabeth to marry the emperor's eldest son, who was also named Ferdinand, had been withdrawn because he refused to repudiate his morganatic marriage.[27] To negotiate the potentially embarrassing switch from elder to younger brother in a world where order of birth had significant hierarchical and financial implications, Breuner and de Quadra used a series of diplomatic evasions. To further complicate their task, the French, who were actively trying to obstruct an alliance between England and their Hapsburg rivals for control of Europe, convinced Elizabeth "that the Archduke had a head larger than that of the earl of Bedford." Just how large was that? Nobody said, though de Quadra assured Elizabeth that Charles was not a "monster," as she had been told, but a "comely" young man who was "more likely to please her than the other" because he "possessed extremely good and fitting qualities which I recounted at length. She was a long while demurring and doubting" but "was quite satisfied about this by your Majesty's letter (wherat, as I thought, she was pleased)." Perhaps Elizabeth *was* pleased. De Quadra was certainly pleased with himself, even though "she went back again to her nonsense and said she would rather be a nun than marry without knowing with whom and on the faith of portrait painters."[28] Elizabeth also said "she has taken a vow to marry no man whom she has not seen, and will not trust in portrait painters."[29] Elizabeth may have chosen the trope of the "nun" and the formulation of a "vow" because she thought that would convince de Quadra, a Roman Catholic bishop vowed to celibacy, to respect the sanctity of her words. Her rhetorical strategy failed to have the desired effect, however, for de Quadra's dismissive comment, "she went back again to her nonsense," suggests that he had heard much the same thing from Elizabeth a number of times before and that he had little respect for her position.

Royal marriage negotiations generally involved the exchange of formal portraits, but Elizabeth repeatedly declared that she would "not trust in portrait painters."[30] She was well aware of the unshakable aversion her father felt when his fourth bride, Anne of Cleves, arrived from Flanders looking far less attractive than the formal portrait Hans Holbein painted during the marriage negotiations. Henry's marriage to Anne was annulled when she agreed, in return for a generous financial settlement, to say that it had not been consummated. Determined to avoid her father's bitter disappointment, Elizabeth told both de Quadra and Breuner that she would only consider marrying "a man of worth whom she had seen and spoken to."³¹ To make sure that they got it, she reiterated the point, saying that she "was determined to see and know the man who was to be her husband." Since de Quadra had already told her she should not allow her personal desires to affect her political decisions, Elizabeth could not tell him why she wanted to "see and know" her future husband.

On May 30 Breuner also reported that Elizabeth compared herself to a nun. Tempting as it might be to conclude that Elizabeth was already imagining and representing herself as the Virgin Queen, we should not leap to this familiar presupposition. Instead, we need to look more closely at how Elizabeth used the trope and to what purpose. When we put the "nun" back in her habit—both in the immediate context of Elizabeth's conversations with the ambassadors and in the larger biographical and historical context of Elizabeth's first year in office—the analogy takes a surprising turn. Here is Breuner's version:

> She also would not that it be assumed that she had forsworn marriage entirely, for she was but human and not insensible to human emotions and impulses, and when it became a question of the weal of her Kingdom, or it might be for other reasons, her heart and mind might change. It is true that she had found the celibate life so agreeable, and was so accustomed to it, that she would rather go into a nunnery, or for that matter suffer death, than marry against her will.³²

In this intricate, complexly layered series of conditions and qualifications, Elizabeth restates the position she articulated in her 1559 parliamentary speech. She had not forsworn marriage altogether, she informed the newly arrived Austrian ambassador, though she would not be rushed or forced to marry for expediency alone. For the time being, she was enjoying her life as a single woman—a life that was chaste and honorable, she assured them by mentioning her celibacy. Yet she might still decide to marry—and here she confides in Breuner what she had not felt free to tell the bishop—if a suitor presented himself who aroused "her human emotions and impulses" and who would preserve "the weal of the kingdom."

As this brief summary of what was no doubt an even more intricate discussion suggests, Elizabeth was balancing a number of interrelated considerations, personal as well as political. Even allowing for the fact that we are dealing with a translated summary of a reported conversation, Elizabeth's final, absolutely blunt declaration that she would not "marry against her will" asserts that she intended to make her own decision about marriage based not only upon political considerations, although she certainly planned to take them seriously, but also upon her "human emotions and impulses."

Elizabeth's declaration that she would "rather go into a nunnery, or for that matter suffer death, than marry against her will" anticipates the choice Duke Theseus offers Hermia in *A Midsummer Night's Dream*:

> Either to die the death, or to abjure
> For ever the society of men.

> Therefore, fair Hermia, question your desires,
> Know of your youth, examine well your blood,
> Whether (if you yield not to your father's choice)
> You can endure the livery of a nun,
> For aye to be in shady cloister mew'd,
> To live a barren sister all your life,
> Chanting faint hymns to the cold fruitless moon. 1.1.65–73

Like Elizabeth, Hermia responds that she would rather live and die "in single blessedness" than "yield [her] virgin patent up" unto the man her father had chosen for her to marry, "whose unwished yoke / My soul consents not to give sovereignty."[33] This, of course, does not mean that Hermia is dreaming of becoming a nun; rather it means that she would choose not to marry at all rather than accept Demetrius, who was her father's choice, not hers. For Hermia, as for Elizabeth, becoming a nun is the best of the unsavory choices offered her. But why did Elizabeth feel compelled to propose such a set of options for herself?

Elizabeth's language suggests that she (like Hermia) was alluding to a specific, but unspecified, person who had already aroused "her human emotions and impulses." Still, she was anxious for the Austrian ambassador to know that she (unlike Hermia) had not made up her mind to marry that person: "But now she could swear by the salvation of her soul, and as she stood in need of and desired to obtain God's grace on the Day of Judgment, that she to this hour had never set her heart upon, nor had come so far as to wish to marry, anyone in the whole world." When read out of context, this could well be taken to mean that she intended to reign as the Virgin Queen. Yet, the intensity of her words suggests another, quite different subtext. Why, we should ask, at this early point in the negotiations, did Elizabeth feel compelled to "swear by the salvation of her soul" that she had not already set her heart on marrying "anyone"? And why did she protest that she was a pious, virtuous woman who had "never" let the yearnings of "her heart" tarnish her celibacy?

Here, as is usually the case with Elizabeth's prose, the provocative but evasive pronoun "anyone" suggests that she was alluding to someone she could not name without compromising the very honor she was anxious to defend. The "one" possible marriage partner who was on everyone's mind, but whom Elizabeth could not mention without creating diplomatic pandemonium, was, of course, Robert Dudley. It would be three more weeks before Elizabeth's relationship to Dudley acquired a position of prominence in the Austrian diplomatic correspondence, but he was already on de Quadra's mind, for as he mentions briefly, in passing, in the same letter to Philip, "Robert is as highly favoured as usual."[34]

Breuner set out, to the best of his ability, to conduct his diplomatic discussions according to the emperor's instructions. Yet Elizabeth often steered the conversation in an unexpected or unwelcome direction, which placed Breuner in an awkward and even worrisome position. He could not afford to falsify Elizabeth's position, since that would have seriously compromised his own standing with the emperor if the envoys the emperor kept promising to send ever arrived to negotiate a marriage contract. Rather than deception, therefore, Breuner chose circumspection. Whenever Elizabeth's demands were at odds with the emperor's directives,

ARCHDUKE CHARLES OF AUSTRIA
From an oil-painting by an unknown German master in the Vienna Art Museum

Figure 7. Archduke Charles of Austria, by an unknown German master

Breuner became more guarded and selective in what he chose to report. While Elizabeth continued to declare, and de Quadra continued to alert Philip, that she would not agree to marry anyone whom she has not seen, or spoken to, or gotten to know, Breuner procrastinated and prevaricated.

Writing to the emperor on June 7 Breuner chose not to mention Elizabeth's precondition. Instead, he wrote a friendly, chatty, encouraging letter to Charles, also dated June 7 and no doubt sent in the same diplomatic pouch, which began by saying that although Elizabeth had not made up her mind to marry anyone and was not yet willing to bind herself, she might be induced to marry Charles. Then he laid it on: "there is no Princess of her compeers that can match her in wisdom, virtue, beauty and splendour of figure and form." She had "three millions in gold annually" and "several very fine summer residences…richly garnished with costly furniture of silk, adorned with gold, pearls and precious stones." The logical conclusion was blunt but seemingly incontrovertible: "Hence she is well worth the trouble."[35] Charles could not possibly hope to find a more appealing prospective wife, so wouldn't he like to come to England to meet and woo this enticing queen? "I have heard from the Queen that she would much like to become acquainted with you, for, so she told me, she would not take a man whom she had never seen."[36] If Breuner could get Charles excited about the prospect of courting Elizabeth, perhaps Charles could convince his father to let him make the journey. That would solve Breuner's diplomatic problem.

On June 10 Elizabeth invited Breuner to join her on her barge, and Breuner wrote to the emperor to report this extraordinary sign of her favor: "Everybody kept saying such honor had never been shown to anyone but me. On the barge she conversed with nobody else, and often of her own accord began to talk about the Archduke Charles." Then, Breuner summoned his courage to inform the emperor that the success of the negotiations depended on Charles' coming to England. Breuner explained that he had "endeavoured to argue her out of this, and begged her to resolve to give a favourable and final answer," but to no avail.[37]

Meanwhile, de Quadra was collecting as much information as he could. He insinuated himself into the company of Elizabeth's courtiers and advisors and even courted and canvassed her ladies-in-waiting. His assessment of the situation ranged the full spectrum. On May 30 he thought the political situation would force Elizabeth to marry, regardless of her personal inclinations: "yet I cannot help thinking that, so clearly is the need for her to marry being daily more understood by herself and her advisers, notwithstanding her disinclination to say yes, I need not despair of her listening to the proposal."[38] But the next letter, dated June 19, was far more pessimistic. Suspicious that Elizabeth was duplicitous and disinclined, de Quadra wrote:

> She makes her intimates think that she is favourable to the archduke's affair, and her women all believe such to be the case, as do the people at large, but there is really no more in it than there was the first day, and I believe for my part that she is astutely taking advantage of the general opinion to reassure

somewhat the Catholics who desire the match and to satisfy others who want to see her married and are scandalized at her doings. She has told the ambassador how earnestly your Majesty has endeavoured to bring about this marriage with the archduke. She has just given 12,0000£ to Lord Robert as an aid towards his expenses.[39]

There were some things de Quadra was not prepared to put in writing. Perhaps, as a bishop, he found sexuality literally unspeakable, or perhaps he was unwilling to commit anything to writing that might potentially damage the negotiations since ambassadorial dispatches were frequently intercepted. Yet, in the gap between those "others" who were "scandalised at her doings" and de Quadra's ever so circumspect addendum, "given 12,0000£ to Lord Robert," lies an important clue to the larger social context in which these negotiations were taking place, the vast arena of gossip, which was either so speculative or so shocking as to be indescribable, even under the cover of diplomatic correspondence.

"The slander proceeds from many persons," the Emperor wrote his son, the Archduke Maximilian only three and a half weeks after Elizabeth protested the sanctity of her soul. Free to confide in Maximilian what he would not write Breuner, the emperor explained: "the harm done is great, and even though it be granted that it very often happens that a woman of good repute is spoken ill of, I do not wish to waste words on such, but when the outcry is so great, and comes from so many sides and always has the same tenor, it is indeed an awkward matter, and very dangerous."[40] Whereas de Quadra's letters to Philip hint that what was being said was too alarming to report, Breuner had been explicitly instructed by the emperor to discover, report, and assess the rumors circulating at court. His more frank accounts contain information not available elsewhere and help to explain why Elizabeth decided she could not marry Dudley at that time and why she was not prepared either to marry Archduke Charles or to end the negotiations.

Instructed by the emperor to find out whether there was any truth to the rumors, Breuner "made most diligent inquiries into the calumnies that are current about the Queen not only abroad but also here in England." He hired an agent who was on intimate terms with the ladies of Elizabeth's bedchamber and one person, Kate Ashley, who had raised her since she was a child: "They all swear by all that is holy that her Majesty has most certainly never been forgetful of her honour." Still, Breuner felt dutybound to add, "it is not without significance that Her Majesty's Master of the Horse, Mylord Robert, is preferred by the Queen above all others, and that Her Majesty shows her liking for him more markedly than is consistent with her reputation and dignity."[41]

In answer to the emperor's question about Elizabeth's honor, Breuner recounted an anecdote about Elizabeth and Kate Ashley that is repeatedly cited. She

implored her in God's name to marry and put an end to all these disreputable rumours, telling Her Majesty that her behavior towards the said Master of the Horse occasioned much evil-speaking; for she showed herself so affectionate to him that Her Majesty's honour and dignity would be sullied, and her subjects would in time become discontented. Her Majesty would thus be the cause of much bloodshed in this realm, for which she would have to give account to God and by which she would merit the eternal curse of her subjects. Rather than that this should happen she would have strangled Her Majesty in the cradle.[42]

Breuner reported this conversation on August 6, after he had been instructed to get to the bottom of the rumors about Elizabeth's relationship with Dudley; however, I suspect the conversation actually occurred shortly before May 30 because that would explain why Elizabeth was so anxious to tell the ambassadors she'd rather be a nun or even die than be forced to marry someone against her will.

Wasting Words

De Quadra saw himself as Breuner's mentor and supporter, for as de Quadra wrote to Feria, "This ambassador does exactly as he is told, neither more nor less, and he is quite a good fellow, but this must surely be the first negotiation he ever conducted in his life."[43] When Elizabeth's demands were at odds with the emperor's instructions, de Quadra advised Breuner what to say both to Elizabeth and the emperor. When Breuner was at his wits end, de Quadra intervened, both with Elizabeth and with the emperor. By August de Quadra had insinuated himself so successfully that the emperor essentially put him in charge of the negotiations: "we command you again and exhort you to remain in constant communication with the Orator of the August King of Spain," Ferdinand wrote Breuner, for that is "the best means" to "bring this English business to a successful issue."[44]

As the political difficulty of negotiating a major international alliance combined with the personal strain of negotiating an unconventional courtship, Elizabeth's rhetorical and ideological challenge was to maintain the mutual dignity of both choices while defending her right to rule the country herself regardless of which choice she made. The diplomatic correspondence repeatedly spells out what Elizabeth had already told parliament more warily and obliquely: that she would consider a suitor only if he made her desire what (as she put it) she would otherwise have no wish for. "We continued at this for some time wasting words," reported de Quadra, "and at last she said she was resolved not to marry except to a man of worth whom she had seen and spoken to, and she asked me whether I thought the archduke Charles would come to this country that she might see him. . . . I really believe she would like to arrange for this visit in disguise."[45] Elizabeth may have been romantic enough to think that the veil of secrecy would heighten the drama and increase the chance of success, since clandestine courtships were often portrayed in literature as passionate and thrilling. Yet she was also being strategic and politically resourceful, for, as she explained to the ambassador, if Charles came to England in secret and either one of them decided not to go through with the marriage, Charles could return home quietly and no one would face a humiliating public rejection.[46]

Not wanting to create even the appearance of encouraging the Archduke's suit, lest she seem to bind herself in advance, Elizabeth reiterated that she could not make up her mind unless and until she had an opportunity to "see and know" the archduke. The emperor, however, refused to allow Charles to come to England until the marriage was "certain." In that case, Elizabeth replied, "she did not wish the Archduke to come, by any means, as she did not wish to bind herself even indirectly to marry him."[47] De Quadra recounted the conversation to the emperor:

> We were at this for a long time wasting words, and at last she said the following words to me, which I copy here that your Majesty may the better consider them. She said, "Shall I speak plainly and tell you the truth? I think that if the Emperor so desires me for a daughter he would not be doing too much by sending his son here without so many safeguards. I do not hold myself of so small account that the Emperor need sacrifice any dignity in doing it."[48]

This is one of the rare occasions when de Quadra remarks that he was reporting *exactly* what Elizabeth said. Elizabeth's decision to give de Quadra what he wanted, the plain and simple truth, was itself a rhetorical strategy, for it suggested that refusing to recognize her "desire" would itself be an affront to her stature and dignity. The "truth" Elizabeth offered was not what de Quadra wanted to hear. As her conditional syntax ("if...he would...") indicated, to "speak plainly" was to assert the "truth" that diplomatic language needed to be complex enough, or qualified enough, to encompass the contingencies of "sending his son here without so many safeguards."

Throughout this interview, or at least throughout this unusually rich and pivotal letter, Elizabeth never budged from her central bargaining position: "she reminded me that we were to agree that she was not to be bound to marry the Archduke if he came: "She says it is not fit for a queen and a maiden to summon anyone to marry her for her pleasure." Constrained by these maidenly expectations, Elizabeth could only imply what decorum prevented her from saying more directly: that she wanted to meet Charles in order to decide whether being married to him would suit "her pleasure." It does seem as if she would have liked him to come, if the emperor would allow him to do so without a prior commitment from her, for two weeks later, when the ambassadors led her to believe that the visit was imminent, de Quadra reported, "the Queen is very pleased and gay, as she thinks the Archduke is coming, but otherwise as fickle as ever, and as determined to see him before deciding."[49]

Despite Elizabeth's attempt to make her position as plain and clear as possible, de Quadra was unwilling or unable to credit what she said. As a result, this letter contains some of the most blatant discrepancies between Elizabeth's assertions and the ambassador's interpretations:[50]

> she reminded me that we were to agree that she was not to be bound to marry the Archduke if he came, and knowing that this was only dissimulation and that she really means to marry him, as I think, for otherwise she would never consent to his coming which she has always refused hitherto, I agreed to this condition, and said all should be as she wished.... Sometimes again, she said it might be so, but she was not decided one way or the other: in short, if I were to tell your Majesty that I considered the business otherwise than certain, I should be going against my conscience.[50]

Although Elizabeth repeatedly insisted that the outcome was uncertain, de Quadra claimed that he would not encourage Archduke Charles to come to England if he, de Quadra, "considered the business otherwise than certain." Perhaps, de Quadra claimed the outcome was "certain" because the Emperor had already declared that he would send Charles to England only on the condition that Elizabeth's intention to marry him was already "sure and certain"; still, de Quadra would not have risked deceiving the emperor and undermining his own credibility if he hadn't felt the trip was likely to produce the desired results.

From the start and throughout the negotiations Elizabeth remained faithful to her original "vow to marry no man whom she had not seen." On this fundamental point her position remained absolutely consistent and explicit throughout. When de Quadra pressed her, saying the emperor needed "to know whether she would marry the Archduke... her answer was that she did not want to marry him or anybody else, and if she married at all it would only be to a man whom she knew."[51] Did Elizabeth want or intend to remain single? Or was she losing interest in the archduke because she was hoping to marry a man whom she already knew, Robert Dudley? Most likely, Elizabeth herself did not know, for there was no way of determining when or whether Amy Dudley's sickness would kill her, or whether she and Charles would like each other enough to want to marry were they allowed to meet. But rather than acknowledging the uncertainty, de Quadra's letter to the emperor concluded: "It can hardly be believed, moreover, that if she did not mean to marry she would condescend to such vanity as to bring a son of your Majesty here to no purpose."[52] Of course, there *was* a "purpose" in bringing the archduke to England, but de Quadra couldn't or wouldn't acknowledge it. In one sense, however, he was absolutely right: *he* was incapable of believing that Elizabeth would bring the emperor's son all the way to England in order to decide whether she wanted to marry him—or whether she wanted to marry "anyone" at that time.

No matter that she repeatedly told de Quadra that she could not make a decision until she could see and know her suitor. No matter that de Quadra had previously accepted this condition. He was ideologically incapable of believing that she could possibly mean what she said—or that anything that radical and unconventional could possibly be what she meant. Realizing what she was up against, Elizabeth threatened to write out the terms upon which the archduke would be welcome to visit, and to send them to the Emperor herself:

> when I pressed her much she seemed frightened and protested again and again that she was not to be bound, and that she was not resolved yet whether she should marry; but this was after we had agreed about the Archduke's visit. At length, to give me to understand that she was serious in her demand, she repeated what we had agreed upon in order that I should put it in writing, and when I took this as a joke she said she would not trust me as she knew I was deceiving her, and she would write to the King herself.[53]

While Elizabeth's discussions with the ambassadors continued to go nowhere, Elizabeth's intimacy with Dudley continued to provoke rumors. On October 5 de Quadra wrote to tell Philip that Elizabeth said "she did not dare to summon [the Archduke] as she feared he might not be satisfied with her." When de Quadra offered reassurances, Elizabeth "replied that he might not be dissatisfied with what he saw but with what he heard about her, as I knew there were people in the country who took pleasure in saying anything that came into their heads about her. This she said with some signs of shame." Shame, of course, is different from guilt, for shame implies the embarrassment of not complying with public codes of conduct. Whether Elizabeth actually felt shame or whether de Quadra thought that any woman making such a statement should display "some signs of shame," or whether he thought that's what Philip would expect to hear, is impossible to know. Still, de Quadra gave Elizabeth the reassurances she wanted: "if there were anything which the Archduke should not hear or learn, the idea of his coming would not have been entertained by us." With this, de Quadra "saw she was pleased as she no doubt thought that if the Archduke heard any of the idle tales they tell about her (and they tell many) he might take advantage of them to the detriment of her honor if the match were broken off, and, although from this point of view I was not sorry, as the fear may not be without advantage to us."[54] Even malicious gossip could be turned to political advantage, as both Elizabeth and de Quadra clearly recognized.

What kind of a person would speak this way, de Quadra wondered. Since she was not acting the way a monarch was supposed to act, she must be, as he wrote to the emperor, "in short, only a passionate ill-advised woman."[55] Breuner expressed similar reservations about being forced to negotiate with a woman: "Her Highness is after all a woman, influenced by insidious advice and very susceptible to passions"; "I must most humbly beg Your Imperial Majesty to reflect that in order to obtain anything I had perforce to accommodate myself to Her Majesty's headstrong temper"; "We also beseech Your Imperial Majesty to reflect that we have to deal with a woman, and that she herself told us we must not treat with her Councillors."[56] Frustrated by their own failure to cinch the negotiations and annoyed that Elizabeth was not acting according to expected rules of diplomacy and decorum, the ambassadors concluded, "With her all is falsehood and vanity."[57]

Having failed to convince the emperor to allow Charles to come to England, the ambassadors tried to frighten Elizabeth into acquiescence. When that produced nothing but a reprimand from King Philip, they turned their anger against Elizabeth in particular and women in general. To be sure, they had every reason to feel frustrated and even angry. Elizabeth *was* being difficult and exasperating. After all, it was their job to find Charles a wife. Not only did Elizabeth change her position as circumstances changed, she also ignored the rules of the game. Baffled and understandably frustrated by Elizabeth's unconventional behavior, de Quadra wrote Feria that she was quite without moral compunctions and just plain stupid: "Your Lordship's opinion with regard to the Queen's marriage would hold good in the case of a woman of brains and conscience with which this one is not troubled, but as it is, I think she either will not marry, or, if she do, it will only be because she has brought the Archduke here and likes him.... [T]he Queen says the most extraordinary things."[58] Although he admits that a woman with "brains and conscience" could exist in theory, de Quadra's preconceptions about women made him unable to recognize one when he saw her. These men would have been willing to forgive Elizabeth her female sex, if she had been willing to act like a proper female, that is, if she had concealed her passionate desires along with her powerful intelligence.[59] When sustained reiteration finally forced the ambassadors to consider the possibility that Elizabeth was serious about making no predetermination one way or the other *until* she had seen and talked to her suitor herself, they responded with conventional misogynist derision.

Fit for a Queen and a Maiden

Because Elizabeth was not only a monarch but also a queen, the ambassadors judged her words and actions according to the assumptions about women that dominated their world. Misogyny pervades early modern discourse; indeed, it was the default setting, as Shakespeare's comedies repeatedly illustrate. When Rosalind decides to retain her identity as Ganymede so that she can decide whether she really wants to marry Orlando, she invokes familiar misogynist stereotypes, for not to have done so would have made her male disguise completely unconvincing. Misogynist rhetoric pervaded the men's club of international diplomacy just as cuckold jokes permeate the male banter in *Much Ado about Nothing*.[60]

Misogynist rhetoric plays an even more dominant and disturbing role in Shakespeare's tragedies. In *Antony and Cleopatra*, after fleeing the battle of Actium, Antony lashes out at Cleopatra, calling her a "triple-turn'd whore" (4.12.13) to cover up his own defeated manhood. Tormented by his own delay in fulfilling his dead father's injunction and isolated by his mother's remarriage and Ophelia's sudden decision to return his love letters and tokens as *her* father commanded, Hamlet projects his feelings of rejection onto all women. He tells Ophelia to "get thee to a nunn'ry" (3.1.136–137) because "Frailty, thy name is woman" (1.2.146). When Goneril and Regan send Lear off to the heath to suffer the ravages of a storm-beaten body and storm-filled mind, he too blames his misery on female sexuality: "Down from the waist they are Centaurs, / Though women all above; /.../ Beneath is all the fiends': there's hell, there's darkness" (4.6.124–27). Shakespeare's plays are full of such agonizing moments, but that doesn't make Shakespeare a misogynist, because his plays repeatedly represent such discourse as mistaken—as the sign of wounded pride or misplaced anger. Shakespeare praises the young man of the sonnets for not being "acquainted / With shifting change as is false women's fashion" (20: 3–4), but that judgment is soon called into question by the young man's own shifty behavior.

It is tempting to criticize de Quadra and Feria for resorting to antifeminist stereotypes, but they were not evil men. They were simply conventional men who could deal with Elizabeth's unconventional rhetoric only by reducing her words and actions to familiar, explicable generalizations. As the negotiations deteriorated, Feria and de Quadra exchanged letters where, free from the constraints of their official diplomatic responsibilities, they expressed their unabashed disdain. Writing on October 14, Feria made no attempt to disguise his derision:

> I should be glad if that woman...were to quite lose her head and bring matters to a point, although when I think what a baggage she is and what a crew she is surrounded by, there is probability enough of my wish coming true. It seems the Emperor up to the present refuses leave for his son to go, and, to tell the truth, I cannot persuade myself that he is wrong, nor do I believe that she will either marry him, or refuse to marry him, whilst the matter at issue is only his visit. Real necessity, however, may make her open her eyes and marry.[61]

Did Feria think Elizabeth would have to be carried away by a fit of passion and "quite lose her head" to betroth herself to the archduke? Or did he think she would be crazy to reject him? Probably the latter, although given the political and religious complications, it is hard to know which would, in fact, have been crazier. What does seem clear, however, is that Feria thought Elizabeth had already all but lost her head. To his way of thinking, any woman who thought she could escape the powerful cultural *psychomachia* that divided women into chaste virgins or faithful wives on the one hand and "baggage" or whores on the other must be mad.

On November 4, the emperor sent an ultimatum: "we have not departed from our determination not to send our son to England until our Orator...shall have given us sure and certain tidings that these negotiations will have the desired result....His Highness cannot travel otherwise than in full publicity with a large retinue."[62] On November 13 de Quadra wrote to Philip,

> I had heard from a certain person who is accustomed to give me veracious news that Lord Robert has sent to poison his wife. Certainly all the Queen has done with us and with the Swede [i.e., Erik, who was also courting Elizabeth], and will do with the rest in the matter of her marriage, is only keeping Lord Robert's enemies and the country engaged with words until this wicked deed of killing his wife is consummated.

A fine choice of words! "The same person told me some extraordinary things about this intimacy, which I would never have believed, only that now I find Lord Robert's enemies in the Council making no secret of their evil opinion of it."[63] De Quadra was too decorous to specify, but the intimations ("some extraordinary things about this intimacy," "their evil opinion of it") are as damning as any particulars could have been.

It wasn't until ten months later, on September 8, 1560, that Dudley's wife actually fell down the stairs of their country house and died. The world was abuzz with rumors that Dudley and Elizabeth had conspired to kill her so that they could marry. The charge was dismissed by an official judicial inquiry and has been generally discredited by modern scholars. Nonetheless, the earlier rumors that de Quadra helped circulate heightened the world's suspicions. Before long, Elizabeth's provocative behavior was spawning widespread rumors of illegitimate children. In 1560 Mother Anne Dowd was tried for treason and imprisoned for "openly asserting that the Queen was with child by Robt. Duddeley."[64] Dionisia Deryck said the Queen "hath already had as many children as I, and that two of them were yet alive, one a man child and the other a maiden child, and the others were burned...my Lord of Leicester [Dudley] was the father and wrapped them up in the embers in the chimney which was in the chamber where they were born."[65] Though egregious charges against the queen's honor were subject to trial and punishment for treason, the scandalous gossip proliferated.

As the possibility of Charles' visit dwindled, the ambassadors' frustration and disappointment turned to exasperation and anger. Mary Sidney warned de Quadra that he would only scare Elizabeth off altogether if he became too aggressive, but he nonetheless thought he could frighten her into acquiescence. Accordingly, he wrote Philip on February 3 that the "way to ensure our business and decide the Queen to this marriage was to keep her in doubt as to your friendship, and even in a state of fear and alarm."[66] Much as de Quadra had initially thought Elizabeth could be induced to adopt a more naïve and simple view of diplomatic discourse, he now assumed she would be susceptible to terror tactics because she was a weak, vulnerable woman. Once again he miscalculated.

Being a woman, and a relatively young woman at that, Elizabeth felt bullied. Intimidation made her face her all-too-real vulnerabilities. She reacted not by becoming pliant or susceptible to manipulation but by becoming anxious and defensive. Then, calling upon the reserves of strength she had developed while being incarcerated in the tower and held under house arrest at Woodstock, she became positively regal, asserting her right to rule the country herself whether or not she decided to marry. In what amounted to a climactic showdown, Elizabeth told de Quadra that

> nothing would suffice to make her think of marrying, or even treating of marriage; but the person she was to marry pleasing her so much as to cause her to desire what at present has no wish for, and if this was not the case it was no good thinking that she would ever marry at all. If the Emperor thought it did not suit him to send his son until she had expressed her desire, she, for her part, did not choose to declare it until she had seen the person she was expected to love.[67]

Adopting an uncharacteristically confessional tone ("the reason why she did not marry was really only because"[68]) and using the discourse of "love" and "desire" more boldly than ever before, Elizabeth told de Quadra point blank that she would not marry unless or until she met a man who aroused her desire. On this note, the negotiations came to an end.

The Most Difficult Thing in the World

The diplomatic dialogues we have been examining comprise a complex web of assertion and interpretation, calculation and surmise, hopeful self-promotion and defensive self-justification. Language was the medium of exchange, but neither side believed that spoken words could be taken at face value. Elizabeth repeatedly expressed concern that her words were being disregarded and misunderstood, and very often they were. She, therefore, continued to elaborate her position, repeating her main points over and over again. "It is her wont to make long digressions," Breuner reported, "and after much circumlocution to come to the point of which she wishes to speak."[69] When the ambassadors seemed skeptical, or resistant, or confused, Elizabeth would elucidate, or qualify, or complicate, or reformulate her position. Sometimes she simplified her language, but more often she tried to find another way to explain why her position entailed complications that necessitated qualifications.

If Elizabeth's assertions seemed variable and even contradictory, that was partially due to the ambassador's failure to understand or credit what she was saying and partially due to the fact that her position did, in fact, change, both to accommodate the constantly evolving political situation at home and abroad and to protect herself from the contradictory messages the ambassadors were themselves giving her. Although the emperor insisted that Elizabeth must make her intention to marry the archduke absolutely "certain" before he would send Charles and an official delegation to England, the emperor was himself uncertain whether he wanted the negotiations to proceed. The more he heard about the reformation of the English Church, or about England's military difficulties in Scotland and France, or about the potentially "dangerous" rumors of Elizabeth's relationship with Dudley, the more hesitant he became, telling de Quadra that it "would not be advisable to push these negotiations too vehemently, or to abandon them entirely, until we know for certain what the Queen and her subjects think of the change in religion, of the proposed marriage, and of other matters in which we are interested."[70]

As the diplomatic conversations unfolded, a wary familiarity, born of proximity and recurrence, developed. To a certain extent Elizabeth felt freer to speak and act as she chose because she had no direct experience in governance or diplomatic proceedings. She was improvising, figuring out what to say and do as events unfolded. Fortunately, she was a quick study. The resulting independence of mind was one of her greatest strengths, for it enabled her to think outside the box and to speak and act in innovative, unconventional ways. By keeping the ambassadors off guard, her novel diplomacy helped her to stay one step ahead of the negotiations. Yet, at the same time, her lack of experience and unconventional tactics were also a limitation because the ambassadors expected negotiations to proceed along predictable and very different channels. As a result, they often felt confused, frustrated, and baffled by her unconventional tactics.

Ultimately, Elizabeth and the ambassadors were divided by basic, intractable differences: national priorities, sexuality and gender, religion, generational attitudes, power, status, and, above all, language. To some extent, the distance between Elizabeth and the ambassadors was a question of translation—of the gap between Elizabeth's English, de Quadra's Spanish, the emperor's Latin, and Breuner's German. Yet the problem was exacerbated by fundamental differences in their conceptions of how the subject, or the self, is represented in language.

Compared to Elizabeth, de Quadra had a relatively simple conception of "intention," "truth," and, above all, "words." Sometimes, it seems, he simply did not grasp what Elizabeth was saying. Sometimes, he may have deliberately chosen to hear or heed only part of what she was saying—a common diplomatic ploy. (Consider, for example, President Kennedy's resolution of the Cuban missile crisis: disregarding Khrushchev's final ultimatum, Kennedy responded instead to a prior, more negotiable communication.) Yet the more Elizabeth insisted she could not decide whether she wanted to marry the archduke until she met him, the more confidently de Quadra discounted her words to maintain his own contrary view of the situation: "I was neither blind nor deaf and could easily perceive that the Queen was not taking this step to refuse her consent after all."[71] Although it is easy to understand and even sympathize with de Quadra's frustration and impatience, his readiness to trust what he "could easily perceive," combined with his need to "be sure about her," meant that he could not "understand her" any better at the end of the negotiations than he did at the beginning, although, no doubt, there were also moments when Elizabeth didn't fully understand herself either.

At times, Elizabeth's words were enigmatic and inscrutable; at other times, they were bluntly insistent. The ambassadors were equally inept at analyzing her language in either case. When she was straightforward, they assumed she was dissembling. When she was elusive, they assumed she was being devious and duplicitous. They were distrustful at the outset, claiming that "her language (learnt from Italian heretic friars who brought her up) is so shifty that it is the most difficult thing in the world to negotiate with her,"[72] and they grew even more suspicious as time went on.

In his first letter to the emperor, de Quadra reported that Elizabeth's advisors were "divided amongst themselves and have a willful woman for a monarch."[73] When negotiations broke down, they complained that she was nothing but a "headstrong," "fickle," unreasonable woman, ill-prepared for the job she had inherited through no merit of her own. As negotiations intensified, they wrote to Ferdinand and Philip in rapid succession, correcting one misperception after another, complaining that Elizabeth's language was "most vague and obscure," "feigned," full of "evasions and subterfuges," and that "nothing has been done here that was not equivocal and hypocritical."[74] The more assertive Elizabeth became, the more they discounted her words as calculating, manipulative, and untrustworthy. Yet, had she recorded her view of the conversations, the ambassadors' words would, no doubt, have seemed equally unreliable. To them, her words seemed like "vanity" and "nonsense," vacillating, evasive, unpredictable, irrational, and ultimately incomprehensible. To her, their strategies must have seemed frustrating, obtuse, simplistic, rigidly conventional, and bullying.

The reported diplomatic conversations we have been examining were at once rhetorical in the Aristotelian or humanist sense of using words and figures of speech to persuade and dialogic in the Bakhtinian sense of anticipating or incorporating an answering response that embodied an entire culture of dissonant voices.[75] Although both sides were carefully choosing and weighing their words, hoping to sway each other's words, that was as far as their shared assumptions went. De Quadra's deep-seated distrust of language reflected his cynical view that words were not what they seemed, but that did not shake his old-fashioned belief that a person's intentions were singular and knowable. When Breuner first arrived, de Quadra described him rather condescendingly as "[t]his good man, however, who is not the most crafty person in the world."[76] De Quadra encouraged Breuner to prevaricate about Charles' religion since "[t]he evil of this is not in saying it, but in doing it....I do not condemn words but only intentions and acts as great good may be done."[77] Perhaps because de Quadra himself believed that successful diplomacy needed to use false and misleading words, he was ready to claim and for the most part seemed to believe he knew what Elizabeth meant, even when his account of what she said contradicted his explanation of what she meant. Elizabeth's words failed to evoke the response or result she desired, at least in part, because the ambassadors were too ready to dismiss what she said as "falsehood and vanity." The ambassadors tried to the best of their ability to understand Elizabeth, for that was their job. Yet, despite the opportunity to "see" her and to "hear" her words, they lacked the analytic capabilities to understand what they were seeing and hearing because they were unable to live with what Keats called "Negative Capability, that is when man is capable of being in uncertainties, Mysteries, doubts, without any irritable reaching after fact & reason."[78]

Elizabeth's vow to marry no man she had not seen proved a partially successful strategy for a new and vulnerable female monarch. Her politics of courtship increased her power by expanding the opportunity to negotiate and maintain relations with foreign powers without committing herself to a marriage that might have displeased or disempowered her. Of course, many male monarchs would also have welcomed the opportunity to see and know their prospective bride before agreeing to marry her, as Elizabeth herself acknowledged when she offered Charles the same right of refusal. Elizabeth's demand would have been a difficult and unusual negotiating position even for as commanding a king as her father, but it was all the more difficult for a queen who was simultaneously combating the widespread assumption that she "would only wed a man who was not only King in name, but would also govern her Royal self and the whole Kingdom."[79]

As Elizabeth's confidence in the validity of her own "will" and the acumen of her political judgment grew stronger, so did her determination to avoid the constraints of an arranged marriage. If the ambassadors were outwitted, they weren't completely outmaneuvered, because Elizabeth herself accomplished only part of what she set out to do. She avoided committing herself to a husband sight unseen, and she established her right to carry on the negotiations and make the decision herself. Yet she failed to convince the emperor to allow Charles to come to England to court her, although the negotiations dragged on so long that Elizabeth herself may have begun to think it would be better for Charles not to come. Ultimately, I suspect, there was nothing she could have said, and nothing the ambassadors could have reported, that would have convinced the emperor to accept her preconditions. Yet, whatever her underlying intentions or ulterior motives, whatever her relations with Dudley, whatever her fears about being subordinated to a husband, Elizabeth remained noncommittal about the archduke for the straightforward reason that she repeatedly stated: she could not possibly know whether she wanted to marry him because she had never met him. This motive was so radical at the time, so contrary to what tradition dictated and good sense seemed to require, that it took months for the ambassadors to credit it.

What emerges from the diplomatic negotiations is a distinctly un-Petrarchan tale of female "desire" and "will." Elizabeth's highly unconventional politics of courtship redefined marriage, not as a foregone conclusion requiring dutiful female subjection to patriarchal power, but as an ongoing conversation about a man who might or might not be capable of "pleasing her so much as to cause her to desire what at present she has no wish for."[80] Negotiations between Elizabeth and Charles would resume in 1563 after Maximilian succeeded his father as Holy Roman Emperor, but the first stage of the courtship reached an impasse in March 1560 due to the irreconcilable differences highlighted in this chapter.

CHAPTER 6

PARLIAMENTARY SPEECHES (1563, 1566) AND THE PSALTER POSY

Then those that daylie see her grace,
Whose vertue passeth euerie wight,—
Her comelie corps, her christall ace,—
They ought to pray, both day and night,
That God may graunt most happie state
Unto that Princesse and her mate.

"A Strife betwene Appelles and Pigmalion"[1]

She Says the Most Extraordinary Things

Elizabeth's refusal either to make an expeditious, politic match or to rule out marriage altogether embroiled the country in a series of prolonged marriage negotiations that dominated the first half of the reign. The rhetorical challenge facing Elizabeth was to maintain the mutual force of both choices, neither precluding marriage altogether nor conceding to a marriage she did not desire. Only thus could she enjoy the personal and political advantages of courtship while maintaining her autonomy and freedom of choice.

When parliament reconvened in 1563, the queen had recently recovered from smallpox, and "the great terror and dreadful warning"[2] of her near demise prompted parliament to present her with two successive marriage petitions, one from the House of Commons and another from the House of Lords. The Commons petition was presented to the queen, both orally and in writing, by the speaker of the House, Thomas Williams, on January 28, 1563. Cognizant of Elizabeth's earlier provisos, the Commons explicitly acknowledged the queen's power and hinted at its fear of offending her: "most high and mighty princess and our most dread sovereign lady." The epithets "high and mighty" and "dread" indicate that, four years after ascending the throne, Elizabeth was, like her father Henry VIII, admired, feared, and held in awe; or at least that is what the Commons thought it would be politic to declare. At the same time, the nouns "princess" and "lady" call attention to her female body, which was, after all, the fundamental issue since the purpose of the petition was to hasten "the most honorable issue of your body" (CW 73).

After humbly acknowledging Elizabeth's authority, the petition stated, in the most explicit terms possible, that choosing a husband and producing an heir were not only the most urgent matters facing Elizabeth as queen but also the country's most pressing concerns:

> And forasmuch as your said subjects see nothing in this whole estate of so great importance to your majesty and the whole realm, nor so necessary at this time to be reduced into a certainty, as the sure continuance of the governance and th'imperial crown thereof in your majesty's person and the most honorable issue of your body, which almighty God send us to our highest comfort, and for want thereof, in some certain limitation to guide the obedience of our posterity. (CW 73)

Secondarily, the Commons urged Elizabeth to limit the succession to prevent pandemonium should she die childless; however, the primary purpose of the petition was to pressure her to marry so that she could give birth to an heir.[3]

The petition asked Elizabeth to consider the situation as her "subjects see" it. From their point of view her refusal to make an expeditious marriage threatened to plunge the country into chaos. Indeed, parliament could not have described the situation more alarmingly:

> the great dangers, the unspeakable miseries of civil wars: the perilous intermeddlings of foreign princes with seditions, ambitions, and factious subjects at home; the waste of noble houses; the slaughter of people; subversions of towns; intermission of all things pertaining to the maintenance of the realm; unsurety of all men's possessions, lives, and estates; daily interchange of attainders and treasons. (CW 73–74)

No matter how successfully Elizabeth governed the country, her female body, open to suitors and traitors alike, fueled national anxieties about foreign invasion and civil disorder. The dangers were no doubt real, but they were neither as imminent nor as inevitable as this hyperbolic prophecy of doom maintains. In the Elizabethan political and gender unconscious, the presence of an unmarried woman on the throne constituted an "unspeakable" threat to the social order.[4]

The dire consequences that would occur should Elizabeth fail to marry and settle the succession provide a strong contrast to the pleasure and comfort that marriage would bring, or so the petition argued:

> your most loving, natural, and obedient subjects do present unto you our most lowly suit and petition. That forasmuch as your majesty's person should come to most undoubted and best heirs of your crown, such as in time to come we would most comfortably see and our posterity shall most joyfully obey, it may please your most excellent majesty for our sakes, for our preservation and comforts, and at our most humble suit, to take yourself some <u>honorable husband whom</u> it shall please you to join to you in marriage. Whomsoever it be that your majesty shall choose, we protest and

promise with all humility and reverence to honor, love, and serve as to our most bounden duty shall appertain. (CW 76)

In presenting themselves as "obedient" and "loving" subjects, the Commons were responding to the doubts about their "love" and loyalty expressed by Elizabeth in 1559. Moreover, by recognizing her freedom to choose her own husband "as it may please" her, the Commons acknowledged and accepted Elizabeth's central contention: that she did indeed have the right to choose a husband according to her own liking. At the same time, however, the Commons hoped it would "please your most excellent majesty" to marry "for our sakes, for our preservation and comforts." That was more problematic: by asking her to put their comforts and desire before her own, the Commons was doing exactly what Elizabeth's 1559 speech warned them not to do: "to take upon you to draw my love to your liking" (CW 57).

When presented with the first marriage petition in 1559, Elizabeth offered a polite but evasive response to the Commons delegation and then wrote a formal speech to be read by the speaker to the assembly. Perhaps because the 1563 petition made the situation seem so urgent and so dire, Elizabeth responded immediately. Since no marriage treaty had been negotiated, she could not announce her engagement on the spot, so how should she respond? Instead of trying to refute the Commons' arguments point by point, Elizabeth chose to confront the underlying cause of their anxiety:

> The weight and greatness of this matter might cause in me, being a woman wanting both wit and memory, some fear to speak and bashfulness besides, a thing appropriate to my sex. But yet the princely seat and kingly throne wherein God (though unworthy) hath constituted me, maketh these two causes to seem little in mine eyes, though grievous perhaps to your ears, and boldeneth me to say somewhat in this matter, which I mean only to touch but not presently to answer. (CW 70)

After four years on the throne, it seems remarkable that Elizabeth still sounds so hesitant: "and boldeneth me to say somewhat in this matter." Say what? Was Elizabeth still struggling to establish her authority? Or was she using the humility *topos,* playing the role of a weak and "unworthy" woman to win sympathy and allay suspicion? Probably, some of both.

This is one of the most widely discussed passages in all of Elizabeth's writing, no doubt because it is one of the few times that she confronted the relation between gender and power so explicitly. Allison Heisch cites this passage in an early and scathing feminist critique, which condemns Elizabeth for believing that a "fear to speak and bashfulness besides" were desirable for all women except herself.[5] Of course, modesty and silence *were* generally expected of Elizabethan women, as John Knox reminded his readers: "a naturall shamfastnes oght to be in womankind, whiche most certeinlie she loseth, when soever she taketh vpon her the office and estate of man." For if God "hath deprived them as before … of speakinge in the congregation, and hath expreslie forbidden them to usurpe any kinde of authoritie above man, howe then will he suffer them to reigne and have empire aboue realmes and nations?"⁶ Elizabeth certainly knew that many members of the English parliament shared this conventional view of women; however, she was not necessarily endorsing such views as suitable or desirable, either for herself or for other women. Indeed, "appropriate to my sex" could mean not only *suitable or proper to my sex* (as Heisch argued and subsequent critics assumed) but also *attached to the female sex by the culture.*⁷

When read in its original historical context, as a response to parliament's petition, Elizabeth's gendered language confronts and queries deep-seated anxieties about female rule. Heisch and most subsequent scholars take Elizabeth's comment that she was "a woman wanting both wit and memory" to mean she thought that she, like all women, was "wanting" or lacking "wit and memory" (CW 70). Yet if that is what her words meant, surely she was speaking ironically, since her parliamentary speeches repeatedly deny any such assumption.⁸

Not only is Elizabeth's main verb a subjunctive contrary to fact ("might cause in me"), but her diction is also riddled with ambiguities and contingencies. By calling attention to what society considered "appropriate" female behavior, Elizabeth's language forces her male subjects to confront their prejudices against her as a woman. Furthermore, as a transitive verb, "want" meant not only *to lack* but also *to be in need of*, and according to the *Oxford English Dictionary,* the two senses were often humorously contrasted. Instead of denigrating herself and all women, I think Elizabeth was suggesting that as a woman she was all the more in need of wit (meaning *the faculty of thinking and reasoning in general; mental capacity, understanding*) and memory (meaning *a recollection of past history* or *a knowledge of government*) to overcome the resistance she faced as a female ruler.

The phrase "wanting both wit and memory" cleverly contrasts Elizabeth's own abundant wit and memory with the widespread misperception that women lacked both. Elizabeth recognized that contradictory assumptions about what women "want," about what they lacked versus what they desired, might still prove "grievous perhaps to your ears," to the ears of her detractors who were chafing at their subjection to her female power. From her vantage point, however, and from the perspective of eternity, such cultural stereotypes were pitifully inadequate, for, as she went on to explain, God's grace "maketh these causes to seem little in mine eyes" (CW 70). She did not say that God's grace made these concerns appropriate for other women but not for her, as Heisch contends. Instead, she said, "in mine eyes": speaking, thanks to God's grace, from an enlightened, transcendent point of view, these widely accepted, conventional assumptions have little force or validity.⁹ This is a direct response to Commons' request that she should accept their view of the situation: "And forasmuch as your said subjects see nothing in this whole estate of so great importance..." By invoking a higher authority, Elizabeth rejected

Commons' "most lowly suit and petition" as unenlightened, or blinded by self-interest. As the Woodstock epigram so pointedly declared, "But all herein can be naught wrought": any meaning can be rendered null by rising above or moving beyond a mistaken, limited, earthly viewpoint. The meaning Heish infers is not the one Elizabeth herself held; rather it is the meaning Elizabeth expected and rebutted in her first parliamentary speech ("my youth and words may seem to some hardly to agree together") (CW 57) and the one she wished once again to face and to nullify here.

By confronting what was considered "appropriate" female behavior, Elizabeth was exposing the pervasiveness rather than affirming the validity of gender stereotypes: "But yet the princely seat and kingly throne wherein God (though unworthy) hath constituted me, maketh these two causes to seem little in mine eyes, though grievous perhaps to your ears" (CW 70). Elizabeth knew, as did her listeners, that God was omniscient and infallible.

Then, in the midst of this comment, Elizabeth's syntax goes askew—generally an indication that she is up to something more complicated than one might at first realize. In mentioning "the princely seat and kingly throne wherein God (though unworthy) hath constituted me," was Elizabeth implying that God Himself was unworthy? Or was she suggesting that she herself was "unworthy"?

The syntactical ambiguity created by the dangling modifier "though unworthy" is the last step in a straw-man argument that invites misprision in order to provoke self-correction. If Elizabeth's listeners rejected the first suggestion that God was "unworthy" (which, of course, they would have to do if they were good Christians) and concluded instead that she was "unworthy" to be the monarch because she was a woman, they would find themselves in deep hermeneutic trouble. God was not only omniscient but also infallible. To think that God had made a mistake in choosing her as his divine representative was sacrilegious; it was also treasonous, since to "say, publish, maintain, declare, or hold opinion that the Queen's majesty…ought not to be Queen of this realm" was an act of treason.[10] By inviting her listeners to entertain this misprision, Elizabeth exposed her male opponents' readiness to leap to dangerous conclusions based on the "unworthy"—in the sense of *unwarranted* or *despicable*—assumption that women lack both wit and memory. Only by bringing these underlying assumptions to the surface could Elizabeth hope to defeat them.

Elizabeth knew that marrying, providing an heir, and limiting the succession were the most important matters confronting her, her government, and her subjects, but she did not agree either with parliament's process of reasoning or with its proposed solution. Whereas the Commons thought it "necessary at this time to be reduced into a certainty" (CW 73), Elizabeth was profoundly uncertain about how best to proceed. The Commons thought only immediate action could prevent "unspeakable miseries." She thought the matter needed careful consideration, which is why she told the Commons delegation, she "[meant] only to touch but not presently to answer" its petition (CW 70).

The Commons cited innumerable precedents from classical antiquity and the Bible as well as English and European history in order to represent her marriage as "this great and only stay of our safeties" (CW 76). Elizabeth thought that the members of parliament were so busy enumerating precedents out of beautiful old books that they failed to grasp the complexities of the situation. Instead of trying to match parliament's argument exemplum for exemplum, Elizabeth chose to tell a story:

> I read of a philosopher whose deeds upon this occasion I remember better than his name who always when he was required to give answer in any hard question of school points would rehearse over his alphabet before he would proceed to any further answer therein, not for that he could not presently have answered, but [to] have his wit the riper and better sharpened to answer the matter withal. If he, a common man, but in matters of school took such delay the better to show his eloquent tale, great cause may justly move me in this, so great a matter touching the benefits of this realm and the safety of you all, to defer mine answer till some other time, wherein I assure you the consideration of my own safety (although I thank you for the great care that you seem to have thereof) shall be little in comparison of that great regard that I mean to have of the safety and surety of you all. (CW 71)

Why flaunt the fact that she could not remember the philosopher's name? Elizabeth was tempting her listeners to respond, "see, you do lack wit and memory." Then, patiently correcting their misprision once again, Elizabeth deftly teased out the significance of the philosopher's advice to show parliament how unwise it would be for her to give them the immediate answer they requested.

Having begun her response to the marriage petitions by eliciting and exposing their prejudices about women's wit, Elizabeth concluded her speech by openly mocking those "restless heads in whose brains the needless hammers beat with vain judgment" (CW 72). Their assumption "that I should mislike this their petition" missed the point, she said. What she misliked was not the petition per se but the "vain judgment," the superficial reasoning and bald presumption that led those "restless heads" to think that such complex matters could be instantly "reduced into a certainty" (CW 73).

To Marry Where It Shall Please You

Modern theories of Elizabethan Petrarchism define subjectivity and desire as inherently male, suggesting that Elizabeth's male subjects depicted her as a Petrarchan lady in order to counter their anxiety and to assert their authority over her female power. Tempting as it might be to apply this theory to the 1563 parliamentary debate, a close examination of the language and the issues shows a very different paradigm emerging, a paradigm that combines Elizabeth's own "loving" expressions of reciprocity for her subjects with her determination to marry only if she and her future husband shared a mutual liking.

The Commons' petition, presented on January 28, urged the queen to marry for her subjects' "comfort" and protection. The Lords presented their own petition on February 1. Like the Commons, the Lords began by presenting themselves as "your faithful, loving, and obedient subjects." With "all humbleness and obeisance," they acknowledged Elizabeth's sovereign power. Yet at the same time their gendered epithets—"good lady and sovereign," "most gracious sovereign lady"—called attention to her female body. The tone of the Lords' petition was more deferential— less alarmist and less vociferously self-seeking than the Commons petition. Whereas the Commons began by elaborating the perils facing the country, the Lords began with two main requests: "The former is that it would please your majesty to dispose yourself to marry where it shall please you, with whom it shall please you, and as soon as it shall please you. The second, that some certain limitation [of the succession] might be made" (CW 81–82). Whereas the Commons acknowledged Elizabeth's conjugal freedom of choice only briefly and in passing, the Lords made it a priority—their first and foremost concern. Using the words "please your majesty" and "please you" four times in quick succession, the Lords made it abundantly clear that they understood and accepted the main point of Elizabeth's 1559 parliamentary speech, that she would marry only someone who "pleased" her enough to gain her "liking" and satisfy her "desire."

When parliament convened in 1563, there were no active, ongoing marriage negotiations with foreign suitors, for Robert Dudley had been preoccupying Elizabeth's attentions. In September 1560 Dudley's wife had fallen down the stairs of their country house and died. Elizabeth would almost certainly have married him at that point, had the incident not generated such damnable rumors. As noted in the previous chapter, there was talk that Robert had his wife murdered so that he could marry the queen. Some said Elizabeth was carrying Dudley's child. Some even claimed that the queen had conspired with her lover to have his wife killed. The official examination of the incident exonerated Dudley, but it did not stop the rumors. Diplomatic correspondence carried daily reports of the scandal. Throckmorton wrote from Paris saying it would be disastrous for Elizabeth to marry Dudley: "God and religion...shall be out of estimation; the Queen our sovereign discredited, contemned, and neglected; our country ruined, undone, and made prey."[11] As the rumors swirled through the country and abroad, Elizabeth decided she could not marry Dudley, at least not then, without making it look as if she were herself implicated in Amy's death.

In 1562 Elizabeth contracted smallpox, and the prospect of her imminent demise led to heated disputes in parliament over the succession. At one moment, the Spanish ambassador reported, Elizabeth awoke from her fever to express her will: Dudley should be given a title and an income of £20,000, and he should be made protector of the kingdom. She said she "loved" him but swore "as God was her witness, nothing improper had ever passed between them."[12] Her bequest of £500 a year to the groom who slept in Dudley's chamber only created further suspicions. Parliament made the logical deduction that Dudley was "her intended." Dudley had powerful allies at court and in parliament, although many resented his intimacy with the queen and distrusted his motives, remarking that he was descended from four generations of traitors. After Elizabeth recovered from smallpox, a consensus seems to have emerged that it would be better

Figure 8. Portrait inscribed Robert Dudley, Earl of Leicester, English School, c. 1586

for her to marry Dudley and bear his child than to remain single and leave the country without a successor.

Of course, the Lords' petition, like the Commons', could not tell Elizabeth whom they thought she should marry, since that was precisely what she forbade them to do in 1559 when she said, "I do well like of and take in good part, because that it is simple and containeth no limitation of place or person. If it had been otherwise, I must needs have misliked it very much and thought it in you a very great presumption" (CW 57). Even though they could not say so directly, the Lords' request for "your majesty to dispose yourself to marry where it shall please you, with whom it shall please you, and as soon as it shall please you" was an implicit endorsement of Robert Dudley, the suitor who had most pleased her, the person Elizabeth said she "loved," and the only man, up to that point, whom it would have seemingly pleased her to marry, circumstances permitting.[13]

It is hard to know what Elizabeth's own feelings about Dudley were at that point, though her hesitation upon being presented with the parliamentary petitions suggests that her reservations had revived with her health. Elizabeth must have begun to think it would not be such a good idea for her to marry him, for on March 24 or thereabouts she suggested to the Scottish ambassador that Mary Queen of Scots should marry Robert Dudley. What a bizarre idea to marry her own favorite to her rival and possible successor! Perhaps, Elizabeth came up with the idea and spoke on the spur of the moment, without weighing the consequences, though that would be uncharacteristic. More likely, she had carefully analyzed the situation and decided the marriage would solve several problems at once. It would give her a trusted ally at the Scottish court, and it would keep Mary from making a match that might prove disastrous to English interests. It would get Dudley off Elizabeth's back and make parliament stop pressuring her to marry him.

Elizabeth was clearly torn about her own feelings for Dudley. She was probably still at least partially in love with him, because even in proposing the idea, she said, "nature has implanted so many graces" in Lord Robert that if she herself "wished to marry she would prefer him to all the princes in the world."[14] But whatever Elizabeth was thinking, politics had once again trumped passion. Perhaps Elizabeth knew all along that the Scottish marriage would come to naught. Yet it was still in the air two weeks later on April 10, 1563, when Elizabeth presented her official response to parliament's petitions at the closing session of parliament.[15]

As in 1559, Elizabeth's speech was read aloud by the speaker. It was brief and to the point, though ambiguities abound. Elizabeth was prepared to discuss the matter of the succession, but as for her marriage she said "a silent thought may serve" (CW 79). Her own plans were still unresolved, and she did not care to declare her intentions or explain her reasons, at least not there, in that august, public arena. The real decision would be made backstage, in private discussions with her most trusted courtiers and councilors or in negotiations with foreign ambassadors.[16]

At this key moment, therefore, Elizabeth had decided once again to use the Woodstock strategy and to say "nothing" that might further confine or constrain her. Yet she felt the need to add a few words to make it absolutely clear that she had *not* taken a vow to live and die a virgin: "And yet, by the way of one due doubt—that I am, as it were, by vow or determination bent never to trade that kind of life—pull out that heresy, for your belief is there awry" (CW 79). To Elizabeth in 1563, a vow of virginity was much worse than "folly," it was "heresy"! Given parliament's express fear of invasion by Catholic powers abroad and traitors at home ("the perillous and intermingling of Foreign Princes with seditious, ambitious, and factious Subjects at home"[17]), a Protestant monarch could not have chosen a more emotionally loaded or politically sensitive term. Elizabeth knew exactly what she was doing; at the outset of the first Elizabethan parliament, after the heated debate over whether she could be the "head" of the church, she had expressly forbidden parliament to use "all contentious, contumelious or opprobrious wordes, as 'heretike', 'schismatike', 'papist', and such like names."[18] The choice of the word "heresy" was Elizabeth's way of declaring that any plans she might be considering would in no way compromise her commitment to the reformed English Church, which had, after all, rejected the Catholic tradition of celibacy by closing the nunneries, removing the beloved statues of the Virgin Mary, ordaining married priests, and transposing the ideal of chastity to marriage.

In the 1563 parliamentary speech Elizabeth asserted her agency and desire even more forcefully than she did in the 1559 speech that it echoes: "being unfitting and altogether unmeet for you to…take upon you to draw my love to your liking or frame my will to your fantasies" (CW 57). Compared to these wary assertions, the 1563 speech bespeaks Elizabeth's monarchical power. The syntax combines a directive speech act, "pull out that heresy" (CW 79), with a performative speech act, "your belief is there awry."[19] The first person nominative pronoun and active verb ("if I can bend my liking to your need") assume full responsibility for the decision. Rather than hiding behind the protection of God's will as she did in 1559, Elizabeth made it clear that she alone could "bend" *her* "liking" to parliament's need.[20]

In the Woodstock epigram Elizabeth defended herself against her foes by saying she had said "nothing" and would say "nothing" that might be used to confirm their suspicions. She used an analogous strategy in 1563: by declaring that she had *not* taken a vow of virginity, she was indeed doing something, she was making "belief…there[in] awry." Then, in a tone at once conciliatory and boldly self-assertive, Elizabeth addressed the heart of the matter: she could not satisfy their request because her marriage was much too murky and complicated a decision to be instantaneously reduced to clarity or certainty. Pestering her further would do no good, on that she also wanted to be absolutely clear.

Indeed, the two sentences that comprise the crux of the answer that was not an answer are as oblique and unresolved as anything Elizabeth had yet written:

> For though I can think it best for a private woman, yet do I strive with myself to think it not meet for a prince. And if I can bend my liking to your need I will not resist such a mind. (CW 79)

The syntax is confusing even with a printed text in hand; it would have been much more puzzling to members of parliament listening to the speech read aloud by the speaker, who was himself not privy to Elizabeth's thoughts and who could not, therefore, clarify the meaning as Elizabeth herself did so successfully in the pre-coronation procession, through eloquent facial expressions, gestures, and meaningful tones of voice.

So what exactly was Elizabeth's answer to parliament's petitions? If "it" refers to virginity, as most scholars assume and as the preceding sentence could suggest, Elizabeth was saying that she thought virginity was "best" reserved for "a private woman," who, unlike a prince, was not responsible for producing an heir to the throne. Yet, even if that was her intended meaning, and I'm not sure it was, the sentence nonetheless signals a sense of internal conflict, of active, ongoing struggle between opposing sides of her character that had not yet been resolved: "yet do I strive with myself." Although it is far from clear what Elizabeth intended to do, her powerful, contradictory feelings about the matter are supremely evident.

As with the Woodstock epigrams, the historical context introduces further, underlying complications that can be gleaned only at the level of the subtext and only through innuendo and double meanings. Given the peculiar intricacies of the historical situation, Elizabeth may have chosen to leave the antecedent of "it" unspecified in order to signal the uncertainty she was struggling to resolve. Let's look at that sentence again: "For though I can think it best for a private woman, yet do I strive with myself to think it not meet for a prince." If she was responding to parliament's desire for her to marry Robert Dudley, the one person she would have married if she had been "a private woman," then "it" might well refer to marriage rather than virginity. With the closing of the nunneries, moreover, "it" was marriage rather than virginity that was deemed "best for a private woman" who lacked the liberty and wealth Elizabeth had acquired by virtue of being a queen. If "it" refers to marriage, as it well might, then the sentence would mean that as "a private woman" Elizabeth would have liked to marry Dudley. Yet, even if parliament thought it "best" for her, as their queen, to marry Dudley and resolve the succession by bearing his child, and even if she herself thought "it" would be "best" for her as a private woman to please herself by marrying him, she was still striving to convince herself that "it" was *not* "best" for her to do so as queen. Clearly, it was these lingering doubts that led her to propose the match between Dudley and Mary Queen of Scots.

Despite her political reservations, Elizabeth could not fully suppress the veiled suggestion that she would have liked to marry Dudley and was still striving to convince herself that it was not a wise political move. That would explain both the syntactical confusion of this pivotal sentence and the surprising disavowal of virginity. Indeed, the handwritten, early draft of the speech, with its numerous corrections and substantial differences from the final version, demonstrates that Elizabeth labored over what to say.[21] Although she did not set out to discuss the mistaken assumption that she was committed to remaining a virgin, that was written into the margin early in the process and remained essentially unchanged throughout the subsequent revisions—stuck there to speak for itself, its connection to what comes before and after left for Elizabeth's listeners to figure out for themselves.

Elizabeth's choice of the impersonal terms, "a private woman" and "a prince," hints that she was thinking not only about herself but also about that other "prince," Mary, Queen of Scots, whose problematic presence loomed over Elizabeth's imagination, even as it shadowed the Elizabethan political unconscious until Mary was finally executed for treason in 1587.[22] Elizabeth's scheme to marry Robert to Mary constitutes the speech's unspoken subtext, the "silent thought" that was far too delicate a matter to be spoken in such a public setting. The situation was complicated. Elizabeth was prepared to remain a virgin should that seem best for the country; that still remained to be determined. However, Mary was far too impulsive and impassioned to remain unwed for long, as her disastrous marriage to Darnley would soon prove. Even if it would be "best" for Mary to wed Dudley rather than someone like Darnley who would create serious problems for Elizabeth and her government, and even if Elizabeth thought it best not to marry Dudley herself, she was still striving with her own lingering "liking" for him, as her "dying" behests had demonstrated so dramatically. The conditional clause, "if I can bend my liking to your need," aptly expresses the strained and somewhat twisted attempt to "bend" her personal "liking" for Dudley to parliament's "need" for a successor.

Thus, while assuring parliament that she would do her "best" to settle the succession, Elizabeth also warned her listeners that her efforts might well come to nothing—that (to cite her poem) "all herein can be naught wrought." After all, Dudley might not share her "liking" for the idea of marrying the Scots queen, or Mary might not share Elizabeth's own "liking" for Dudley. As Elizabeth herself was no doubt keenly aware, she was speaking not only to parliament as a whole but also in particular to Dudley himself, whose "liking" and "need" were as clamorous and complex as her own. Yet, while speaking to him, she could not speak for him—yet another reason why "a silent thought may serve."

At this climactic moment, Elizabeth was torn between her desires as a "private woman" and her responsibilities as queen—a conflict that she would revisit in the equally enigmatic language of "On Monsieur's Departure," the subject of chapter 8. The ambiguity of her language indicates that the situation was far too complex for a single public speech to resolve. Elizabeth was "striving with [her]self" (CW 79) both to think that marriage was not desirable for her as a queen and to think that virginity was not desirable for her as a queen. The result was a confusing combination of persuasion and evasion that we expect from a Shakespeare sonnet but not a political speech. The ambiguous pronoun "it," with its lack of a clear antecedent, poses a grammatical choice that is raised to the level of a hermeneutic principle. Like the dangling parenthetical phrase "though unworthy" (CW 79), the multivalent obliquity of "it" invites Elizabeth's listeners to confront the difficulties that made it impossible to know what was "best" under the circumstances. Enigma and ambiguity simultaneously express and veil what could not be said openly in public. With the strain of these competing imperatives, Elizabeth asked parliament to understand her hesitancy and to respect her uncertainty.

The Windsor Epigram: Your Loving Mistress

The moral discrimination, enigmatic multiplicity of meaning, incisive verbal wit, and self-reflexive form devised in the two Woodstock epigrams became a hallmark of Elizabeth's style. These rhetorical strategies pervade her public speeches, and they became more intricate and sophisticated in her mature poems, such as the epigram written in her psalter, or psalm book, where the concrete physical images of the opening lines pose deeper questions of perception, judgment, trust, and the process of interpretation itself that had come to dominate the 1563 marriage debate between Elizabeth and parliament.

> No crooked leg, no blearèd eye,
> No part deformèd out of kind,
> Nor yet so ugly half can be
> As is the inward, suspicious mind.
> Your loving mistress, *Elizabeth*[23]

Compared, for example, to Donne's or Jonson's satiric epigrams, this language sounds generalized and impersonal. The initial physical traits provide a contrast with the final moral judgment. The poem does not deny the importance of physical attraction or repulsion. Rather, the final epigrammatic turn declares that mental and moral ugliness are far worse than physical deformity. Yet despite the generalizing diction, Elizabeth clearly intended the poem for a particular person because the autograph text, written in her French psalter, was signed, "Your loving mistress, Elizabeth."

The book is now in the Royal Collection, having been presented to Elizabeth II when she was still a princess by Lord and Lady Melchett on the occasion of her wedding, November 20, 1947. The final page of the psalter containing Elizabeth's handwritten poem can be seen online: http://www.royalcollection.org.uk/eGallery/object.asp?searchText=elizab eth+I+french+psalter&x=4&y=14&object=1051956&row=0By

By concealing this brief little poem or posie at the end of the psalter rather than inscribing it on the opening pages, Elizabeth made it into a secret missive of the sort that became popular during her reign.[24] Posies were short, epigrammatic poems that were typically written in a book or on a napkin or ring or mirror, where they could be found by whomever they were intended for. Posies were generally unsigned and unaddressed to protect the author or the addressee, should the text be discovered by someone other than the intended audience. Elizabeth follows the conventions of the genre by discreetly omitting the name of her addressee, as well as any identifiable references to his person. If someone else discovered the poem in the psalter, it would have seemed like an abstract, ethical speculation on the relative importance of body and mind rather than Elizabeth's private judgment of the specific person for whom she wrote the posy.

The puzzling disjunction between the impersonal diction and the intimate signature constitutes the poem's primary interpretive crux. The signature complicates the tone, making it not only trenchant but also conciliatory. "Mistress" meant both *lady-love* and *a woman with power over someone else*; hence the signature reminds Elizabeth's private lyric audience—as she had repeatedly reminded parliament, and as her lyric "Ah, silly pug, wert thou so sore afraid" would later remind "Sir Walter Ralegh"—that *she* was the only one with the power to decide whether a particular suitor or courtier was pleasing or displeasing to her, and whether she was presently and would continue to be his "loving mistress." The signature reveals, moreover, that the epigram was written to and for someone Elizabeth cared about so deeply and knew so intimately that she could read—and sway—his inward mind.

Just as the 1563 parliamentary speech contained a "silent" plea to Dudley, the posie contained a private message for the unidentified person to whom it was addressed. If Elizabeth showed him the poem or, more likely, if she sent or gave him the psalter with a hint to look within, the words would have contained a pointed, veiled reference to a recent interaction—to some sort of unspecified tension or disagreement known to them both. Elizabeth clearly wanted to reassure her private lyric audience that she was still his "loving mistress," even as she felt compelled to warn him that unless he changed his behavior, he would sacrifice her good opinion of him.

The editors of Elizabeth's *Collected Works* suggest that "[t]his may be the 'obscure sentence' referred to by Cecil as written by the queen in 'a book at Windsor' when she was 'much offended with the earl of Leicester' in August 1565" (CW 132).[25] That seems likely for a number of reasons. First, the epigram is a sentence in both senses of the word: both a single grammatical sentence and a maxim, or *sententia*.[26] Second, it *was* actually written by Elizabeth in a book, her French psalm book, which is still extant in the Royal Library at Windsor Castle.[27] Third, the handwriting suggests an early date, and Robert Dudley, who became the Earl of Leicester in 1564, was one of the few people the youthful queen loved and chastised in this way.

Although Cecil's journal entry is also a single rather obscure sentence, his wording contains a valuable clue to the function the epigram may have served: "The Queen Majesty semed to be much offended with the Erle of Lecester, and so she wrote an obscure Sentence in a Book at Wyndsor."[28] The logical connective, "and *so* she wrote," suggests that Elizabeth wrote the "obscure sentence" *because* she had been and still "seemed to be" much offended with Robert Dudley, the Earl of Leicester, the very person whom the 1563 parliamentary petitions tried to convince Elizabeth to marry. But are the epigram and the "obscure sentence" one and the same?[29] Do the events cited by Cecil match and shed light on the Windsor epigram? More importantly, what role might the poem have played in the historical drama unfolding at Windsor Castle in August 1565—and in the politics of Elizabeth's courtship that we have been following in this chapter?

Cecil's journal entry offers no further information, but the reports of the Spanish ambassador, Don Diego Guzmán de Silva, provide a detailed account of what was happening at the time.[30] The queen arrived at Windsor on August 10, 1565, more preoccupied than ever with perturbing questions of courtship and marriage. To Elizabeth's great consternation, the marriage she had tried to arrange between Dudley and Mary Queen of Scots had come to naught, and Mary had recently married Darnley, a decision as rash as it was disastrous. While the English court anxiously awaited news from Scotland, Elizabeth was being actively wooed by several suitors. The French ambassador was pressing for an immediate answer to a marriage proposal from Charles IX. The sister of King Erik of Sweden was on her way to England, presumably to urge Elizabeth to reconsider her brother's suit. Elizabeth thought the French match would make her look ridiculous because Charles was only fourteen years old. Furthermore, she had little interest in reviving the Swedish courtship because Erik had failed to spark her interest when the suit was first proposed in 1559. She was more attentive to the Austrian envoy, Adam von Swetkowich, Baron von Mitterburg, who had been sent to England to try to revive marriage negotiations between Elizabeth and Archduke Charles.[31] "She will have no lack of husbands," de Silva commented.[32]

On July 4, however, Emperor Maximilian sent an uncompromising letter claiming that Elizabeth rather than Charles should provide a dowry since the woman always provided the dowry, and declaring, moreover, that Charles' household expenses should also be paid by her because she was the monarch. Maximilian also demanded certain political prerogatives for his brother, including the right to dispense patronage. Most problematic of all, Charles must be allowed to practice his Catholic religion.[33] Meanwhile, Dudley began jockeying to see whether Elizabeth might still be persuaded to marry him. While doing everything he could to support the Archduke's suit, de Silva believed Elizabeth would marry Dudley or no one.

As we have seen, Elizabeth had repeatedly assured parliament that she would never make a match that was detrimental to the country, as her cousin Mary, Queen of Scots, had just done. Elizabeth's husband would not be granted any political prerogatives; that was not negotiable. She was willing to discuss the possibility of allowing Charles to practice his Catholic religion in private, yet, as she had insisted from the start of the reign and as we have already seen repeatedly, she would not be compelled to marry for pragmatic reasons alone. To that end, she had taken a vow to marry no man whom she had not seen. True to her word, in August 1565 Elizabeth once again refused to commit herself to marrying the archduke—even if the religious, financial, and political differences could be resolved—until he came to England so they could discover whether a mutual liking would develop.

On one level, the Windsor epigram explores the difficult judgments that courtship and courtiership entailed. While the English and Austrian governments were trying to hammer out a marriage agreement, Elizabeth was pondering what qualities were important in a potential husband. Sexual attractiveness and physical deformity may have been on Elizabeth's mind because she had been told earlier that Charles "had a head bigger than the earl of Bedford's."[34] She was much relieved to learn that his head was not, in the words of the epigram, a "part deformèd out of kind." On July 13 de Silva reported, "[we] spoke of the Archduke's person, his age, his good parts, and she evidently felt pleasure in dwelling upon the subject."[35] Elizabeth may also have been thinking about misshapen body parts and marriage because Jane Grey's sister Mary, who had some claim to the succession and whom de Silva described as "little, crookbacked, and very ugly," was living in the queen's household when, on August 20, it "came out ... that she had married a gentleman named Keyes.... They say the Queen is very much annoyed and grieved thereat. They are in prison."[36]

Relations between Elizabeth and Dudley were strained during the entire month of August. Toward the end of July, de Silva noted that Dudley "seems lately to be rather more alone than usual, and the Queen appears to display a certain coolness towards him. She has begun to smile on a gentleman of her chamber named Heneage, which has attracted a good deal of attention."[37] Dudley became increasingly jealous of Heneage, and an argument broke out between the two men. Meanwhile, Throckmorton urged Dudley to find out whether he was still a lively candidate for the queen's hand by pretending that he had fallen in love with one of the ladies of the court and observing Elizabeth's response when he then requested permission to leave court and return to his own lodgings. Dudley began ostentatiously flirting with the Viscountess of Hereford, "one of the best-looking ladies of the court," according to de Silva. "The Queen was in a great temper and upbraided him" for fighting with Heneage and flirting with the viscountess.[38] Heneage was sent away, and Robert returned to his own apartments where he remained for three or four days while Cecil and Sussex sought to broker a reconciliation. At the beginning of September de Silva wrote, "both the Queen and Robert shed tears, and he has returned to his former favor."[39]

The posie's reference to an "inward, suspicious mind" would have struck Dudley with particular force. By flirting with the viscountess and fighting with Heneage, Dudley had not only displayed an "inward, suspicious mind" but also made himself "suspicious" to Elizabeth. Like the double meaning of "suspected by" invoked by the Woodstock epigram, "suspicious" meant not only *open to or deserving of suspicion* but also *disposed to suspect evil, mistrustful.* Indeed, Dudley's whole life had been clouded by suspicions. To begin with, "No part deformèd out of kind" refers—since the word "kind" could refer to birth or family—to lingering feelings that Dudley's honor was tainted because both his father and grandfather had been attainted for treason. Then too, Dudley, like Elizabeth herself, had been imprisoned in the Tower of London on suspicion of treason during Mary's reign. But even more to the point, rumors that he had his wife killed raised such troublesome suspicions about Dudley's mind and character that Elizabeth decided she could not marry him, even though she loved him and was physically attracted to him. By 1565 the gossip had receded, but many of Elizabeth's subjects and allies continued to harbor their own inward suspicions about Dudley's mind and character.

There is also good reason to associate the "inward, suspicious mind" with Elizabeth herself since the very word "suspicious" alludes to and builds upon the key term in the Woodstock epigram, "Much suspected by me, / Nothing proved can be." While at Woodstock, Elizabeth outwitted her foes by countering their suspicions with inward suspicions of her own. The Windsor epigram confronts Elizabeth's fear of being plagued by the inward suspicious thoughts that both tormented and protected her at Woodstock, that propelled her first parliamentary speech, and that recurred, to her distress, whenever she was faced with a potential betrayal.[40]

By writing the Windsor epigram and suggesting that Dudley (or whoever the poem was intended for) was the object of her suspicion, Elizabeth was expressing her own suspicious or mistrustful thoughts. That is precisely what makes this brief little posie at once so challenging a piece of writing and so intriguing an outward and visible sign of Elizabeth's inward preoccupations. But, one might well ask, was it fair for Elizabeth to admonish her private lyric audience for a quality of mind that she herself shared and that her own behavior may well have provoked? If Dudley's schemes incited Elizabeth's suspicions, she had herself given him good reason to be suspicious: only two years ago she had tried to marry him to Mary Queen of Scots, and more recently, she had been showering attention on Heneage while encouraging the archduke to come to England to woo her. Upon learning that Dudley had been trying to provoke her jealousy by flirting with the viscountess, moreover, Elizabeth "was in a great temper and upbraided him."[41] Their reconciliation, complete with tears (or "bleared eyes") on both sides, reaffirmed their mutual affection. As de Silva's account indicates, Elizabeth herself had behaved badly, but she was not wont to apologize. If, as the signature suggests, Elizabeth wrote the epigram to confront and work through her anger, the implicit acknowledgment—both to herself and to her private interlocutor—that her own inward, suspicious mind had led her to behave in an "ugly" way may have been instrumental in bringing about a reconciliation.

Since the poem neither attributes "the inward, suspicious mind" to any particular individual nor addresses her private lyric audience directly, Elizabeth may have originally written the poem *about* Dudley but not *for* Dudley; however, it seems more likely that she was thinking about how it would strike him because the abstract language provides a tactful way of admonishing him without criticizing him directly. The choice of the penultimate verb, "Nor yet so ugly half can be" suggests that "the inward, suspicious mind" is a danger to beware, a condition, unlike a crooked leg or a deformed body part, that "can be" resisted even if it cannot be entirely avoided. Although the poem raises objections that "can be" made in the past or future, its formal structure, when read along with the "loving" signature, implies that Elizabeth was no longer as "offended" as she "seemed to be" before writing the epigram.

In the autograph copy the rhyme words appear as the first word in line 2, the second word in line 3, the third word in line 4, and the last two words in line 5. Elizabeth was not a professional scribe. She may have simply miscalculated the space required, but the result is interesting nonetheless. Like the mirror text written on the window at Woodstock, the outer deformity of the apparently unrhymed lines conceals an internal pattern that the poem invites the reader to discover. Despite appearances, there is an inner harmony that secretly links Elizabeth and her private lyric audience together, much as the internal rhymes transform the four-and-a-half-line sentence into a quatrain.

Although questions about the signature and the date remain, the remarkably close correlation between the language of the poem, events at Windsor in August 1565, and the complications associated with Dudley's lingering courtship make it highly likely that this was indeed the obscure sentence Elizabeth wrote in a book at Windsor. If Elizabeth wrote the poem in her French psalter when she "semed to be much offended" with Leicester as Cecil notes, the pointed critique articulated by the epigram's final lines but tempered by the loving signature could have been a pivotal intervention in the historical situation: a way of telling Dudley (without reigniting the quarrel) that his attempts to manipulate and deceive her by pretending to be in love with the viscountess were uglier than any sort of physical deformity, but that she was willing to forgive him as long as he didn't make such behavior a regular habit of mind. If so, the epigram would have served a dual function: at once gentle admonition and tacit apology, it offered them both a face-saving pose that made reconciliation possible.

When we reconsider the epigram as a whole, the apparent dichotomy between physical and mental traits becomes a continuum that interrogates the very distinctions upon which the poem rests. This larger hermeneutical challenge pivots on the word "ugly," which alludes back to the physical deformity of the previous images, even as it anticipates the morally offensive loathsomeness of "the inward, suspicious mind." The "bleared eye" refers initially to someone whose eyes are inflamed with infection or swollen with tears; upon rereading, the "bleared eye" also refers proleptically to someone who is mentally blinded or deceived by mistrust (as both Dudley and Elizabeth were wont to be). Similarly, "[n]o part deformèd out of kind" evokes, first of all, a body part twisted out of its natural shape, but in retrospect, it also describes a part of one's mind or character that is "deformèd out of kind"—deformed as a result of birth, or family, or a manner that is natural or habitual to a person, or an obsession with a single part of a much larger problem—a mind haunted by the kind of personal history and anxieties that troubled both Dudley and Elizabeth not only in August 1565 but throughout their courtship.

Under the circumstances, even "[t]he crooked leg" begins to look less literal and more symbolic, embodying the twisted movements of an "inward, suspicious mind." The penultimate line suggests that the distinction between body and mind is a matter of magnitude rather than kind: "[t]he inward, suspicious mind" is related to but much worse than any of those previous traits because it encompasses them all, perverting all one's actions and distorting all one's perceptions, even at times capable of causing physical ailments. As the literal and figurative meanings merge, the "bleared eye" begins to perceive—even as it comes to symbolize—just how easily the process of perception, judgment, and interpretation "can be" distorted by deceit and distrust. Thus even if the epigram is rooted in the August 1565 events at Windsor, it transcends them, for it not only epitomizes the inward suspicions and outward doubts that prevented Elizabeth from marrying Dudley when the 1563 parliament urged her to do so, it also invokes the personal history that was so deeply embedded in both Elizabeth's style and character and in Dudley's words and actions.

The 1566 Parliamentary Speech: I Shall Do No Otherwise Than Pleases Me

When the 1566 parliament convened, Elizabeth's marriage was once again the principal matter of state business. According to most sources including Camden, Neale, and Elton, the ensuing battle over "those two great businesses, touching her Majesties Marriage, and Declaration of her next Successor" was not only the bitterest but also the most important of the reign.[42] Upon hearing that parliament was preparing to present another marriage petition, the queen took preemptive action and summoned a parliamentary delegation. The speaker need not attend, she said, since she intended to be the speaker. And speak she did: "the Commons, she said, were very rebels," and "would not have dared to act thus in her father's life time."[43]

After confronting the issue of her sex head on, Elizabeth concluded by asserting her freedom and authority in the plainest terms she could muster: "My Lords, do whatever you wish. As for me, I shall do no otherwise than pleases me. Your bills can have no force without my assent and authority."[44] Elizabeth sounds positively regal. Most remarkable of all is the unhesitating assertion of will: "I shall do no otherwise than pleases me." Since, after all, the point of contention was marriage, it does not require too great a leap into the unspoken to infer what she meant by "pleases me." She might just as well have reminded the delegation that marriage "can have no force"—that is, it can neither be consummated nor produce the desired heir—"without my assent."

Equally interesting rhetorically is the command "do whatever you wish"—a performative speech act that makes whatever parliament chooses to do the result of her decree. The power of her speech highlights the powerlessness of their "bills," which "can have no force without my assent and authority." Citing this remark—Elizabeth's most powerful declaration of power to date—Neale comments: "Thus the monarch was left in isolation, the greatest peril that could befall a prince." Then, already beginning to build his case for parliament's victory and Elizabeth's defeat, Neale concludes, "The regiment of a woman displayed its inherent weakness."[45] That's not how it looks to me. I think we need to reexamine the evidence.

As if to prevent any notion that the regiment of a woman was bound to display "its inherent weakness," Elizabeth proceeded to assert her liberty and strength, both as a monarch and as a woman: "and though I be a woman, yet *I* have as good a courage answerable to *my* place as ever my father had. *I* am your anointed queen. *I* will never be by violence constrained to do anything. *I* thank God *I* am indeed endued with such qualities that if *I* were turned out of the realm in *my* petticoat, *I* were able to live in any place in Christendom" (CW 97). The italics are mine, but the bold face is Elizabeth's.

The petticoat, a sign of Elizabeth's womanhood, strikingly associated here with freedom of action rather than shameful exposure, is what makes this moment of self-fashioning so symbolically significant. Elizabeth dared the Lords to imagine her in her petticoat and to face what they most feared: lo and behold, beneath the robes of power she *was* a woman and, worse yet, she declared, implying that arranged marriage would be equivalent to rape, she was a strong and independent woman who would "never be by violence constrained to do anything."[46] She was not wearing the emperor's new clothes. Rather, she maintained, even if she were cast ashore by shipwreck—like Shakespeare's Viola—she would remain resourceful and undaunted.

By flaunting her female body and calling up an image of herself in intimate female garb, Elizabeth was putting on her femininity with a vengeance—as feminist theory reminds us, "To put on femininity with a vengeance suggests the power of taking it off."[47] Even if she was dethroned and cast out of her kingdom, Elizabeth declared, she would survive, not only with the help of God's grace, of course, but also with her own female courage and wit—a feisty Viola or Rosalind rather than a pathetic Lear. Having symbolically stripped herself both of the official robes of power and the cultural restrictions imposed on her as a woman, having risked hypothetical violence and survived mythic exposure as a poor, bare, forked female, there was little more to fear.

When Elizabeth was first crowned queen, the original Elizabethan parliament, afraid of upsetting the patriarchal social order, debated whether or not to allow her to use the title her father claimed for himself, Supreme Head of the Church of England. After a heated discussion, parliament decided upon the less symbolically loaded term *governor*. Recalling that slight now, Elizabeth concluded her diatribe by claiming the male titles "Prince" and "head of all the body" (CW 105), and thus asserting the symbolic power that her male subjects had tried to retain upon their own sturdy, male shoulders: "I will deal therein for your safety and offer it unto you as your prince and head, without request. For it is monstrous that the feet should direct the head" (CW 98).

In *The First Blast of the Trumpet against the Monstruous Regiment of Women*, John Knox had argued that "this monstriferouse empire of women, (which amongest all enormities, that this day do abound upon the face of the hole earth, is most detestable and damnable)."[48] But monstrosity, like beauty, resides in the eyes and ears of the beholder—and the culture. To Elizabeth, to her ears and eyes, what was monstrous was not "the bodie of that commonwelth, where a woman beareth empire"[49]—not a female ruler speaking with the bold authority generally reserved for men, claiming "wit and memory" that was not considered "appropriate to my sex" (CW 70)— but, as she put it, "men of wit [who] can so hardly use that gift they hold" (CW 93).[50] In this classic example of symbolic inversion—of "behavior which inverts, contradicts, abrogates, or in some fashion presents an alternative to commonly held cultural codes, values, and norms be they linguistic, literary or artistic, religious, social and political"[51]—Elizabeth's rhetoric redefines cultural norms from a female point of view, declaring that the monstrous or the grotesque that "designates the marginal, the low and the outside from the perspective of a classical body situated as high, inside and central by virtue of its very exclusions,"[52] applied not to her female body but to that classic male body, the parliament, which, by renouncing its head and flailing about without its wits, was in danger of becoming a disorderly, erupting body politic.

Scholars generally depict the 1566 parliamentary debate as a battle over the ancient liberties of parliament. When Elizabeth told parliament that they could not discuss her marriage, they charged her with denying them their constitutional freedom of speech. Yet for Elizabeth it looked more like a battle over her right as a woman and monarch to exercise the liberties, the authority, and the performative power of speech heretofore reserved exclusively for men. Only three years earlier, Elizabeth had apologized for speaking in private to a parliamentary delegation, expressing "some fear to speak and bashfulness besides, a thing appropriate to my sex," wishing "a silent thought [might] serve" (CW 70, CW 79). In the first Parliament she said, "I must needs have misliked it very much if it had been otherwise" (CW 57). Since then, events had made it clear that neither bashfulness nor "a silent thought" would serve her purpose.

After the speaker finished reading her prepared text, Elizabeth declared her intention to address parliament. Then speaking in her own voice in those hallowed chambers for the first time, she said, "I have a few words further to speak unto you. Notwithstanding that I have not been used, nor love to do it, in such open assemblies, yet now, not to the end to amend [the lord keeper's] talk, but remembering that commonly princes' own words be better printed in the hearers' memory than those spoken by her commandment, I mean to say thus much unto you" (CW 107).

Only seven years had passed since the first Elizabethan parliament decided that Elizabeth could be the governor but not the head. Having survived her most heated and difficult parliamentary struggle, Elizabeth asked her subjects to reconsider the matter: "As to liberties, who is so simple that doubts whether a prince that is head of all the body may not command the feet not to stray when they would slip?" (CW 105). Far from being a sign of insecurity, this rhetorical question supplied its own scathing answer. Obviously, she was the head, for she was commanding those straying parliamentary feet.

Most scholars have declared a resounding victory for parliament and an embarrassing defeat for Elizabeth, but why? Elizabeth urgently needed funds to carry out her policies, and parliament threatened to insert a promise to marry as a preamble and prerequisite to passing the subsidies bill. Upon hearing of the plan to limit her liberty, Elizabeth exploded, and parliament backed down. To be sure, Elizabeth assured parliament that she was planning to marry if the remaining obstacles could be overcome. Yet to my mind she neither "lost a head-on clash with Parliament" nor suffered an "unprecedented defeat" for she did not alter the conditions she had insisted on since the beginning of the reign.[53] She would not allow either parliament or a husband to rule for her or over her, nor would she agree to marry someone she had not met and did not desire.

Marriage negotiations with the Austrian archduke heated up but soon came to naught for the very same reasons that the previous marriage negotiations with Austria failed. Emperor Maximilian was appalled that Elizabeth intended to maintain all political power for herself: "For it would be derogatory to the dignity and esteem not only of His Love, but also of our glorious House of Austria, if His Love were to be excluded from all share in the governance, and were nothing more than a shadow or figurehead in the realm."[54] The emperor was even more outraged that Elizabeth "still abides by her former resolve to marry no one whom she has not previously seen." That was "entirely novel and unprecedented, and we cannot approve of it." As a result, the emperor concluded, a satisfactory marriage contract with the archduke remained "very dubious and questionable."[55]

Perhaps, Elizabeth insisted upon defining courtship in terms that seemed "very dubious and questionable" to Emperor Maximilian and to many members of her own parliament because she knew she could only be satisfied with an "entirely novel and unprecedented" marriage. Or, perhaps, she was stalling, having discovered that courtship gave her political leverage, both at home and abroad, that marriage to Charles might threaten if not destroy. But whatever her reasons, the debate with the 1566 parliament "boldeneth [her] to say" that she would "do no otherwise than pleases me."[56]

Elizabeth had unequivocally become a political actor and speaker. Parliament never again acted so peremptorily. There were no more parliamentary delegations sent to issue ultimatums about her marriage. When the question was raised again by the 1576 parliament, the tone of the discussion was decidedly less combative and more solicitous.

CHAPTER 7

POPULAR DEBATE AND COURTLY DIALOGUE: ALWAYS HER OWN FREE WOMAN

they were to her most devoted, and she was alwayes her owne free woman, and obnoxious [or subject] to no one.

William Camden, *The Historie of the…princesse Elizabeth*[1]

Sexual Politics

The parliamentary debate over Elizabeth's marriage constituted "politics" in the classic sense of the term, but it also redefined politics to include sexual politics. Elizabeth's commanding presence—for she "g[ave] her orders and ha[d] her way as absolutely as her father did"[2]—and her insistence upon the right to rule the country herself and to remain single or to marry according to her own "will" and "liking" challenged the dominant ideology, which required women to be chaste, silent, and obedient.

Within two years of Elizabeth's climactic confrontation with the 1566 parliament there appeared in print three remarkable texts that extended the debate about women's liberty and equality to Elizabethan society at large: (1) *The copy of a letter, lately written in meeter, by a yonge Gentilwoman: to her unconstant Louer: With an Admonitio[n] to al yong Gentilwomen, and to all other Maids in general to beware of mennes flattery by Is. W.*; (2) *A Letter sent by the maydens of London, to the vertuous matrones & mistresses of the same, in the defense of their lawfull libertie. Answering the mery meeting by us Rose, Jane, Rachell, Sara, Philumias and Dorothie*; (3) *A brief and pleasant discourse of duties in Mariage, called the Flower of Friendshippe* by Edmund Tilney.[3] These texts span the social spectrum, from a young gentlewoman addressing her erstwhile fiancé and all other unmarried women, to serving women seeking common cause with their wealthy, powerful mistresses, to a courtly dialogue dedicated to the queen and printed for all the world to read. Together, they demonstrate that, like the queen, Elizabethan women were actively defending their liberty, wit, and pleasure and that Elizabethan men were joining the debate.

Deterred from venturing into print by the ideology of silence, Elizabethan women primarily wrote religious writings or translations of male authors. It is all the more significant, therefore, that Isabella Whitney and the maydens of London went public, using the power of the press, the strongest weapon available to them, to urge all women, regardless of social or marital status, to join together to fight for the rights and freedoms that Elizabeth herself was actively defending. Whitney's letter and admonition, the first original, secular poems written and printed by an Englishwoman, turn private experience into public discourse and provide an instructive example for all women conducting their own courtships.[4] The maydens' letter bids women of all social ranks to join together to defend their legal rights—to go freely about the city, to attend the theater, and to marry (or not) as they chose. Tilney's courtly dialogue represents men and women from the educated upper ranks debating the questions of courtship, marriage, and female liberty articulated by Whitney, the maydens, and their queen. Dedicated to Elizabeth, *A brief and pleasant discourse* is a bid for patronage that sets out to define marriage in ways that would please Elizabeth and that would simultaneously provide intellectual support for her position in the ongoing marriage negotiations with Archduke Charles. Significantly, Tilney's boldest, most outspoken proponent of female liberty and equality is named Isabella, the Spanish form of Elizabeth.

Elizabeth did not control the ways in which the controversy over women, courtship, and marriage played itself out, for power does not work cleanly from the top down, from monarchs to subjects. Nonetheless, Elizabeth's bold defense of her "wit" and "liberties" catalyzed the public debate over her marriage and what was "appropriate to [her] sex," which in turn generated or merged with a wider popular controversy over freely chosen marriage, female sexual desire, male rule, and women's subordination.

Whitney's Poetry of Courtship

Whitney's letter claims an active, vocal role in her own courtship, while her admonition exhorts other Elizabethan women to do likewise. Writing *"in meter"* and citing numerous biblical and classical precedents to establish her authority, Whitney claims the conventional male roles of poet, scholar, suitor, and counselor to assert the conjugal freedom of choice that Elizabeth defended so vehemently in her parliamentary speeches. The title, *The Copy of a letter to her Unconstant Lover,* announced what the text asserts, that Whitney wrote the letter when she heard her betrothed was secretly planning to marry someone else: "As close as you your wedig kept / yet now the trueth I he[ar]." Whitney had hoped her poetic persuasion would demonstrate her worth, convince her betrothed that "the promises be kept, / that you so firmly made," and regain his love: "And yet it is not so far past, / but might againe be wonne." Yet, like her queen, Whitney insists that she wants to marry only if there is mutual liking: "But if I can not please your minde / for wants that rest in me: / Wed whom you list."[5]

Whitney artfully shapes her letter as an autobiographical *cri du coeur,* which is no doubt how it was read. By publishing a copy of her letter along with an admonition to other women, Whitney defends her good name and makes her unconstant lover's "falsenes manifest." Drawing on the personal experience recounted in her letter, Whitney's admonition sets out to teach other Elizabethan women the critical and interpretive skills they need to conduct their own courtships and to avoid similar betrayals: "Trust not a man at the first sight, / but trie him well before."[6] It was, Whitney declares, terribly important for women to test their suitors "before." Before what? Presumably, before having intercourse, since a promise to marry followed by coitus constituted a legally binding common law marriage. Elizabethan couples often began sleeping together as soon as they were betrothed, but clandestine marriage contracts were often broken, as ecclesiastical court records demonstrate.[7]

An Admonition addresses Elizabethan women whose hearts are raging with love: "Ye virgins [that] from Cupids tentes / do beare away the foile / Whose hartes as yet wth raginge love / most painfully do boile. / To you I speake: for you be they, / that good advice do lacke." Given the prevailing code of ethics, it is hard to know what was more daring: Whitney's kinship with and respect for other women's boiling, "raging" libidinous urges or her claim to be a judge of men and a teacher of women. Premarital sex was not the sort of thing "a Yonge Gentilwoman" was supposed to discuss—never mind write about in print. Whitney's advice was not only "good counsel" but it was also precisely the kind of advice Elizabethan women desperately needed, "[w]hich if you do observe, it will / some of your care redresse."[8]

A Letter Sent by the maydens of London

With a single extant copy, *A Letter sent by the maydens of London* is one of the rarest books in the English language. It may have had a limited circulation and short shelf life, but it may have filled such an important need in women's lives that it was literally read to pieces. Either way, it made enough of a mark to be attacked and parodied by Thomas Nash two decades later, as we shall see at the end of this chapter.

The maydens' letter, now once again in circulation, was part of a lively Elizabethan social debate.[9] As the title, "Answering the Mery Meeting" indicates, it was conceived as a refutation of an earlier, no longer extant pamphlet, which contemporary sources attribute to the lawyer Edward Hake.[10] Although we cannot rule out the possibility that a Letter was written by a cross-dressed Elizabethan John Stuart Mill, the text presents itself, and was surely read as a bold defense of female liberty written by and for Elizabethan women—and in all probability that's what it was.[11] Although the title page, *"by us Rose, Jane, Rachell, Sara, Philumias and Dorothie,"* could have been an artful fabrication by a writer who hoped to capitalize on the publicity generated by Hake's tract, the text identifies the authors as well-educated gentlewoman serving women—to be more precise, six such women—and the detailed account of the daily lives of serving women sounds as if it was indeed written by and for women.

Elizabethan servants spanned the social hierarchy, replicating the larger social order from aristocrats on down. If the maydens felt personally defamed by Hake's attack, as their letter declares, they would necessarily have "scribbled" their response "in haste," not only because, as they point out, serving women had only half a day off each week, but also because they felt urgently compelled to defend their character and rights before Hake's slanders and proscriptions could gain traction.

Like Elizabeth's first parliamentary speech or Whitney's letter and admonition, the maydens' letter derives much of its force from personal testimony. Drawing on their experiences as serving women, the maydens retort that Hake provided no evidence to support his claim that Rose and Jane spent too much money on food and drink: "he hath but said a thing that he hath not proved, and so have we the lesse to say therein… For when *Rose* would have sent for wi[ne], *Jane* wold not suffer hir…"[12] The particular names cited on the title page recur throughout the text, showing how foolish Hake was to attack all serving women for what six particular women may or may not have said or done.

The maydens argue that Hake, being a lawyer, should stick to what he knows, the law: "After his serious study he wold have found out some honester recreation, and medled in maters meter for his vocation, wherein also his skill and knowledge had bene greater: and in that the common law is his studie & profession, he might farre better have written of some Writte, as *Supersedeas*, or *Corpus cum causa*, or *De Idiota inquirenda*, or of some suche like argument."[13] Parodying Hake's penchant for alliterative and pretentious legal language, the maydens' satire packs a powerful punch. *Supersedeas*, meaning a writ staying a proceeding, articulates the maydens' goal: to stop the unjust proceedings initiated by Hake's attack. *Corpus cum causa* (a writ of *Habeas corpus cum causa* which transferred a case from one court to another) suggests that Hake had wrongly transferred the maydens' case from the household, where their behavior should be judged, to the court of public opinion. Since he chose to go public, that was the courtroom in which the maydens would present their rebuttal. The maydens' third legal Latinism, *De Idiota inquirenda*—a writ whose purpose was to inquire whether a person was an idiot—mockingly suggests that Hake was a fool for meddling in affairs he did not understand: he "doth so much invey against our overmuche libertie, in that he writeth that hee knoweth not, and medleth of that he hath no skill off."[14] Much as Elizabeth told the "witless" members of the 1566 parliament that their attempt to reduce the complex political decision of her marriage to simple certainty was "unmeet" and uninformed, the maydens argue that Hake had no business preaching to or about London's serving women since he was neither a preacher, nor a serving woman, nor the person they served.

The maydens' letter parallels Elizabeth's language and arguments in a number of telling ways. Elizabeth derided those "men of wit [who] can so hardly use that gift they hold" in order to rebuff parliament's marriage petition and to declare, "As for me, I shall do no otherwise than pleases me." Similarly, the maydens mocked Hake's witless attempt to curtail their liberty: "Yet when he hath sayd what he can: he can shewe no good cause why our liberties should be restrained, as he so earnestly desired...he hath no lesse declared his little wit, than he hath uttered his small skill & learning in the handling of it."[15] Elizabeth used the power of print to publicize her responses to the city fathers, the bishops, and the members of parliament who sought to subordinate her will to their masculine authority. So too, the maydens also used the press to answer Hake's attempt to curtail their independence.

Early modern women became servants primarily to promote their matrimonial prospects. They set aside their wages to defray the significant costs of setting up an independent household when they married. If they came from a more privileged family, they took positions in one of London's great houses to receive an elite education, polish their social skills, mingle with high society, and meet eligible men. Handmaids, chosen from a social network of family and friends, provided companionship, accompanied their mistresses to the theater, and joined in the various household activities. The most trusted servants helped raise the children and run the household. Since the average age of marriage was 26 for women and 28 for men, and since most serving women worked until they married, the maydens were probably approximately the age of their queen; thus they would have identified with her struggle to defend her freedom of choice against parliament's marriage petitions.

Although early modern prescriptive texts insist that women should remain safely at home within the protective walls of their husbands', fathers', and masters' houses, foreigners visiting London reported that Englishwomen were remarkably free to go out on the town. Indeed, prescriptions and circumscriptions such as Hake's typically become more urgent and insistent when traditional social mores are eroding. The maydens' letter defends women's right to go freely about the city, whether doing the marketing for their mistresses, attending the theater, or just enjoying their free time, drinking together in a tavern and getting to know the men upon whom their future happiness and well-being as wives would depend. Thus the maydens claimed for themselves the freedom of movement and marital freedom of choice that Elizabeth, too, so jealously protected. Refusing to remain safely ensconced in the palace, she set tongues wagging by galloping about the countryside, reveling in the company of Robert Dudley, and she appalled the ambassadors and alienated the emperor by insisting that she would sign a marriage contract only if and when a "mutual liking" occurred.

The language the maydens use "in defense of their lawfull libertie" bears a striking resemblance to Elizabeth's own rhetoric. Elizabeth assured parliament that she would not make an unwise decision based on passion alone, but she also rejected the notion of a marriage arranged solely for pragmatic reasons. Similarly, the maydens recognize that a husband must provide the requisite "goods and money," but they reject the notion of a marriage arranged for wealth or status alone. Like their queen, they knew how important it was to consider the "qualitie" of a suitor, not only his rank or position in society, although that was of great importance in Elizabethan England, but also his ability, mental or moral attributes, and accomplishments.

The maydens contend that marriage should be based, above all, on love: "And sith love should be the principall cause in mariage, why shold we be blamed, for chosing wher we most love and fansie?" In this regard as well, the maydens' defense of their "lawfull libertie" resembles Elizabeth's language. Elizabeth told parliament that it was "unfitting and altogether unmeet for you... to take upon you to draw my love to your liking or frame my will to your fantasies" (CW 57), and she told the Spanish ambassador that "she, for her part, did not choose to declare it until she had seen the person she was expected to love."[16] Much as Elizabeth took a vow to marry no man she had not seen, the maydens refuse to "be coupled in mariage with such as are lothsom to looke upon," and they defend their right to "refuse such olde doting fooles as sometimes ar procured by our paretes to be suters to us, & have a thousand worse impedimentes, and nothing but their goods and money to mary them."[17]

Since female servants were poorly paid, the maydens argue that women would simply refuse to work in London if they were denied the freedom that provided a valuable compensation for their hard work and low wages: "when such as are born in the countrey shoulde choose rather to tarie at home, and remaine there to take paines for a small stipend or wages with libertie: and such as are Citizens borne, shoulde repaire also to the country, or to other Cities where they might be free, than to abide as slaves and bondewomen in London."[18]

The maydens also argue that the servant/mistress relationship must be mutually profitable and warmly supportive, fulfilling the needs and desires of both parties. The maydens' affective view of the organic household—in which they, "being free borne," freely offer their loving care as long as their mistresses continue to "cherishe them, and make muche of them" in return—mirrors Elizabeth's penchant for declaring her loving relationship to her loving people.[19] During the pre-coronation procession, Elizabeth was so eager to "show her most gracious love toward the people in general" that she turned her passage through the crowded streets of London into a "wonderful spectacle, of a noble hearted princess toward her most loving people" (CW 53). Similarly, Elizabeth instructed the lord keeper to inform the members of the first Elizabethan parliament that she would be "careful" of them as long as they were "careful" of her, and she continued to assert this mutual "care" and "careful" reciprocity throughout her reign.

The maydens deploy an analogous rhetorical strategy when they represent themselves and their mistresses as integral, interdependent members of a common household body: "For as ye are they that care & provide for our meat, drinke and wages, so we are they that labor and take paines for you: so that your care for us, and our labor for you is so requisite, that they cannot be separated: so needeful that they may not be severed."[20] The maydens' promise to "care" for their mistresses posits a muscular reciprocity of needs and rewards held together by sinews "that cannot be separated" as long as their mistresses show loving solicitude for their serving women. The maydens maintain that the household will thrive only if mistresses and serving women alike understand, love, and respect each other.

John Knox contended that a female head of state would disrupt the gender hierarchy upon which the social order rested:

> For who wolde not judge that bodie to be a monstre, where there was no head eminent above the rest, but that the eyes were in the handes, the tonge and mouth beneth in the belie, and the eares in the feet.... And no lesse monstruous is the bodie of that common welth, where a woman beareth empire.[21]

Having been denied the title Head of the Church, Elizabeth declared herself the head of those witless parliamentary feet: "I will deal therein for your safety and offer it unto you as your prince and head, without request. For it is monstrous that the feet should direct the head" (CW 98). Like their queen, the maydens transformed the traditional patriarchal polity to suit their own strategic purposes.

Indeed the maydens' version of the classic patriarchal analogy is remarkable for its organic, non-hierarchal structure. Since they do not even mention the husband, the traditional head of the household, one might expect the matrons and mistresses to be the head of this all-female body. Not so: "we are to you very eyes, and hands, feete & altogether."[22] The maydens are not only the feet to carry out their mistresses' requests and the limbs to wait on them hand and foot but also the heart to satisfy their mistresses' desires, the eyes to foresee their wants, and the brains to assure that the household body continues to run smoothly. The maydens were not lowly servants busily scrubbing floors and emptying bedpans. Rather, they were important administrative assistants, who helped their mistresses run a large, complex household.

The maydens were not anarchists, but their rewriting of the traditional patriarchal body was deeply subversive in its own way. Rather than giving each member of the household a predetermined place in the hierarchy, the maydens placed the lowliest servant, the most respected gentlewoman attendant, and the most powerful mistress "altogether" on equal ground. By constructing a household body where women share service and governance, the maydens rendered their subordination to men all but moot. The maydens' letter, like late twentieth-century feminist discourse, "constitutes a discursive space which defines itself in terms of a common identity; here it is the shared experience of gender-based oppression which provides the mediating factor intended to unite all participants beyond their specific differences." By inviting their female readers to join a potential army of "above sixe thousand," the maydens transform symbolic action into political action.[23] Regardless of whether the author was a woman, a group of women, or a man (which is possible though unlikely given the virtual erasure of men except for the bumbling know-nothing author of *The Mery Meeting*), this rare text urges all Elizabethan women to join together in defense of their common liberty, not only in the household but in society at large.

Good Conversation

In 1568, two years after Elizabeth's climactic debate with parliament and a few months after the maydens and Whitney published their letters and admonition, there appeared in print Edmund Tilney's *A brief and pleasant discourse of duties in Mariage, called the Flower of Friendshippe*. The dedicatory epistle, addressed to "the Noble and most Vertuous Princesse, Elizabeth," identifies the queen as the dialogue's principal audience and most important judge. It also indicates that Tilney presented Elizabeth with a private manuscript of the discourse before it appeared in print. Tilney's epistle asks Elizabeth to "receive these fewe simple lines" as "my simple Present unto your Highnesse" and hopes she will accept his "gift" among other "Noble presentes of more higher estate." In Elizabethan England the word "present" denoted an *offering* or *gift*, but it still carried its original meaning, *a person's presence*. Tilney was connected by birth to all the most powerful families at court and was himself a distant cousin of the queen. His dedicatory epistle asserts his personal kinship with the queen and his even closer ties to those with direct access to her. William Howard, the Lord Chamberlain and the chief officer at court, who had access to the queen's eyes and ears on a "dailye" basis, was a close relation of Tilney's.[24] Clearly, Tilney was hoping that his "present" would help him gain access to the queen's presence and patronage.

After briefly affirming Elizabeth's virginity and purity (the "Noble vertues" that flow from "a pure Fountaine"), Tilney compares Elizabeth, our "Alexandra," to Alexander the Great, who graciously accepted the gift of poems offered him. To acknowledge Elizabeth's "great knowledge" and to impress her with his own learning, Tilney peoples his treatise with the great humanist commentators on marriage, including Vives, Castiglione, and Erasmus whose works had recently been translated into English. However, Tilney's principal spokesman for companionate marriage, Pedro di Luxan, wrote a treatise on marriage that had not been translated into English. Since Elizabeth was not as fluent in Spanish as she was in French and Italian, Tilney could make a genuine contribution to "the learned labors of [those] more excellent authors" by making Pedro's views available in English.[25]

Like most works produced by courtly authors, *A brief and pleasant discourse* was originally written for private manuscript circulation. The dedicatory epistle does not mention print or a wider public audience, and it is only at the very end that Tilney explains he decided to publish the dialogue at the urging of Lady Isabella. The name Isabella may have alluded to Isabella

Whitney, whose recently published letter makes many of the same arguments as Tilney's Isabella. It almost certainly alluded to the queen since (as noted above) Isabella is the Spanish form of Elizabeth.²⁶ The first edition of Tilney's dialogue no longer exists, but the words *"cum privilegio"* (meaning that the printer had a license from the crown) appear on the title page of the second and subsequent editions, which suggests that Tilney's publication may have received official approval.

The epistle begins by combining its praise for the queen's "great knowledge" and "noble mind" with protestations of Tilney's own humble unworthiness. Anxious to find words that would gain the queen's attention without sounding presumptuous, Tilney explained that he gathered the nerve to present his "Present" to Elizabeth only after "dailye perceiving the clemencie of your highnesse most noble mind." Conscious of the gap between "your Majesties highe dignitie, and the lownesse of my estate, with my simple skill," Tilney explains that it was Elizabeth's own "heavenly humilitie matched with [her] great knowledge" that "boldened [him] to presume so farre" as "to put this my base stile to the hearing either of your Majesties reverent eares, or to the judgment of your skilfull eyes."²⁷

Tilney's claim that he was emulating Elizabeth's own combination of humility and learning recalls the 1563 parliamentary speech where Elizabeth said that "the weight and greatnes of this matter might cause in me, being a woman wanting both witt and memory, some feare to speake, and bashfulnes besides, a thing appropriate to my sex. But yet the princely seate and kingly throne wherin God, (though unworthy) hath constituted me, maketh these two causes to seme litle in mine *eyes*, though grevous perhaps to your *eares*, and *boldeneth me* to saye somewhat in this matter."²⁸ Tilney's mention of "eares" and "eyes" along with his choice of the verb "boldened" emulate Elizabeth's own language, signaling his appreciation for her point of view.

True to its title, *A brief and pleasant discourse* presents a friendly dialogue or conversation about marriage: the first day's discourse discusses the duties of husbands, the second, the duties of wives.²⁹ The organic form follows the movement of the sun from one day to the next, making the discourse read more like an unfolding drama or tale than a didactic sermon or prescriptive treatise. The dramatic immediacy and dialogic structure invite the reader to entertain and choose from a variety of contrasting viewpoints.

The dialogue proper begins with a narrative frame, which explains that Tilney was out for a walk in the countryside with "a friende of mine, called Maister *Pedro di luxan*" when the mid-day heat prompted them to seek shelter at Lady Julia's country estate where they are invited to join her guests for a mid-day meal. After they finish dining, the "jollye companie assembled togithers, both Ladies and Gentlemen," begin to discuss possibilities for the afternoon's entertainment. Since physical sport would exclude the ladies, Master Pedro proposes an intellectual discourse, "both pleasaunt and profitable," like those practiced "in the courts of Italie." Such dialogues were, the narrator pauses to explain, taking place at Elizabeth's court as well: "and some much like to them are practiced at this day in the English court, wherein is not only delectation, but pleasure joined with profit, and exercise of the wit."[30]

Pedro selects Lady Julia to preside over the day's discourse, thereby paying tribute to Book 3 of Castiglione's *The Courtier*, probably the best-known and most influential Renaissance dialogue. Translated into English by Sir Thomas Hoby in 1561 and reprinted three times during Elizabeth's reign, *The Courtier* is a courtesy book that describes the ideal courtier and court lady and offers practical advice about how to behave at court. Castiglione selects a female sovereign, Lady Emilia, to preside over the dialogue, but her power is more symbolic than real because she and the other Italian court ladies have very few speaking lines. By comparison, Tilney gives his English women characters substantial speaking roles, and he further empowers his female sovereign by naming her Julia after Castiglione's most eloquent and learned spokesman, Lord Julian. By combining the roles of Lord Julian and Lady Emilia, Tilney underlines his dedicatory epistle's tribute to his own female sovereign's great learning.

Elizabeth's symbolic position overarching the dialogue is depicted by the sweet briar, or eglantine, which covers the arbor where the dialogue takes place.[31] As Roy Strong writes, "Everyone in the court circle and beyond it knew of the Queen's use of eglantine as especially her flower. She *was* the eglantine."[32] Strong associates the eglantine's white color with Elizabeth's virginity; however, its vigorous growth, abundant red hips, and tendency to seed itself freely also make it a sign of the fertility and fruitfulness evoked by Tilney's title: *A brief and pleasant discourse of duties in Mariage, called the Flower of Friendshippe.* By reminding his readers that female sovereignty and intellectual conversation between the sexes were daily facts of life at Elizabeth's court, and by situating the dialogue beneath an arbor festooned with Elizabeth's flower, Tilney linked his humanist discussion of marriage in general to the current debate over Elizabeth's own marriage negotiations with the Austrian archduke Charles.

A brief and pleasant discourse was Tilney's bid for patronage, not only from the queen but also from his Howard relatives, the queen's cousins who played an active role in court politics, including the debate over Elizabeth's marriage. Thomas Howard, First Baron of Effingham, had originally supported Dudley's ambition to marry the queen but by 1566 had shifted his allegiance to the powerful group of courtiers advocating Elizabeth's marriage to Archduke Charles. Although Dudley was trying to derail negotiations with Austria in order to protect his own position as the queen's favorite, Elizabeth's own sympathies had, it seemed, swung to Archduke Charles. Indeed, it was Charles that Elizabeth had in mind when she told the 1566 parliament that she would marry unless the person she hoped to marry proved unavailable or unacceptable.

Upon becoming Holy Roman Emperor in July 1564, Maximilian reopened marriage negotiations with the English queen, which had stalled six years earlier. Still concerned about the gossip over Elizabeth's relationship to Dudley, the emperor instructed his envoy, Adam von Zwetkovich, Baron von Mitterberg, to "ma[k]e diligent inquiries concerning the maiden honour and integrity of the Queen." Zwetkovich provided the requisite reassurances about the queen's virtue and character. Tilney's dedication provides similar assurances that Elizabeth's honor and reputation remained unsullied: "within your Majesties sacred breast, wisedome, adourned with Noble virtues, is only harbored. From whence as from a pure Fountaine, doth flowe, the deedes of a Noble hart."[33]

Elizabeth herself assured Zwetkovich, as he reported to the emperor, that she was more serious about the match than ever before: "the Queen becomes fonder of His Princely Highness and her impatience to see him grows daily. Her marriage is, I take it, certain and resolved upon."[34] After a series of setbacks, Elizabeth's ambassador Thomas Radcliffe, Earl of Sussex, finally arrived in Austria in May 1566 and Elizabeth was pleased by his report that the archduke was not deformed, as she had been led to believe earlier by the French ambassador who hoped to scuttle the alliance between England and Austria. Less encouraging was the news that Charles attended Catholic services every day and was far more serious about his Catholic faith than the former Austrian ambassador Casper von Breuner, Baron von Rabenstein, had led Elizabeth to believe in 1559. Worse yet, Charles refused to meet the English ambassador, and the emperor rejected the terms proposed by the Privy Council.[35] First regarding finances, the English wanted Austria to provide a dowry and to pay Charles' household expenses. Maximilian replied that Elizabeth, being the monarch, should pay her husband's expenses and, being a woman, she should also provide the dowry. Second, on the question of religion, the English argued that there was nothing to prevent Charles from attending the Church of England, since everything in the English church service had been taken from Holy Scripture. Maximilian replied that Charles should be given a church of his own where he could publicly celebrate the Catholic mass. But that was out of the question, so the English ambassador proposed a compromise, which still needed official approval: Charles could receive the mass in private, as long as (1) he agreed not to discuss his religious views publicly and (2) Elizabeth's subjects were not allowed to attend, since that would undermine the religious conformity required by English law. Finally, there was the question of political power: the emperor demanded the title of king, equal dignity with the queen, and joint governance of the country, since, he said, it was customary for men to rule. That too was unacceptable and nonnegotiable: Elizabeth was adamant that she would retain all political power. Finally, on the question of the marriage treaty, Elizabeth would not finalize the terms until Charles came to England, for, as discussed in chapter 5, she had taken a vow to marry no one she had not seen. Religious differences would provide a face-saving excuse should a mutual liking fail to develop during Charles' visit. But like his father, Maximilian refused to let Charles come to England until "greater and surer certitude can be given that our beloved brother will not return with his object unaccomplished." As Maximilian wrote to Zvetkovich, the marriage was "still very dubious and questionable, for the illustrious Queen, who had formerly declared that she did not desire to marry, still abides by her former resolve to marry no one whom she has not previously seen. Among Kings and Queens this is entirely novel and unprecedented, and we cannot approve of it."[36] On that note, negotiations came to a standstill for the very reasons that stymied Elizabeth's negotiations with the ambassadors when the marriage was first proposed in 1559.

Taking his cue from Elizabeth's 1566 parliamentary speech, Tilney does not explicitly mention Elizabeth's marriage to Charles. Nonetheless, the marriage negotiations between England and Austria comprise the dialogue's subtext. To maintain the dramatic fiction that he was merely describing "[t]he rites of divers Nations in marrying," Tilney includes a few exemplary tales that could have no possible bearing on Elizabeth's marriage, such as the story of the Scottish "Lorde of the Soyle" who "had the first fruites, of all the Virgins, within his Lordship."[37] Yet, with the exception of a few such screamingly irrelevant tales, Pedro's argument and exempla support the English negotiating conditions: (1) Elizabeth and Charles should be free to decide for themselves whether or not they wanted to marry; (2) Elizabeth need not provide a dowry simply because she was a woman; (3) It was Charles's duty as the husband to pay his own household expenses, and (4) Charles' authority as husband need not impinge upon or impede Elizabeth's authority as queen.

Eager to provide counsel without offending her "Majesty's high dignitie" "with my simple skill" or "the lownesse of my estate," Tilney assigns himself the role of narrator, expatiating upon the opinions of the other characters while maintaining a tactful silence about his own views. The dialogue's main spokesman and the narrator's supposed friend and walking companion is the highly regarded Catholic humanist scholar Pedro di Luxan. By drawing his principal arguments from a contemporary Spanish writer, Tilney appeals to the Hapsburg bond between Spain and Austria that played such a central role in the 1559 marriage negotiations between Elizabeth and Archduke Charles. Pedro's advice about selecting a marriage partner implicitly prefers Charles to both Dudley and Prince Henry of France and provides historical, biblical, and classical precedents that could be used to defend England's position in the marriage negotiations.[38]

Much as Tilney begins his dedicatory epistle with a brief allusion to Elizabeth's virginity before invoking her response to parliament's marriage petition, Master Pedro begins his presentation by first "setting virginitie aside, as the purest estate," and then proceeding to his main argument that marriage is "more honorable," "more just," more "humaine," and "more holy." Indeed, he says, nothing is "more necessarie than Matrimonie, which containeth the felicity of mans life... the preservation of Realmes, the glorie of Princes, and that which is, most of all, it causeth immortalitie." Pedro does not mention Elizabeth by name, but Tilney's choice of words alludes to her marriage, which was, as the 1563 parliamentary petition expressly pointed out, crucial to "the preservation" of the realm. Elizabeth's marriage to Charles would create an alliance between two international powers, thereby increasing "the glory of [two] princes," Elizabeth and Charles. As Cecil observed, "no Prince ever had less Alliance, than the Q. of England hath; nor any Prince ever had more cause to have Friendship and Power to assist her estate."[39] By producing a much-desired heir to the throne, Elizabeth's marriage would secure "immortality" not only for Elizabeth herself but also for the Tudor dynasty.

Early modern English marriage manuals typically argue that it was important to select a mate of equal age, rank, and wealth. Pedro's particular version of this conventional advice advantages Charles over Elizabeth's other suitors: "equalitie is principally to be considered in this matrimoniall amitie, as well as yeares, as of giftes of nature, and fortune. For equalness herein, maketh friendlinesse."[40] Dudley was Elizabeth's equal in age, and Elizabeth apparently found his physical attractiveness, his "gifts of nature," equal to her desires. Yet he was certainly not her peer in status and wealth. Prince Henry, whom the French proposed as soon as the Austrians reopened negotiations, was more Elizabeth's equal in terms of rank, but the difference in age was a problem: Elizabeth had little interest in marrying an adolescent boy eighteen years younger than herself. Pedro mentions ancient philosophers who argued that a man should be considerably older than his wife "bicause in that time, the man should be best able to rule his householde."[41] This implies what Tilney is too diplomatic to state directly—that Elizabeth would be less likely to be subjected to her husband's power and better able to rule both the household and the country herself if she married Charles who was seven years younger than herself, but not so much younger as to be ridiculous. In fact, Elizabeth's only other foreign suitor to receive serious consideration was François, the Duke of Alençon and later Anjou, who was also younger than Elizabeth.

The question of whether or not to marry was a common assignment for students learning rhetoric.[42] Yet Tilney specifically links Pedro's discussion of marriage to Elizabeth by referring to "the preservation of Realmes, the glorie of Princes" and to Alexander the Great who "being Lorde of the whole worlde could finde no equall match in respect of his greatnesse." As noted above, Tilney's dedicatory epistle describes Elizabeth as "our Alexandra." Moreover, the 1563 marriage petition invoked the example of Alexander to demonstrate the disasters that would ensue if Elizabeth failed to marry and settle the succession: "what ensewed the death of great Alexander, when for want of certeine heires by him begotten or appointed," his successors ruined "his dominions" with "warres and slaughters."[43] With the 1563 marriage petition and Tilney's dedication to "our Alexandra" as the subtext, Pedro's remark that the woman Alexander chose to marry was "not farre his inferior, both in parentage, and substance," implies that Elizabeth should marry Charles rather than Dudley because Charles was "not far" her "inferior in parentage and substance."[44]

At this point, Lady Isabella interrupts the discussion to express her personal objections to marrying a much older man: she "woulde never marry, rather than to take such old crustes, whose wi[v]es are more occupied in plaistering, than in enjoying any good conversation." Much like the maydens who refuse "to be coupled in mariage with such as are lothsom to looke upon," Isabella expresses the sentiments Elizabeth expressed when she told parliament that "nothing would suffice to make her think of marrying, or even treating of marriage; but the person she was to marry pleasing her so much as to cause her to desire what at present she has no wish for."[45] Like Elizabeth, Isabella would rather forgo marriage altogether unless it meant "enjoying...good conversation"—a word commonly used to describe not only the open exchange of ideas promoted by *A brief and pleasant discourse* but also sexual intercourse. Isabella is not only physically repulsed by the idea of marrying an old crust of a man but she is also determined to marry only someone who could match her wit and respect her unconventional views. Later in the dialogue, Isabella's radical defense of female liberty and equality is qualified by her mother Lady Julia, but here Pedro backs Isabella up, remarking, "You say truth." Pedro agrees with Isabella that it is the husband's duty to win his wife's love by being courteous and gentle in conversation, a view that stands in marked contrast to Erasmus's colloquy on marriage, which was translated into English and published just one year earlier, where the "good wife" teaches the shrewish wife to temper her tongue and subordinate her every wish to her husband's will.

As Tilney's subtitle announces, *the Flower of Friendshippe* is the principal goal and essential prerequisite for marriage. Pedro's historical survey of marriage customs provides a plethora of supporting evidence for the importance of companionate marriage. In France, for example, parents invited a number of young men whom they "thought fittest" for their daughter to a banquet so that the maiden could choose for herself whom she wanted to marry: "him, to whom the maide gave first water, by that signe she chose for hir husband." The Chaldeans betrothed themselves by touching a fire kindled by the priest. If one of them later had a change of heart, they could let the fire go out and "so were they as free, as ever." The flower of friendship could develop only little by little over an extended period of time, Pedro argues, but it would never even begin to put down roots unless the husband was "merie, and pleasant with the wife, to make hir the more in love with him at the beginning."[46] Pedro's claim that a marriage needs to get off to a loving start if it is to succeed validates Elizabeth's refusal to finalize the marriage treaty until Charles came to England to see whether a "mutual liking" would develop.

Most Renaissance marriage manuals were written by ministers or religious educators who maintained that equality or commonality of religion was an essential prerequisite for marriage. By omitting religion from his list of equalities, Tilney supports Elizabeth's express wish to leave the question of religion in abeyance until Charles came to England. At the same time, Tilney's treatise implies what cannot be said openly in a country where religious conformity was required by law: that Charles' Catholic religion need not preclude his marriage to Elizabeth, as long as he was "secrete," and "discreete," "dissembling" rather than openly disagreeing.[47]

In addition to offering precedents and reasons for Charles to come to England to secure Elizabeth's love, Pedro provides support for England's monetary demands. Elizabeth wanted Maximilian to pay Charles' household expenses, but Maximilian thought she should pay; Pedro argues at length that it is the husband's duty to provide for the household, and the wife's to govern it: "the husband is, to maintaine well his livelihood, and the office of the woman is, to governe well the houshold." England asked Austria to pay a dowry, but Maximilian responded that it was customary for the woman to provide the dowry. Pedro offers the counterexample of the Babylonians who "maried their Maides without Dowries."[48]

Proponents of the Austrian match argued that Charles was the best choice precisely because, as the son and brother of the Holy Roman Emperor, he was as close as Elizabeth could come to finding an equal.[49] While equality was the principal argument in favor of Elizabeth's marriage to Charles, it was also the main impediment because the English were offering Charles only a nominal appearance of "equality": the title of king without a share in governing the country. The emperor wanted genuine equality: "the King's share in the governance of the country, whether he by virtue of this marriage will be placed on an equality with the Queen as regards honour and the royal title, and [should] assist her in ruling over this realm and its dominions."[50] Pedro offers the English negotiators a way to hold firm while appearing to grant Maximilian's request. By suggesting that it was the husband's duty to serve as his wife's counselor in "secret in that, wherein he is trusted, wise in giving counsaile, carefull in providing for his house," Pedro implies that Charles can, as Maximilian requested, "assist her in ruling over this realm and its dominions."[51]

The husband's traditional religious and legal power over his wife posed the most serious impediment to the marriage negotiations, for how could Elizabeth rule over her subjects, if her husband ruled over her? A marriage based on "friendship" and "equality" could finesse but not totally resolve the patriarchal assumptions underlying Maximilian's demands, as Pedro acknowledges when he says that "the civil law giveth the man the superiority over the wife." Pedro proceeds, however, to say that the husband ought "not to offende or despise [his wife], but lovingly to *reform* her."[52] This could mean that it is the husband's duty to *correct* or *reprove* his wife's insubordination since, as "The Homily on Marriage" puts it, "the woman is a weak creature, not endued with like strength and constancy of mind; therefore they be the sooner disquieted, and they be the more prone to all weak affections and dispositions of mind, more than men be; and lighter they be, and more vain in their fancies and opinions." But Pedro does not proceed to argue, as the homily and prescriptive texts conventionally did, that women need to be corrected and constrained because they are naturally weak, vain, inconstant, and irrational. Indeed, the misogynist rhetoric that pervades early modern prescriptive writing is strikingly absent from Pedro's discourse; instead, he explains that a relationship based on love, friendship, and mutual regard obviates the need for subordination: "For whome the wife hateth, in feare she serveth, but whome shee loveth, she gladly cherisheth."[53] Pedro could easily have said, "whom she loveth, she gladly obeyeth," but he finesses the question by saying instead, "she gladly cherisheth."

Pedro uses the humanist theory of companionate marriage not to subordinate the wife but to "reform" the institution of marriage; the word "reform" meant not only to *correct* or *reprove*, but also to *put a stop* or *end to an abuse by enforcing or introducing a better procedure or conduct*; *to repair or redress a wrong*. Not only does Pedro argue that the husband "must not be rigorous" and must never use force, but he also warns that a husband may forever sacrifice his wife's love and friendship if just "once he reprehend" her "sharply."[54] "The Flower of Friendshippe" redresses social abuses sanctioned by law, religion, and tradition that were, Tilney's dialogue suggests, morally wrong.

Pedro offers a secular analogy to the traditional spiritual union of marriage, which mystically transforms two bodies into one soul, when he advises the husband to "steal away her private will, and appetite, so that of two bodies there be made one onelye hart." Disturbed by the stealthiness of the verb "steal away," Valerie Wayne argues that this passage surreptitiously reasserts the husband's power over the wife.[55] Perhaps, but I doubt it, because Pedro's recommendations are far more liberal than traditional versions of this familiar argument. John Knox, for example, argued that after the fall, the woman was forevermore "made subject to man by the irrevocable sentence of God...Thy will shall be subject to thy husband, and he shall beare dominion over the[e]...He shall be Lord and gouernour, not onlie ouer thy bodie, but even over thy appetites and will." Tilney's language is much closer in spirit to the passage in *The Courtier* where Lady Emilia instructs the male lover to satisfy his mistress's desire: "He that taketh in hande to love, muste please and applye himself full and wholy to the appetites of the wight beloved, and accordinge to them, frame his owne."[56]

Tilney's subtitle, *the Flower of Friendshippe,* contains a barely veiled allusion to the sexual amity that enables marriage to flower and produce children because the word "flower" was a common circumlocution for both menses and hymen.[57] I think Tilney chose the verb "steal away" not to stealthily introduce the wife's subjection to her husband but to express something that could be mentioned only covertly. With its associations of secrecy, "steal away" intimates that the flower of friendship will blossom and grow to fruition only if the husband is initiated into the arcane mysteries of female sexual pleasure. Indeed, the Renaissance interest in the classics led to "the rediscovery of the clitoris." In 1559 the Italian anatomist Colombo described the clitoris as "the principal seat of women's enjoyment in intercourse, so that if you not only rub it with your penis, but even touch it with your little finger, the pleasure causes their seed to flow."[58] As noted in chapter 4, it was widely believed that female orgasm was vital to conception; this medical belief had important implications for Elizabeth's marriage negotiations. If Elizabeth was to produce the much-desired heir to the throne, and if a husband was not permitted to force himself upon his wife as Pedro expressly declares, and if female orgasm enabled conception, it followed, as the fruit follows the flower, that Elizabeth's husband needed to learn how to "steal away" his wife's "private will and appetite"—or to use Elizabeth's own words, to satisfy her "will" and "liking."

The second part of Tilney's dialogue, where the lords and ladies reassemble to discuss the wife's duties, references book 3 of *The Courtier,* where the men set forth ideal standards of female behavior. The powerful, highly educated ladies who people Castiglione's dialogue facilitate and judge the conversation, inserting witty gibes but rarely expressing their own views at any length. Thus, when Lord Octavian and Lord Gaspar speak ill of women, Lady Emilia calls on Lord Julian to defend women. Moreover, when M. Unico asks "what pleaseth women," Lady Emilia responds that he is himself "most acceptable to women," so "it [is] pardee meete for [him] to teach it."[59] By contrast, Tilney's Elizabethan women express their opinions and articulate their desires as freely and fully as the men.

Lady Julia teaches her daughter Isabella what much of the dialogue about the wife's duties strives to teach its female readers: that women are bound to "obey our Husbandes. God commaundeth it, and we are bounde so to doe." This dictum provokes a response from Isabella that is remarkably undeferential: "I know not, quoth the Lady *Isabella*, what we are bound to do, but as meete is it, that the husband obey the wife, as the wife the husband, or at the least that there be no superioritie betwene them, as the auncient philosophers have defended. For women have soules as wel as men, they have wit as wel as men, and more apt for procreation of children than men. What reason is it then, that they should be bound, whom nature hath made free?" Isabella's declaration that women are the spiritual and intellectual equals of men recalls the moment in *The Courtier* where Lord Julian defends women's judgment and learning: "what ever thinges men can understande, the self same can women understande also."[60] Yet Isabella goes much further, arguing not only for equality of understanding but also for the equality of speech and action that Elizabeth claimed for herself.

Isabella bravely disagrees with her mother to whom she owes deference and obedience in order to argue that women are no more bound to obey men than men are to obey women. Declaring that "nature hath made [women] free," Isabella contends that women's subordination was not natural or divinely ordained but constructed by men for their own benefit. Her radical claim repudiates the assumptions underlying a patriarchal theory of government and society: that "women are commanded to be subject to men by the lawe of nature," as Knox put it, "Because in the nature of all woman, lurketh suche vices, as in good governors are not tolerable."[61] Isabella thus extends Elizabeth's defense of her female wit and liberty to all women and anticipates later even more outspoken defenses of women, from Æmelia Lanyer (1611)—who declares, "Then let us have our Libertie againe, / And challendge to your selves no Sov'raigntie"—to modern feminists who define gender and "reality as social constructs that can be dismantled and reconstructed in new and perhaps more egalitarian ways."[62]

Isabella's radical pronouncement prompts Master Erasmus to give a brief sermon invoking religion to justify the universal subordination of women: "For in deede both divine, and humaine lawes, in our religion giveth the man absolute aucthoritie, over the woman in all places." This is essentially the argument made by Knox when he declared that "It is a thing moste repugnant to nature...that a woman shuld be promoted to dominion or empire to reigne over men."[63] It is also what the English bishops argued when they insisted that Elizabeth could not be named the head of the church because St. Paul said, "Let women be subject to their husbands, as to the Lord. For the husband is the head of the woman, as Christ is the head of the church" (Ephes. 5: 22–23). In 1565, Thomas Smith resuscitated the argument when he wrote *De Republica Anglorum*: "we do reject women, as those whom nature hath made to keep home and to nourish their familie and children, and not to meddle with matters abroad, nor to beare office in a citie or common wealth."[64]

Lady Julia seems to agree with these arguments, for she responds, "Then what blame deserve those men that doe permit their wives to rule all, and suffer themselves to be commaunded for company." Yet, upon more careful examination, Julia actually sides with Isabella against Erasmus when she goes on to say, "the man being as he is, most apt for the soveraignetie being in governement, not onely skill, and experience to be required, but also capacity to comprehende, wisdome to understand, strength to execute, solicitude to prosecute, pacience to suffer, meanes to sustaine, and above all a great courage to accomplishe, all which are commonly in a man, but in a woman verye rare."[65] While acknowledging that the "skill," "experience," and "capacity" needed to govern were "common" in men and "verye rare" in women, Julia recognizes that there are exceptional women, such as Elizabeth, who have the qualities a sovereign needs to rule effectively. In so doing, she supports Isabella's rejection of the essentialist argument that women were by "nature" unfit to rule.

Lady Isabella represents one end of the political spectrum; Lord Gualter represents the other. Although Gualter's conventional misogynist sentiments echo those expressed by Castiglione's Lord Gaspar, Gualter's anger is fueled and intensified by what he sees happening all around him in Elizabethan England: "they be shrewes all, if you give the simplest of them leave to daye to treade upon your foote, to morrow shee will tread upon thy head." Gualter's explosive outbursts betray barely contained tensions between the sexes and the generations.[66] Yearning for the unquestioned male authority of days past and positively bristling with resentment about women's empowerment "to daye," Gualter's diatribe epitomizes male resentment of Elizabeth's female power. His images of the head and the foot recall the bishops' 1559 arguments that Elizabeth should not be declared "head of the church." Even more immediately, they echo Thomas Smith's *De Republica Anglorum*, which argues that women should never be granted sovereignty over men and seeks to curtail Elizabeth's power by encompassing it within the larger, overriding authority of parliament: "parliament (which is the whole universall and generall consent and authoritie aswell of the prince as of the nobilitie and commons, which is as much to say of the whole head and bodie of the realme of England) and also of the prince, (which is the head, life and governor of this common wealth)."[67]

Smith's argument provoked the debate over liberties that caused Elizabeth so much difficulty with the 1566 parliament, prompting her to respond: "As to liberties, who is so simple that doubts whether a prince that is head of all the body may not command the feet not to stray when they would slip?" (CW 105). Tilney reduces Smith's argument to the brief misogynist outbursts that cause Gualter to be marginalized and mocked by Pedro and the women: "This sawcie foole, quoth Madame *Aloisa*, woulde be well beaten, and banished our company. For he is still pratling against women...No, no, quoth Maister *Pedro*, he increaseth our sporte."[68] Elizabeth answered parliament's marriage petition by deriding the witless feet that would lead her astray if she followed their bidding, and the maydens of London answered Hake's hostility to women with a satiric writ inquiring whether he was an idiot. So too, Tilney's courtly men and women answer Gualter's misogyny with mocking laughter.

The extreme positions represented by Isabella and Gualter, positions that we would call feminism and anti-feminism, mark the boundaries of the Elizabethan debate.[69] Misogyny did not suddenly disappear simply because Elizabeth ascended the throne. Elizabeth could not suppress conservative voices such as Lord Gualter, or the bishops who invoked the Bible to discredit her as head of the church, or Thomas Smith who argued that no woman should rule. She could, however, surround herself with counselors, courtiers, and intellectuals who would contest and reject such views—flexible, progressive men such as Edmund Tilney and the liberal humanists who people his *Discourse.*

Tilney's dialogue not only redefines marriage as a less intransigently patriarchal institution but it also provides a model for amicable, mutually rewarding relations between a female monarch and her husband, or a female monarch and her male subjects. Just as a husband is advised by Master Pedro to win his wife's affection by treating her with loving care, so too the men in Elizabeth's court and government would be well advised, Tilney implies, to seek Elizabeth's favor and trust, not by trying to "command whose duties are to obey," as Elizabeth put it in her first parliamentary speech, but by accepting her power, respecting her learning and judgment, and recognizing her will and liking. When Pedro argues that a loving, discreet husband has the qualities necessary to become a circumspect and valuable counselor, he expresses what the treatise seeks to demonstrate: that Tilney himself has the learning, judgment, and discretion to become a trusted member of Elizabeth's government.

Tilney's contribution to the debate over Elizabeth's marriage is so deftly woven into the discussion of marriage in general that modern scholars have not perceived the connection. Yet that is precisely what makes *A brief and pleasant discourse* such a brilliant bid for patronage. By writing a dialogue on marriage in general that echoed and supported Elizabeth's own view of marriage, and by constructing a well-developed, coherent argument in the voice of a highly regarded contemporary Spanish writer that Elizabeth could use to defend her position in the marriage negotiations with Austria and its ally Spain, Tilney hoped to win Elizabeth's favor. Moreover, by assembling so many precedents from history, the classics, and the Bible, he provided Elizabeth with exemplary precedents that she could use to disprove Emperor Maximilian's claim that her position was "entirely novel and unprecedented," and that therefore "we cannot approve of it."[70]

A brief and pleasant discourse demonstrates Tilney's sophisticated sense of what was and was not an appropriate way to intervene in court politics. Having dedicated the discourse to Elizabeth, Tilney assumes the role of narrator, allowing male and female voices equal credibility and authority. Just as important, the discourse expresses Tilney's appreciation of Elizabeth's esthetic. By discussing her marriage indirectly, under the cover of a dialogue on marriage in general, Tilney demonstrates an understanding and mastery of the "flowers" of rhetoric that Elizabeth herself valued and deployed: ambiguity, enigma, irony, analogy, all the strategies of indirection and concealment subsumed under Puttenham's "courtly figure *allegoria.*" Yet, Puttenham's reductive and duplicitous view of "his place and profession of a very courtier, which is, in plain terms, cunningly to be able to dissemble" replaces the surface meaning with another, equally reductive meaning. By contrast, Tilney's discourse sustains multiple levels of meaning, working both as a general treatise on marriage and as a covert intervention in Elizabeth's marriage negotiations. Moreover, by transforming a debate about monarchy and marriage into an engaging, dramatic narrative, Tilney showed that he had the ability to provide entertainments such as "are practiced at this day in the English court wherein is not only delectation but pleasure joined with profite, and exercise of the wit."[71] In short, *A brief and pleasant discourse* demonstrated that Tilney was well qualified to become master of the queen's revels, with the dual responsibility of arranging entertainments for the queen and her court and approving or censoring plays for the public theater.

Tilney was appointed master of the revels in 1578, thanks to the patronage of his cousin and contemporary Charles Howard, the son of William Howard who was Lord Chamberlain when Tilney dedicated *A brief and pleasant discourse* to Elizabeth. Tilney built the Revels Office up from a state of disrepair, where bills remained unpaid and disorganization prevailed, to a major force in Elizabethan culture and society.

Moreover, in 1581 when the Spanish ambassador was angry at being denied access to Elizabeth, she apparently sent Tilney as her envoy to the king of Spain.[72]

A brief and pleasant discourse reveals an intricate connection between theory and practice, court politics and popular debate.[73] Pedro's and Isabella's progressive, egalitarian visions of marriage echo and apply the models of governance set forth by Elizabeth in her coronation procession, in her parliamentary speeches on marriage, and in her negotiations with foreign ambassadors. Furthermore, *A brief and pleasant discourse* suggests that Elizabeth could marry and rule over her household as she ruled over the country by freely offering her husband and subjects the love and respect she expected from them in return. The dedication to Elizabeth, "our Alexandra," and the repeated allusions to Alexander the Great indicate what the narrator declares at the outset: the humanist debate about marriage, with its classical, biblical, and historical precedents, has a direct bearing on conversations that were taking place "at this day in the English court."[74]

Although we do not know how or whether Elizabeth responded to Tilney's presentation copy, ultimately his attempt to please her and win her patronage had a powerful impact on popular views of marriage. *A brief and pleasant discourse* was printed in 1568, and it became an immediate bestseller.[75] The first printing sold out immediately, and two more appeared the same year. A total of seven editions were published within the decade, making it one of the most influential Elizabethan treatises on marriage. Tilney's dialogue acquired a second life when substantial portions of it were incorporated into Henrie Smith's *Preparative to Mariage* (1591), which became a popular and influential Elizabethan marriage manual in its own right, being reprinted four times within the first year. Through Tilney's narrative, therefore, Elizabeth's reciprocal views of marriage permeated Elizabethan society, moving beyond the court to the culture at large.

The formal narrative frame—both the introductory description of the discourse as "a pleasant and profitable" way to pass the time and the final claim that Tilney was transcribing a dialogue that actually occurred—places the dialogue squarely in the context of the larger social debate about courtship, marriage, and female liberty, much as the Maydens' letter, by explicitly *"Answering the Mery Meeting,"* adds its defense of women's "lawfull libertie" to the popular controversy over courtship and women's rights. The second part of Tilney's dialogue includes the classic argument for female subordination, but it also gives voice to an Elizabethan woman of the younger generation who claims for all Elizabethan women the liberty and equality that Elizabeth demanded for herself. The dialogue form allows Tilney's readers to choose amongst the conflicting views that it represents, but it makes Gualter's hostility to women seem retrograde and laughable.

Together Whitney's letter and admonition, the maydens' letter, and Tilney's discourse show Elizabeth's politics of courtship merging with the popular controversy about courtship and rapidly acquiring a controversial life of its own. The maydens' letter applies the rhetoric of courtship to urban, working women, attributing the "defense of their lawfull libertie" not to a single author who might have seemed isolated and marginalized but to a group of outspoken, like-minded, and altogether typical Elizabethan women—"by us Rose, Jane, Rachell, Sara, Philumias and Dorothie." By transforming a courtly dialogue written for and dedicated to the queen into a printed text that reached Elizabethan society, Tilney's discourse extended the courtly debate over Elizabeth's marriage to a debate over marriage in general. He probably decided to go public, as his final comments imply, because Elizabeth herself encouraged him to do so, hoping that the printed dialogue would win further support for her position in the marriage negotiations with Austria.

A direct bid for the queen's patronage, *A brief and pleasant discourse* shows how Elizabeth's presence on the throne tempered patriarchal rhetoric, marginalized stridently misogynist voices, and encouraged Elizabethan women to speak out in defense of their liberty and equality. As the political negotiations over the queen's courtship merged with the popular controversy over marriage, the debate became general across England.

Their Argument Is Social, Political, Personal

The controversy over courtship, poetry, and women's "lawfull liberty" escalated in 1579 with the publication of Stephen Gosson's *School of Abuse, Containing a Pleasant Invective against Poets, Pipers, Players, Jesters, &c.* Gosson reiterated some of the charges made by Hake and answered by the maydens twelve years earlier. In particular, he denounced the theater for encouraging Elizabethan men to consort with prostitutes and for encouraging Elizabethan women to behave like prostitutes. Gosson also argued that Elizabethan poets, taught by Ovid, that "amarous schoolmaister," and his "trumpet of bawdrie, the Craft of Love," had debased the art of poetry, pretending to make art while surreptitiously making love: "pul off the visard that poets maske in, you shall disclose their reproch, bewray their vanitie, loth their wantonnesse, lament their folly, and perceive their sharpe sayinges to be placed as pearles in dunghils, fresh pictures on rotten walles, chaste matrons apparel on common curtesans."[76]

The debate over the poetry, politics, and practice of courtship escalated in 1589 when Puttenham's *Arte of English Poesie* was finally printed along with Nash's *The Anatomie of Absurditie, Jane Anger her Protection for Women,* and John Stockwood's *A Bartholmew Fairing for Parentes.* Punning on Stubbes' name, Nash titled his treatise *The Anatomie of Absurditie* in order satirize Phillip Stubbes' *Anatomie of Abuses* for "pretending foorsooth to anatomize abuses, and stubbe up sin by the rootes."[77] Probably alluding to Sidney's *Defence of Poesie,* Nash asked, "Are they not ashamed in their prefixed posies to adorne a pretence of profit mixt with pleasure, when as in their bookes there is scarce to be found one precept pertaining to vertue, but whole quires fraught with amorous discourses kindling *Venus* flame . . . alluring even vowed *Vestals* t[o] reade awry, inchaunting chaste mindes, and corrupting the con[t] inenst."[78] Nash was distressed by the widespread use of poetry for courtship and seduction, not only in learned, courtly circles but in every bar and tavern: "Hence come our babling Ballets, and our new found Songs and Sonets, which every rednose Fidler hath at his fingers end, and every ignorant Ale Knight will breath foorth over the potte, as soon as his braine waxeth hote."[79]

Nash complained that Elizabethan poets were concealing their ulterior motives beneath paeans of praise, yet his own attack on poetry was a thinly disguised excuse to vent his vitriol against women. Nash's misogynist rhetoric is so familiar that it doesn't bear examining here. What is worth noting is that Nash not only anatomized Gosson and Sidney but also satirized *A letter sent by the maydens of London to the Matrones & Mistresses of the same, in the defense of their lawfull libertie*: "Is this correspondent to the modestie of maydens, and the maners of Matrons, nay, rather it seemes that law is turned to libertie, and honest civilitie into impudent shamefastnes." The maydens' letter had been published twenty-two years earlier. Yet Nash still found it disturbing enough to take on its principal contentions. The maydens defended their right to have drinks at a tavern and to stroll freely about the city. According to Nash, that made them little better than prostitutes: "But wemen through want of wisedome are growne to such wantonnesse, that uppon no occasion they will crosse the streete, to have a glaunce of some Gallant, deeming that men by one looke of them, shoulde be in love with them, and will not stick to make an errant over the way, to purchase a Paramour to helpe at a pinche." Six themselves, the maydens invoked an army of "above sixe thousand" women ready to join their political campaign. Nash responded witheringly, "But perhaps Women assembling their senate, will seeke to stop my mouth by most voices." Nash was particularly incensed by Elizabethan men who were writing their own defenses of women—"even so they by compiling of Pamphlets in their Mistresse praises, to be called the restorers of womankind"—in order to win their mistresses' favor. Mocking the maydens' letter, Nash directs his satire more broadly at the growing number of boldly outspoken women writers: "View their workes, and know their vanitie, see the Bookes bearing their name, and smile in thy sleeve at their shame. A small ship in a shallow River, seemes a huge thing, but in the sea a very litle vessell, even so each trifling Pamphlet to the simpler sorte, a most substantiall subject, whereof the wiser lightly account, and the learned laughing contemne." Nash complains bitterly that women "will not be content to be a wife, but will be a Maister or Mistresse, in commaunding, chiding, correcting & controlling."[80]

For all his scornful dismissiveness, Nash's distress reveals that *A Letter sent by the maydens of London, to the vertuous matrones & mistresses of the same* had prompted other Elizabethan men and women to write *"defense[s] of their lawfull libertie"* and that they were having a significant impact on contemporary social mores.

Nash's dedicatory epistle alludes to the "obscured cause" that "hath compelled my wit to wander abroad unregarded in this satyricall disguise":

> Onely this shall my arguments inferre, and my anger averre, that constancie will sooner inhabite the body of a Camelion, a Tiger or a Wolfe, then the hart of a woman: who predestinated by the father of eternitie, even in the nonage of nature, to be the Iliads of evils to all Nations, have never inverted their creation in any Countrey but ours. Whose heauenborne Elizabeth, hath made majestie herselfe mazed, and the worlds eye sight astonied.

Ironically, by implying that his own anger was caused by a woman's betrayal, Nash affirms the maydens' claim that hostility against women is the result of spurned love. Donne's irreverent female speaker makes the same satiric claim in "Confined Love":

> Some man unworthy to'be possessor
> Of old or new love, himself being false or weak,
> Thought his pain and shame would be lesser,
> If on womankind he might his anger wreak.

Nash apparently realized that misogynist invective was not the best way to curry favor in Elizabethan England. Before proceeding to describe "the abusiue enormities of these our times," he pauses to praise the "heavenborne Elizabeth" promising his "feruent zeale shall be the vncessant attendant on her weale."[81]

In the same year, 1589, *Jane Anger her Protection for Women* set out to answer the kind of misogynist invective Nash promulgated, although Nash may have been responding to Anger when he wrote "Onely this shall my arguments inferre, and my anger averre."[82] Challenging the very stereotypes—"the weaknesse of our wits, and our honest bashfulnesse"— that Elizabeth worked to overcome at the outset of her reign, Anger's dedication urges all Elizabethan women to join her—"and herein I conjure all you to aide and assist me"—in defying the ethical codes that equated women's honor with modest bashfulness and dutiful subordination: "your wits are sharp and will soone conceive my meaning." Anger's barbed wit and barely contained fury show how much the popular controversy over marriage and women had escalated since Whitney and the maydens published their far more decorous letters in 1567. As Anger points out, "the scandalous reportes of a late Surfeiting Lover" were only the most recent provocation "among the innumerable number of bookes to that purpose."[83] Some scholars argue that Anger is a pseudonym for a male writer whose covert goal was to contain female sexuality and curtail female liberty. Yet the profound similarities between Anger's *Protection*,

Whitney's *Admonition*, the maydens' letter, and Elizabeth's speeches suggest instead that the author was an Elizabethan woman provoked to publication by the rash of attacks on the burgeoning defenses of women's liberty and wit.

Anger was primarily concerned about the deleterious impact of male rhetoric that denigrated, deceived, and injured Elizabethan women—rhetoric such as Nash's derisive attack on Elizabethan women for "deeming that men by one looke of them, shoulde be in love with them." Anger turned the blame back upon Elizabethan men who were vaunting about their own sexual prowess:

> It is a wonder to see how men can flatter themselues with their own conceites: For let us looke, they wil straight affirm that we love, and if then Lust pricketh them, they will sweare that Love stingeth us...Nay, some of them are so carried away with conceite, that shameles they wil blaze abroad among their companions, that they have obteined the love of a woman, unto whom they never spake above once.

Anger censured rapacious men—"ravenous haukes, who doe not onley seize upon us, but devour us"—for using the rhetoric of love to deceive and ruin Elizabethan women: "wee take all the griefe from man: we languish when they laugh, we lie sighing when they sit singing, and sit sobbing when they lie slugging and sleeping."[84] As Anger's colloquial diction suggests, Elizabethan men could have casual sex and walk away, "slugging and sleeping" to their hearts' content, but a woman who trusted an unscrupulous, deceitful suitor could be ruined for life.

Instead of advising Elizabethan women to preserve their chastity so that their fathers could choose husbands for them, Anger—like Whitney, the maydens of London, and Tilney's Isabella—defends women's liberty and wit, urging her female contemporaries to "use our wittes well, as they [men] can their tongues ill." Anger, like Whitney, warned women conducting their own courtships to think critically and act advisedly: "Though love be sure and firme: yet Lust fraught with deceit, / And mens fair wordes do worke great wo, unless they be suspected." Above all, women must defend themselves both by being skeptical of men's rhetoric and by expressing their own viewpoint more forcefully. Seduction thrives on female credulity—"The greatest fault that doth remaine in us women is, that we are too credulous," and misogyny exploits the code of female silence: "the time wherin [men] have lavished out their words freely, hath bene so long that...they thinke we wil not write to reproove their lying lips."[85] The ideology of silence was unacceptable and deleterious to women, Anger declared, urging women to speak out in their own defense.

The last of our texts published in 1589—John Stockwood's *A Bartholmew Fairing for Parentes, to bestow upon their sonnes and daughters, and for one friend to give unto another: Shewing that children are not to marie, without the consent of their parentes, in whose power and choise it lieth to provide wives and husbandes for their sonnes and daughters*—might look, from the discursive title alone, like a conventional assertion of patriarchy. Actually, it is an impassioned diatribe against the growing numbers of Elizabethans who were rejecting the time-honored custom of arranged marriage: "Sonnes and daughters, as now a daies (the more is the pitie) in too great multitudes betroth themselues in mariage without the privitie, nay against the will of their fathers and mother." In alarmist language reminiscent of the 1563 parliament's doomsday prophecies, Stockwood warned that the unprecedented numbers of children rebelling against parental authority were "bring[ing] in al confusion and disorder, in altering and changing Gods owne course, to set up and establish their owne unbrideled lust and lawles affection."[86]

While Stockwood was issuing dire warnings that unrestrained lust would destroy the social order, other Elizabethans were arguing that the real threat to family and society was arranged marriage. "What is the cause of so many housholde breaches, devorcements, and continuall discontentmentes, but unnaturall disagreementes by unmutuall contractes?" John Lane asked in 1593, appealing directly to "the Gentlewomen and others of England."[87] To these Elizabethans, the large numbers of freely chosen and clandestine marriages represented the happy prospect of a society where the relationship between the sexes could be reconstructed not as it was but as it should be. If arranged marriage was the older generations' and higher orders' way of preserving past privilege, freely chosen courtship and mutually desired marriage were the daughters' and the sons' means of exercising their "lawfull libertie" to shape their own lives. If, in the process, they reshaped the social order, so much the better, Tell Troth suggested.

By 1595 Phillip Stubbes was so distressed by the growing numbers of Elizabethans rebelling against authority that he added a dedicatory epistle to the 1595 edition of *The Anatomie of Abuses* that asked "The Christian Magistrates and godly Governors of England," "Was there ever seene lesse obedience in Youth of all sortes, both men-kinde and women-kind, towardes their superiours, Parents, Masters and governors?"[88] As Elizabeth's reign drew to a close, many Elizabethans were asking precisely that question.

During the first half of the reign, the prolonged marriage negotiations between Elizabeth and parliament and between Elizabeth and the foreign ambassadors placed a vocal female voice at the center of political debate, giving relations between the sexes an unprecedented public visibility and import in England and abroad. By the last decade of the reign, when Shakespeare's dramas of courtship and marriage were being staged and many of the greatest English love poems were being written and circulated in manuscript, Elizabeth was no longer involved in marriage negotiations. By then, her politics of courtship had merged with a wider social and literary conversation about courtship, marriage, and women. For Anger, Whitney, the maydens, and Elizabeth herself—as for Hermia and Helena, Rosalind and Celia, Hero and Beatrice—the solution was not the silencing of women, or the suppression of female desire, or the elimination of conjugal freedom of choice, but a savvier grasp of the subtle, multivalent ways in which rhetoric could be deployed, not only in private persuasions to love but also in public debates about social change, which may explain why so many of Shakespeare's female characters (think of Hermia, Hero, Beatrice, Helena, Desdemona, and Cleopatra) are called upon to defend their private desires in a public forum.

On Monsieur's Departure

I grieve and dare not show my discontent;
I love, and yet am forced to seem to hate;
I do, yet dare not say I ever meant;
I seem stark mute, but inwardly do prate.
      I am, and not; I freeze and yet am burned,
      Since from myself another self I turned.

My care is like my shadow in the sun—
Follows me flying, flies when I pursue it,
Stands, and lies by me, doth what I have done;
His too familiar care doth make me rue it.
      No means I find to rid him from my breast,
      Till by the end of things it be suppressed.

Some gentler passion slide into my mind,
For I am soft, and made of melting snow;
Or be more cruel, Love, and so be kind.
Let me or float or sink, be high or low;
      Or let me live with some more sweet content,
      Or die, and so forget what love e'er meant.

                    Elizabetha Regina.[1]

CHAPTER 8

THE QUEEN OF ENIGMA AND MONSIEUR'S DEPARTURE

There will be time to murder and create,
And time for all the works and days of hands
That lift and drop a question on your plate;
Time for you and time for me,
And time yet for a hundred indecisions,
And for a hundred visions and revisions...

T. S. Eliot, "The Love Song of J. Alfred Prufrock"[2]

Poetry and History

As we have seen repeatedly in the course of this book, for Elizabeth and the Elizabethans poetry was the preferred medium for exploring complex thoughts and feelings that could not be expressed straightforwardly or openly. Elizabeth's most important poem, "On Monsieur's Departure," is intensely personal, surprisingly erotic, and deeply rooted in the messy contingencies of an unusually distressing personal and historical crisis.[3] It is also remarkably enigmatic, even for the queen of enigma. The missing direct objects, the switch to the passive voice, the undefined verbs of being and doing enact both the open-ended interpretive possibilities the poem privileges and the constraint the poem embodies. Although Elizabeth insists that *she* knew what she "meant," that is the interpretive dilemma the poem poses for its audience. The radical indeterminacy makes "On Monsieur's Departure" deeply characteristic of Elizabeth's poetry in particular and Elizabethan lyric in general.

Elizabeth's opening lines make little effort either to situate the speaker or to assist the reader, which suggests that the poem was either written for Elizabeth herself or for a private lyric audience which was privy to the underlying events. It is only from the title, which appears in three of the five extant manuscripts, that we can infer the dramatic situation: the departure of Elizabeth's last serious suitor, François de Valois, Duke of Alençon, who became the Duke of Anjou and was known as Monsieur Frère du Roi after his brother was crowned Henry III, King of France, in 1574. Elizabeth came closer to marrying Monsieur than she did to any of her previous suitors, except perhaps Robert Dudley. The courtship began as an opportunity for England to forge an alliance with France and to

Figure 9. Portrait presumed to be Hercule-Francois de France, Duke of Alençon, by Francois Clouet, c. 1560

Figure 10. Queen Elizabeth I: The Pelican Portrait, by Nicholas Hilliard, c. 1574

check the threat of Spanish attacks on the Netherlands, Portugal, Ireland, Scotland, and England itself. Negotiations dragged on for years, embroiled in international politics and the competing needs of two governments and two complex personalities. Most biographical and historical studies of the courtship either mention the poem in passing or ignore it altogether. Literary critics have done little with the poem, even less with the context. No one has analyzed the poem closely enough to figure out either how the historical situation illuminates the poem or how the poem illuminates the historical situation.[4] This chapter follows my own process of discovery—a roller coaster ride that became more gripping as the final twists and turns came into view.

The Marriage Debate Escalates

Monsieur visited England twice. Since scholars have attributed the poem to both of Alençon's departures, before proceeding we need to determine which departure the poem represents. Monsieur came to England the first time during the last two weeks of August 1579.[5] It was over two years later, on October 31, 1581, that he arrived on his second visit. He finally left the country, after a long drawn-out departure, in February 1582.

Years of negotiation had gone into bringing Alençon to England. The French first requested permission for the seventeen-year-old prince to court the English queen in 1571. At the time, Elizabeth was not enthusiastic about the possibility of an adolescent husband, but the proposal laid the ground for the Treaty of Blois, a mutual defense pact against Spain signed by England and France in April 1572. A French envoy arrived in June 1572 to explore the possibility of opening marriage negotiations, but discussions were abruptly terminated when French Protestants were brutally slaughtered in the streets of Paris on August 24 during the St. Bartholomew's Day Massacre, which many Elizabethans blamed upon the Queen Mother and her son Henry. There was another hiatus in the negotiations when the duke was fighting with his mother and brother who held him under virtual house arrest at court. After considerable hesitation on both sides, more active discussions resumed in 1578, when the marriage presented a possible solution to England's problems in the Netherlands and when rumors that King Philip of Spain was planning to claim the Portuguese throne made the alliance look more politically desirable to both France and England.

In 1578 Elizabeth was forty-five years old. Alençon looked like her last chance to marry and bear an heir to the throne. Yet the prospect posed a number of serious questions for Elizabeth and her councilors. Would Monsieur's Catholicism be a catalyst for plots against the queen and the English church? Would he try to gain control of the government, or would he bankrupt the English treasury to support his own military goals in the Netherlands? If Monsieur inherited the French throne, would he desert Elizabeth and try to subject England to French rule? These political, financial, and religious questions gave everyone including the queen pause.

There was also some lingering concern about discrepancies in age and power. Would Monsieur willingly spend the rest of his life humoring an aging queen? Would Elizabeth be too old to bear a child by the time the marriage was finally negotiated? If she failed to produce a child and heir, would Monsieur try to annul the marriage, as Elizabeth's own father had done? Conversely, would Elizabeth find Monsieur satisfactory? Having been the most desirable match in Europe for two decades, Elizabeth's standards were as high as her visibility. Monsieur was a younger brother with limited financial assets and no power. Moreover, his eyes bulged. His complexion was scarred by smallpox. His nose was large, heavily veined, and disfigured, probably by syphilis. His mother denigrated him. His brother, the king, distrusted him and, at times, even warred with him. His contemporaries mocked him, calling him dwarfish. Was this the man, Elizabeth's advisors wondered, to make the queen "desire" a marriage she had evaded for nearly two decades?

Elizabeth, though, was willing to give it a try, especially after being wooed by Monsieur's charming envoy, Jean de Simier, "a choice Courtier, a man thoroughly versed in Love-fancies, pleasant conceits, and Court-dalliances."[6] Yet, she continued to insist, as she had during negotiations with the Austrian archduke Charles, that she would not agree to marry a man she had not seen. In February 1579, Simier had been in England for a month when Dudley reported: "If the person adventure without condition to come hither, and if she then like him, it is like she will have him."[7] Lengthy negotiations ensued. The Privy Council discussed the matter at length, and "utterly rejected and denied" the request that Monsieur be given "Conjunction with hir Majesty in Disposition of all Thyngs perteaning to hir Crown," just as they had refused to allow Archduke Charles to share Elizabeth's power when negotiations with Austria failed in 1568. To satisfy Elizabeth's vow to marry no man she had not seen, it was agreed that Monsieur would come to England secretly to see whether a mutual liking would emerge, and that the religious differences would be held in abeyance "untill that Monsieur shold come to hir Majesty, and upon their mutuall lykyng the same should be concluded." Thus, "if ther war no mutual lykyng," the failure of the negotiations could be attributed to religious differences.[8]

Thus the preconditions that the Holy Roman emperor had scoffed at became the grounds upon which marriage negotiations with France proceeded. The French received reassurances that Monsieur could withdraw from the marriage without losing face should no mutual liking occur. In return, they agreed, Elizabeth could call off the match without damaging relations with France. Elizabeth had once again taken charge, as she had earlier during negotiations with the ambassadors for Archduke Charles. As the Spanish ambassador Don Bernardino de Mendoza reported: "this marriage affair is being conducted by the Queen herself, we can only judge by appearances and her own words."[9]

Elizabeth had finally succeeded in negotiating the conditions she had been fighting for ever since the beginning of her reign: first, to decide for herself, guided by God but moved by her own mind and heart, whether or not to marry; second, to rule the country herself regardless of whether she married. On August 17, 1579, Monsieur Frère du Roi arrived in Greenwich incognito. The secrecy, or at least the pretense of secrecy, heightened the drama and marked the courtship from the outset with subterfuge and role-playing. During one lavish banquet, Monsieur was concealed behind a hanging where he could play the voyeur as Elizabeth conversed vivaciously and danced gracefully.

Despite the earlier, discouraging reports about Monsieur's person, Elizabeth was pleased by his princely bearing, charmed by his sophisticated

French manners, and flattered by his amorous attentions. "The Queen is delighted with Alençon, and he with her, as she has let out to some of her courtiers," Mendoza wrote. As the Spanish ambassador, he had every reason to hope that this new threat of a marital alliance between England and France would come to naught. Yet he nonetheless felt compelled to report that she "was much taken in by his good parts, and admired him more than any man. She said that, for her part, she [would] not prevent his being her husband."[10] The Privy Council met for over a month, spending long hours discussing the pros and cons.

Meanwhile, Protestant opposition was mounting. The day after Monsieur's arrival John Stubbs published *The discoverie of a gaping gulf whereinto England is like to be swallowed by another French marriage*.[11] The hyperbolic title was just the beginning of the political and religious cataclysm that Stubbs prophesied, should Elizabeth decide to endanger English Protestantism and invite Catholic insurgency by giving the country a Roman Catholic king.

Then Stubbs got personal. Elizabeth was too old to win Monsieur's love or to bear his child. As a woman, she was incapable of making a wise choice. Moreover, Monsieur was unworthy, and Stubbs thought it was foolish to trust Elizabeth, a woman who needed male guidance to make such an important choice: "He should hardly be the man, that choice man of choice in all respects to content both eye and mind."[12] Elizabeth was not pleased. On September 27, 1579 she issued a proclamation banning the book and recalling all extant copies. Then, ignoring the advice of her legal counsel, she insisted that Stubbs and the printer be tried for treason. They were found guilty and sentenced on October 30. On November 3, as they faced their punishment, Stubbs addressed the crowd, saying "Pray for me, now my calamity is at hand." It was a brave pun: after his right hand, his writing hand, was severed with three blows of a cleaver, Stubbs removed his hat with his left hand and said, "God save the Queen!"[13] The punishment was brutal and unusual, even for an age when public executions and dismemberments were popular entertainment. Instead of providing a deterrent, Stubbs' heroism and loyalty won the crowd's sympathy and galvanized Protestant opposition to the match.

Elizabeth's poem does not match the circumstances of Monsieur's first visit. At the time of his first departure, Elizabeth had clearly not turned him away as the poem implies she had: "Since from myself another self I turned." Nor was she afraid to say she ever "meant" to marry him ("yet dare not say I ever meant"). Indeed, she went to extraordinary lengths to punish Stubbs, silence Protestant opposition, and proclaim her interest in the marriage.[14] The poem refers to the end of a long-standing, intimate relationship ("His too familiar care doth make me rue it"), but the courtship was in its infancy on the occasion of Monsieur's first departure. While the Stubbs debacle was brewing, Alençon was flushed with the success of his visit. He sent Elizabeth three letters from Dover while waiting to set sail, another from aboard ship, and three more upon landing in Boulogne, all tied in pink ribbon. Elizabeth cherished the letters, keeping them as her own private love tokens and refusing to turn them over to Cecil to be included amongst the state papers.

For the next two years Elizabeth and Monsieur continued to exchange letters heavy with the language of love. Yet Protestant opposition grew so strong that in July 1581 Elizabeth proposed a political alliance with France instead of a marriage, instructing her ambassador, Sir Frances Walsingham, to

> beseech [Monsieur] not altogether to look to his private affection of the love he bears us, but to weigh these reasons which withdraw us from such a disposition to marriage as that if we also only regarded our love to him we should readily assent to it; but we have also to look to the consequences of a marriage so ungrateful to all our subjects that it is better for us both to have none at all than to have it with the general misliking of them, who will nei-ther joy in us nor in him, and so we ourselves should lack the comfort that marriage ought to bring with it.[15]

Monsieur was not pleased. On August 4, 1581 he wrote to Elizabeth saying that, without intermission, for five or six years, he had courted her ardently, refusing all other overtures and options: "car sans intermition durant sinc ou sis annees je le poursuyvi tres ardanmant, refuzant et negligant toutes autres ouvertures et parties."[16] Henry III rejected Elizabeth's proposal for a political alliance and sent Secretary of State Claude Pinart to pursue the marriage negotiations.

Contracted by Promise

Monsieur Frère du Roi, arrived in London for a much more tumultuous second visit on November 1, 1581. Hoping to obtain financial support for his military exploits in the Netherlands, he stayed in England for two months. On November 22, the court was bustling with the annual Accession Day festivities when Elizabeth surprised everyone by publicly betrothing her-self to Monsieur. Camden describes the scene: "The force of modest Love in the midst of amorous Discourse carried her so far, that she drew off a Ring from her Finger, and put it upon the Duke of Anjou's, upon certain Conditions betwixt them two. The Standers-by took it, that the Marriage was now contracted by Promise."[17] Mendoza sent Philip a more detailed report:

> The Queen and Alençon were walking together in a gallery, Leicester and Walsingham being present, when the French ambassador entered and said that he wished to write to his master, from whom he had received orders to hear from the Queen's own lips her intention with regard to marrying his brother. She replied, "You may write this to the King: that the duke of Alençon shall be my husband," and at the same moment she turned to Alençon and kissed him on the mouth, drawing a ring from her

own hand and giving it to him as a pledge. Alençon gave her a ring of his in return.[18]

This was a stunning moment and, as Elizabeth's poem demonstrates, its reverberations shaped everything that followed. We shall dwell further on this, but first a few words about our narrator. Here, as in the earlier negotiations with Archduke Charles that we examined in chapter 5, it is the Spanish ambassador who provides the most detailed account of events as they were unfolding at the English court.

Mendoza proceeded to offer a lengthy explanation of why he believed the betrothal was "only an artifice to draw Alençon on, and to make him believe that the men who were openly opposed to it are now openly in favor." Much as the French had tried to scuttle the alliance between England and Austria in 1559 and 1563 by telling Elizabeth "that the Archduke had a head larger than that of the earl of Bedford,"[19] the Spanish actively opposed an alliance between England and France. Although some modern scholars have accepted Mendoza's skeptical assessment of the betrothal, it seems extremely unlikely that Elizabeth's act was only a ruse because a promise to marry, made in the present tense in front of witnesses, without conditions or preexisting impediments, had the force of law, committing a man and a woman to marry each other and none other. The exchange of rings provided corroborating legal evidence that the marriage had indeed been contracted by both parties.[20]

A close reading of the documents suggests a far more complicated state of affairs. First of all, as Mendoza himself reported, "people in London consider the marriage as good as accomplished, and the French are of the same opinion."[21] Monsieur also seems to have taken Elizabeth at her word: he immediately sent a messenger to inform his brother that the marriage was now certain to take place. Moreover, when Elizabeth returned to her chambers and described what she had done, her ladies were horrified and urged her to reconsider. According to Camden, "The Queen's Gentlewomen, with whom she used to be familiar, lamented and bewailed, and did so terrifie and vex her Mind, that she spent the Night in Doubts and Cares without Sleep among those weeping and wailing."[22] Her most intimate and trusted courtiers also treated the betrothal seriously. Sir Christopher Hatton told her with tears in his eyes that her subjects might well depose her if she married Monsieur. Dudley, after "ask[ing] her whether she was 'a maid or a woman'," warned Elizabeth that the betrothal would spark a Protestant uprising that would endanger her life. Visibly shaken by these alarming predictions, Elizabeth agreed to send Monsieur a message "saying she had been thinking about the ring, and she was sure that if she married him she would not have long to live."[23]

Instead of retracting her promise to marry Monsieur, however, Elizabeth postponed it, saying, "He was a witness to the dissatisfaction of the English people at her attachment to him, which dissatisfaction she hoped he did not wish this to be fatal to her. For this reason, she would be grateful if he would allow her to defer the marriage." Anjou "replied with much gentleness that all he had said and done was to please the Queen, whose death not only did he not desire, but he would venture his own life to give her pleasure, as he had often done, and indeed was doing now, to save her from annoyance, by pressing his suit with less ardour at her request."[24] The language of "pleasure" and "ardour" suggests a considerable degree of intimacy. To protect herself from the political or legal consequences of a betrothal, Elizabeth claimed that the betrothal had always been conditional upon resolving the political differences between the two countries.

I Dare Not Say I Ever Meant

The poem's dramatic situation parallels the historical events in the days following the betrothal, when Elizabeth felt "forced" to "mute" her feelings and "dare[d] not say" she "ever meant" to betroth herself unconditionally, even as she continued to tell Monsieur in private (as both the poem and contemporary documents suggest) that she did still "love" him and would cherish him until death. Although both the poem and the historical situation allow an alternative, more complicated or skeptical interpretation that we will consider later in this chapter, we first need to understand just how fully the poem conveys Elizabeth's regrets at being forced to defer the betrothal.

The opening lines sound as if they could have been written not long after November 22, when the memory of promising to marry Monsieur and then denying she ever "meant" her words to constitute an unconditional contract *de praesenti* weighed heavily on Elizabeth's "breast." By continuing to say "I do" while simultaneously acknowledging the ensuing constraints, "yet dare not say I ever meant," Elizabeth recreates the moment of betrothal even as she laments the deferral she was "forced" to make shortly thereafter. The intensity and immediacy of the present tense verbs ("I grieve," "I love," "I do," "I freeze and yet am burned," "Follows me flying, flies when I pursue it"), along with the insistent first person "I," reinforce the sense that Elizabeth is still actively committed to Monsieur in her heart and breast.

After betrothing herself, Elizabeth essentially "turned" Monsieur away, although both her letters and the last line of the first stanza ("Since from myself another self I turned") insist that it was not easy for her to do so, either politically or personally. As a conjunction, "since" implies that the act of turning away was the precipitating event that set the poem in motion. As an adverb, "since" suggests that the emotional "discontent" and verbal constraint the poem struggles to comprehend and contain occurred after Monsieur was "turned" away. As the poem's only past tense verb, "turned" acquires further causal force that seems all the more definitive due to its place at the end of the stanza's final, rhyming couplet. The indefiniteness of "another self" multiplies the line's significance, suggesting that by turning Monsieur away Elizabeth "turned" away part of herself or another conception of *herself*, a self who continues to "love"—a self who nourished the prospect of a child and heir, yet "another self" the betrothal might have produced.

By comparison, the second stanza sounds tumultuous and anxious:

> My care is like my shadow in the sun—
> Follows me flying, flies when I pursue it,
> Stands, and lies by me, doth what I have done.

Although the words "doth what I have done" might sound even more vague and superfluous than "I do, yet dare not say," or "I am, and not," they too acquire particularity and weight from the immediate political situation. Together the present tense "doth" and the past perfect "have done" allude to and obsessively reiterate the traditional words of betrothal, the central defining event that set the poem in motion. The word "care" evokes the care cloth that was traditionally held over the heads of the bride and groom as they knelt to say the words "*I do* thee wed." It is not only Monsieur, that "other self" who "doth what I have done," but also Elizabeth herself who reenacts that past—"doth what I have done"—letting the lyric present do and undo the immediate past, over and over again.

As noted in previous chapters, Elizabeth regularly used the word "care" to refer both to her love for her subjects and to her responsibility as monarch. Beginning with her pre-coronation procession and continuing until her last Golden Speech, Elizabeth built a power base by declaring her love for her subjects and eliciting their loving support in return. The letters Elizabeth wrote to Anjou, as well as the letters her negotiators wrote to their French counterparts, repeatedly reiterate that she "dare not" "do" anything that would jeopardize her subjects' love and care. The poem makes this point when it implies that her "care"–meaning, *both her responsibility to* and *her love for*—her subjects conflicts with her "care" for Monsieur. The frenzied turns and returns of lines 7–9 suggest that Elizabeth's political cares preoccupy her day and night, denying her even a moment's peace of mind. The verb "stand," commonly used in the phrases "to stand one's friend" or "to stand good prince to," depicts Elizabeth torn between standing companion to Monsieur and standing good prince to her people. The alternating pursuit and flight enact Elizabeth's frustration with her government's failure to support the marriage. When parliament and the Privy Council pressured her to marry earlier in the reign, she resisted. Now that she "pursue[s] it," the members of her own government fly from her, loath to provide the support she needs.

Although she has been "forced" to deny and conceal her love for Monsieur, her choice of words suggests that, in the privacy of her "breast" and the privity of the poem, her commitment to him "stands" as firm as ever. Since "My care" (meaning, *the object of one's affection or concern*) can also refer to Monsieur himself, lines 7–9 also imply that he "Stands, and lies by me, doth what I have done." After the betrothal was resoundingly attacked, Elizabeth publicly maintained that she was not legally or morally obligated to marry him. Yet in private she continued to act as if she was in love with and betrothed to him, as numerous contemporary sources attest. For example, the Duke de Nevers noted in his memoirs that Elizabeth entertained Anjou with new demonstrations of her love, accompanied by kisses, intimacies, caresses, and endearments common to lovers ("par de nouvelles démonstrations, accompagnées de baisers, privautés, caresses et mignardises ordinaires aux amants").[25] Happy to report anything that might shed a disparaging light on the courtship, Mendoza also relayed the rumors: "My confidant tells me that the Queen frequently sees Alençon alone."[26]

The blatantly sexual double entendres of "Stands, and lies by me," along with the allusion to present and past reciprocities ("doth what I have done"), evoke the erotic "pleasure" (to use Monsieur's word) they were accustomed to giving each other as well as the conjugal consummation they had promised each other. The more intimate meaning of "care" (*regard arising from desire, liking*) leads directly to the next line: "His too familiar care doth make me rue it." The feminine rhyme softens the line, which can be construed to mean: because we have been so intimate with each other for so long, that is why I regret being "forced" to suppress my promise to marry Monsieur. The stanza ends by declaring that Elizabeth can find no means "to rid him from my breast," the breast being the bodily part associated with the affections, the source of mother's milk that would have flowed had they married, and, even more intriguingly, the location of private thoughts and secrets. Thus the words of the second stanza repeatedly imply that Elizabeth still "stands" by Monsieur, even though she cannot admit it in public, and that she fully intends to keep her promise "Till by the end of things it be suppressed"—or in the conventional language of the marriage vow, until death do us part.

The reading of the betrothal and the poem that I have constructed up to this point is supported by a recurrent pattern of words and actions stretching back to Elizabeth's very first parliamentary speech, by her insistence that Monsieur should come to England to court her in person so that they could see whether a "mutual liking" would develop, and by Cecil's handwritten memoranda, which state that Elizabeth will marry Monsieur only if it pleases her to do so: "If hir Majesty shall lyk of the Conditions and Person of Monsieur, as without which no Mariadge can be allowed, hir Majesty then shall have that Comfort in hir Liff, that ordinarely is to be looked for of Mariadg."[27]

Cecil's notes repeatedly stipulate that the determining factor, the sine qua non, was neither the Privy Council's approval, nor Parliament's vote, nor differences between England and France, although clearly these would have to be resolved for the marriage to take place, but the queen's "contentation" or "discontentation." These wonderfully evocative (and sadly outmoded) words imply that Elizabeth would marry Monsieur if, and only if, he satisfied her moral or rational faculties, if he gave her physical satisfaction and pleasure, and if he allayed her scruples and doubts. The word "contentation" shares its etymological root with the words "content" and "contentment," words that run like a leitmotif through Elizabeth's letters to Anjou,[28] and, even more importantly, with the words that anchor Elizabeth's poem: "discontent" and "sweet content," meaning primarily *satisfaction, pleasure, delights,* as well as the more steady *contentment* that marriage could provide. The continual references to "contentation," "contentment," and "content" by both Elizabeth and Cecil provide a forceful reminder that the courtship was shaped by amorous "pleasure" and "ardor" as well as domestic politics and international relations.

During the debates over her marriage that preoccupied the first three Elizabethan parliaments, Elizabeth repeatedly defended her freedom of choice by insisting that the Privy Council and parliament should stop telling her to marry forthwith, and under no circumstances should they tell her whom to marry. Rather, she would make her own choice according to her own "liking," guided by God alone. By the time the Privy Council met to discuss the Anjou courtship in October 1579, these principles had been established as the premises upon which Elizabeth's marriage negotiations would proceed. One memorandum, written in Cecil's hand and dated October 6, 1579, summarizes the Privy Council's discussion of the marriage treaty and concludes that the final decision would be made by the queen: "No man doth move hir Majesty to marry without perceaving in hir some Dispositon therto." Moreover, Cecil noted, "if God shall move hir hart to Mariadg, than hope is, that she may prosper therein."[29] In Elizabeth's official statements—in the parliamentary speeches, letters, and marriage negotiations examined in preceding chapters—Elizabeth repeatedly justified her freedom of choice by invoking her reliance on God's guidance. It is all the more notable, therefore, that in the privacy of the lyric Elizabeth never once refers to God, not even when the allusion to "the end of things" might easily have led her to do so.[30] Instead, the poem's language is entirely secular and remarkably sensuous, echoing the language of love that pervades the letters Elizabeth and Monsieur wrote to each other during the two-year interval between his first and second visits.

Allusions to lovers' intimacies occur throughout the poem. The conventional Petrarchan oxymoron of the first stanza—"I freeze and yet am burned"—suggests that Elizabeth has been "burned," both aroused and pained, by the betrothal and its aftermath. The ongoing present tense of "yet am burned," followed by the sexual innuendo of "Stands, and lies by me," implies that Elizabeth's passion for Monsieur still ("yet") burns as hot as ever. This veiled erotic subtext reaches a climax in the final stanza:

> Some gentler passion slide into my mind,
> For I am soft and made of melting snow;
> Or be more cruel, Love, and so be kind,
> Let me or float, or sink, be high or low,
> Or let me live with some more sweet content,
> Or die and so forget what love e'er meant.

Since women were commonly referred to as both the gentler sex and the weaker vessel, the words "soft," "melting snow," and "gentler passion" make Elizabeth seem vulnerable, surprisingly feminine, and full of desire.

Elizabeth uses images of feminine weakness in her public speeches, but she balances them with assertions of masculine strength. In the speech to the troops at Tilbury, when the Spanish Armada was looming and Elizabeth had received intelligence of plots to assassinate her, she memorably declared, "I know I have the body of a weak and feeble woman, but I have the heart and stomach of a king" (CW 326). Despite the feminine connotations of "soft," "On Monsieur's Departure" comprises an equally bold affirmation of authority and agency, especially when we remember that poetry in general and the language of love and desire in particular were conventional male discourses. If Elizabeth's final explanation ("For I am soft, and made of melting snow") lacks a countervailing assertion of power, it acquires form and strength from the very act and agency of writing the poem.

To understand how unconventional Elizabeth's language is, we need to put the poem in context. Like Elizabeth's response to Ralegh, which we examined in chapter 2, "On Monsieur's Departure" uses the traditional language of Petrarchan poetry to critique conventional assumptions about women. Rather than allowing herself to be constructed and defined by the ways in which her male courtiers and poets portrayed her, Elizabeth constructs herself, even as she constructs the poem, to represent a distinctly anti-Petrarchan lady and a decidedly unconventional queen. Petrarch finds pleasure in a pure and unflagging love that remains the same, always desired and always unattainable, even after his angelic Laura ascends to heaven. By contrast, Elizabeth bristles with impatience, eager to alter her situation, anxious to trade her current "discontent" for "some more sweet content."

Hoping to find relief from the circularity and stasis that made Petrarchist poems into stale reproductions of their predecessors, Elizabeth tears the traditional oxymorons into their constituent elements in order to examine the alternatives available to her. Elizabeth could, like an exalted Petrarchan lady, choose to live up to her "high" station and "float" above her "low" desires, finding pleasure in "the more sweet content" of her loving courtiers and devoted subjects. She could "do" that, but at this crucial turning point in her life, she prefers not to. As the statement "For I am soft, and made of melting snow" makes all too clear, she would rather "sink" below these heavenly heights to the earthly sexual desires Monsieur has aroused in her "breast."

The pervasive erotic subtext suggests that "the gentler passion" and "more sweet content" refer not only to her public "love" and "care" for her subjects but also to her lingering "inward" desire to trade her current "discontent" for the sweeter pleasures of "love" and "care" that she and Monsieur promised each other when they betrothed themselves. If these desires are traditionally seen as "low" or common, so be it. The final line, "Or die, and so forget what love e'er meant," sounds like a last resort to be chosen only if all else fails. Yet because its logical connection to the previous alternatives remains so loosely defined, it also hints that Elizabeth would like to pursue her love for Monsieur even if it proves fatal, as Hatton and Dudley told her it would when they pressured her to rescind or at least postpone her promise to marry Monsieur.

Elizabeth's private admission that she was willing to face death itself to maintain her love for Alençon introduces another erotic double entendre that poses an even more radical challenge to Petrarchism's eternally deferred desire. As anyone familiar with Donne's love poetry knows, "die" was a common circumlocution for sexual consummation because it was believed that reaching orgasm shortened a person's life by a day. Alluding back to the erotic subtext of "Stands, and lies by me," Elizabeth's final line intimates that if the choice were a matter of her desires alone, she would choose to marry Monsieur and consummate their marriage with a distinctly anti-Petrarchan death, "and so forget what love e'er [in the sense of *previously or* always] meant" in conventional love poetry.

The contraries that comprise Elizabeth's final stanza echo the familiar Petrarchan oxymorons, the "living deaths, deare wounds, faire stormes, and freesing fires" that the great Elizabethan poets parodied and lesser poets endlessly reiterated.[31] Like Sidney, Spenser, Donne, and Shakespeare but unlike less talented Petrarchists who littered the literary landscape with their tedious iterations, Elizabeth does not simply repeat and endorse Petrarchism's endless, oxymoronic stasis. Instead, she uses conventional Petrarchan tropes to critique Petrarchist ideology, for, as the final stanza asserts, she would rather expire than live the rest of her life as an icy Petrarchan lady.

In her reply to Ralegh, which was written a few years later and which we examined in chapter 2, Elizabeth again expresses her impatience with the manipulations and evasions of conventional Petrarchist rhetoric; as she acerbically declares there, "her mind" was no more controlled by fortune than by Ralegh's poem. "On Monsieur's Departure" comprises a telling critique of the pageants, pastorals, and lyrics that sought to convince Elizabeth *not* to marry her French Catholic suitor by casting her as an innocent pastoral shepherdess, too pure for marriage, or an icy Petrarchan lady, too "high" and exalted for the "low" desires of the flesh.[32]

"On Monsieur's Departure" rejects the passive role of the cold, distant, heavenly Petrarchan lady who is little more than a reflection of male desire or a pawn of male poetic power. Instead, Elizabeth represents herself as a passionate poet/lover, constrained by the responsibilities and cares of monarchy, which pressed upon her, day and night. As the author and subject of her own lines, Elizabeth insists upon her own agency, yet, she is also, she must admit, subject to emotional, social, and political forces beyond her control. If Elizabeth conceived "On Monsieur's Departure" as a response to representations of her as a Petrarchan lady and Virgin Queen which were just beginning to emerge as a way of preventing the French marriage, she kept it to herself because, as the poem explains, events forced her to conceal her "love." Before she could join that more public lyric debate, Monsieur's departure became so pressing and distressing that it cast those disputes into the shadows.

Before we turn to the even murkier final phase of the courtship, we need to consider the fate of Elizabeth's manuscript. Did she keep the poem for her own private pleasure as she kept Anjou's love letters, or did she write it in the hope of creating "some more sweet content" ("content" also refers to the contents of a piece of writing), not only for herself but also for that most "familiar" interlocutor, Monsieur himself?

Elizabeth's Private Manuscript

"On Monsieur's Departure" begins as a private meditation: the first stanza, with its insistent first person pronouns, announces itself as a self-reflective act, while the second stanza refers to Monsieur in the third person ("his too familiar care"), making him the subject of the poem and the object of Elizabeth's loving "care." But in the third stanza, in the poem's most jarring line, Elizabeth's stance and tone of voice shift: "Or be more cruel, love, and so be kind." Scholars have dismissed this as conventional Petrarchan rhetoric, which it is, but it acquires a more specific and unsettling meaning when we consider what was happening with Elizabeth's betrothal and Monsieur's departure.

Elizabeth might have been exhorting herself to "be more cruel" by turning Monsieur away once and for all, "and so be kind" rather than continuing to create unrealistic hopes that would make the courtship drag on as endlessly as a Petrarchan sonnet sequence. We will return to this possibility shortly, but there are two other options to consider. First, the line could be an apostrophe to Cupid, that impish God of Love, whom Renaissance poets/lovers were wont to blame for all their woes. As Philip Sidney explains in *Astrophil and Stella*, "It is most true, what we call *Cupid's* dart, / An image is, which for ourselves we carve; / And, fooles, adore in temple of our hart" (5:5–7). But that seems like a stretch, since Elizabeth's lyric contains none of Cupid's conventional trappings, and mythological allusions were not her mode, even though she was well schooled in the classics. Second, the apostrophe to "love" could be addressed to Monsieur himself, which seems at once more likely and more potentially enlightening.

The three other genres Elizabeth favored, letters, parliamentary speeches, and prayers, all address a specific audience, whether human or divine. Moreover, unlike poetry today, which is generally written for print and the public, or the web and a global audience, or both, early modern English poetry, as we saw in chapter 2, typically comprises one side, or one moment, in a private dialogue that begins before the poem is written and continues as it is read or heard and then answered by the poet's intended interlocutor.

Elizabeth's poetry is firmly rooted in this oral/manuscript tradition. She wrote poems to reestablish and redefine her relations with both Dudley and Ralegh. "On Monsieur's Departure" probably played a similar defining or shaping role in her relationship with Monsieur. If so, Monsieur's identity as Elizabeth's original private lyric audience, like

Dudley's identity as the recipient of the psalter posy, comprises part of the meaning the poem embodies and simultaneously conceals. Before we consider the ways in which this possibility might enhance or complicate our interpretation of the poem, there are some practical questions we need to address. If Elizabeth sent "On Monsieur's Departure" to Anjou, why was it neither mentioned in their correspondence nor preserved along with her letters to Monsieur?

If Elizabeth sent the manuscript to Monsieur after he left England or entrusted it to anyone else involved with the marriage negotiations, it would almost certainly have been preserved in the archives, amidst the voluminous collections of documents pertaining to the courtship.[33] If it was addressed to Monsieur, therefore, as the direct address "Love" suggests it might well have been, Elizabeth probably recited it to him or showed it to him herself, keeping the manuscript in her possession in order to protect the secrets the poem anxiously conceals. But how could "On Monsieur's Departure" have been part of a private lyric dialogue between Elizabeth and Monsieur if it was written after Monsieur left the country, as the title seems to suggest? "On," in the sense of *regarding* or *concerning*, was widely used in titles to announce the subject of a poem or piece of writing; thus, "On Monsieur's Departure" could mean that Monsieur's departure is the subject of the poem rather than the date of the poem. Furthermore, the temporal meaning of "on" was broader than we might assume, for it implied *motion or direction towards a position* as well as *on the occasion of* or *immediately after*.[34] Consequently, the poem could have been written shortly after the betrothal when Monsieur was making only the slightest motion in the direction of leaving for the Netherlands, or it could have been written during the weeks when his departure was repeatedly announced only to be deferred. It could also have been written on the occasion of his departure itself, though not, I think, after he left because (1) the language is so immediate and pressing and (2) the poem is neither mentioned in their letters nor preserved in the archives. To decide whether Elizabeth's lyric was written on the occasion of or prior to Monsieur's departure, we need to look more closely at both the poem and the historical documents.

If "On Monsieur's Departure" was intended for the Duke of Anjou, why didn't Elizabeth write it in French, since she wrote her letters to him in French.[35] Perhaps, she began composing the poem to explore her own thoughts and feelings and decided, when she got to the third stanza, that she wanted to share her thoughts with him. But it seems more likely that she wrote the poem in English because there was so much she "dare[d] not" say. Writing in English would not only give her more control over the nuances of her language, but it would also enable her to claim that Monsieur had misinterpreted what she "meant," that he had mistaken the meaning or missed the subtleties of her words.

Was Monsieur's English good enough to understand the poem? With a very few exceptions, the words are remarkably simple: "high or low," "float, or sink," "some more sweet content." The verbs are mostly in the present tense, and the sentences are comprised of short, main clauses.

Significantly, the poem does not use the intricate subordinate clauses that complicate Elizabeth's other poems and parliamentary speeches, nor is there any ornate rhetoric, archaic poetic language, or inverted syntax. The complexities—and they are considerable—are presented as a series of simple oppositions. Thus the reader can grasp a single, straightforward thought before moving on to an opposing idea. Even if Monsieur could not understand the darker subtexts that we will explore shortly, the primary meaning sketched above would have been comprehensible to a native-speaking Frenchman with a limited knowledge of English. Moreover, Elizabeth had been honing her skills as a translator since adolescence, so she could easily have explained anything she wanted him to understand. After all, that is one of the primary advantages a private lyric dialogue has over print—though, of course, an interlocutor who is "familiar" with the poet can also raise problems or objections the poet might have preferred not to acknowledge or confront.

What rhetorical purpose could the poem have served? If it was addressed to Monsieur after the betrothal was hedged about with conditions, Elizabeth could have written "On Monsieur's Departure" for some of the same reasons she wrote the Woodstock epigrams, the psalter posy, and the reply to Ralegh: to address the "discontent" that was troubling her and her interlocutor; to soothe hurt feelings, resolve differences, and make amends; finally, to hedge her meaning—for the sum of its parts is much more complicated than any of the individual elements—so that she could later say, if necessary, "but that's not what 'I meant' at all."

His Too Familiar Care Doth Make Me Rue It

In the days and weeks following the betrothal, Elizabeth was anxiously trying to convince Monsieur that she could not marry him because her subjects were vehemently opposed to the match. Mendoza reported the events along with his customary suspicion about Elizabeth's guile: "she rather prefers to let it appear that the failure of the negotiations is owing to the country and not to herself, as it is important to keep him attached to her."[36] As we have already seen, this is the primary message the poem tries to convey from its initial declaration ("I love and yet am forced to seem to hate") to its ensuing regrets ("From myself another self I turned," or "his too familiar care doth make me rue it"). The allusions to Monsieur's sexual potency and their mutual sexual pleasure would have flattered his ego and mollified his hurt feelings, while the promise that she would care for him as long as he lives would have provided the reassurances he needed to leave the country without feeling like a reject.

Certainly the poem was an "elaborate artifice," to borrow Mendoza's assessment of the betrothal, to make Elizabeth's love look sincere; however, her anxiety and difficulty in breaking off the courtship suggest that it probably was far more sincere than Mendoza was willing to believe. Yet, true or not, her declaration of love would have been more convincing to Monsieur since the poem claims to provide direct access to her "inward" thoughts and feelings. That would explain why the poem begins as a private meditation and turns to address Monsieur directly only in the third stanza.

For an interpretation of a poem to be not only plausible but also compelling, it must be compatible with the poem as a whole, in *all* its intricate, multifaceted detail. Hence we need to ask not only whether there is sufficient evidence to support a particular reading but also whether there are alternative interpretations of the details we have already considered and, moreover, whether there are details we have not yet considered that might undercut or complicate our reading. In short, we need to ask ourselves not only whether our interpretation can be proved but also whether the opposite can be proved. All the details of "On Monsieur's Departure" are consonant with the consoling reading I have constructed up to this point; however, as I've already hinted, there are a number of darker shades of meaning that complicate and disturb both the poem and the events that unfolded between the time the betrothal was postponed on November 23 and the time Monsieur finally departed in early February 1582.

While the opening lines recall and affirm the "love" Elizabeth expressed when she betrothed herself to Monsieur, they also hint at grievances that emerged after she "turned" him away. To begin with, according to the *Oxford English Dictionary* the word "grieve" was not used in its modern sense, *to feel grief for someone*, until sixteen years after Monsieur's final departure. In Elizabethan England, "grieve" was a cognate for the word grievance, meaning *to do bodily harm to a person; to be angry or vexed; to cause anger, pain or vexation*. Since "discontent" also means *a grievance or cause or occasion of discontent*, the poem's opening line, "I grieve and dare not show my discontent," contains another, more disturbing meaning: that Monsieur himself may have said or done something to cause Elizabeth's "discontent," and that she was angry or vexed with him. If so, the opening lines could mean, alternatively, that Elizabeth did not "dare" show her vexation to Monsieur himself lest she inflame his anger, heighten his discontent, and complicate or prevent his departure.

In the days and weeks following the betrothal, Monsieur's continually deferred departure was one of the most pressing political concerns facing Elizabeth, the Privy Council, and the country as a whole, and it had far-reaching political, military, and economic implications for England, France, Spain, and the Netherlands.[37] Elizabeth was trying to placate Monsieur by expressing her own unhappiness at having been "forced" by her subjects to turn him away; however, she was also becoming increasingly vexed with Monsieur's own behavior, not right away when his response was extremely loving and empathetic but a bit later when he began to realize that she really "meant" it when she "turned" him away.

Their mutual grievances emerged in stages, punctuated by angry, explosive encounters that became more violent and more disturbing the longer Monsieur's departure was delayed. The difficulties began when Elizabeth told Anjou, as Dudley convinced her to do, that she could not go through with the betrothal because it would incite rebellion and endanger her life. Persuaded that marriage was impossible for the moment at least, Monsieur was amenable when the Privy Council offered him a considerable sum of money in exchange for releasing Elizabeth from her betrothal. This was the one time during Monsieur's second visit that Elizabeth's councilors acted on their own, without consulting or informing her, and she was furious—furious with them for acting independently and furious with Monsieur for being so readily persuaded to take her money and call it quits.[38] The resulting quarrel between Elizabeth and Monsieur was explosive and nasty. Mendoza, pleased that the marriage was exploding, reports the fallout: "As Alençon thought fit to forget her in exchange for her money, she would neither marry him nor give him any money, and he might do the best he could. She sent at once for him, Alençon, and told him this very angrily, to which he replied in a similar way, and they parted very ill friends."[39]

From this point on, relations between Elizabeth and Monsieur deteriorated. The ensuing tensions and resentments help explain the poem's dark shadows:

> My care is like my shadow in the sun,
> Follows me flying, flies when I pursue it,

Since "care" means not only *affection* and *responsibility* but also *mental suffering, grief, trouble,* these lines suggest that Elizabeth was grievously upset about the state of affairs. The constant role reversals and frantic shifts in direction, signaled by the trochaic inversions, make the situation these lines describe seem disruptive and unsettling. The clauses seem to have a will or motion of their own. When she runs away, care follows; when she turns in pursuit, care flees. Elizabeth seems driven, riven by anxiety, unable to take a firm stand or to escape the distress that follows wherever she turns. Since "care" refers not only to her responsibilities as queen but also to Monsieur himself for whom she continues to care, this mini-allegory suggests that they have been constantly changing positions. When she pursues him, he flees. When he pursues her, she flees.

The lack of a clear antecedent in the phrase "doth make me rue it" heightens the ambiguity, complicating the more consoling meaning that Elizabeth wishes she hadn't been "forced" to turn Monsieur away with the more distressing thought that she should have never promised to marry him since that created such anxiety and "discontent." As we've already noted, "His too familiar care" sounds tender and intimate, even as the words "doth make me rue it" sound loving and regretful. Yet, if her discontent was caused by Monsieur's behavior, then his "too familiar care" begins to seem more oppressive and burdensome.

Monsieur continued to delay his departure. Perhaps, he still hoped Elizabeth would marry him. He certainly hoped to extort additional funds for his military exploits in the Netherlands. The longer he delayed, the more anxious Elizabeth was to be "rid" of him: "she complained greatly of the annoyance that she felt at Alençon's pressing her so closely, saying that she could not *get rid of him* without danger, or entertain him further without inconvenience" (my emphasis).[40] Since Monsieur was beginning to irk Elizabeth by behaving badly, the couplet that ends stanza 2—"No means I find to rid him from my breast, / Till by the end of things it be suppressed"—could be hinting at another, more worrisome possibility that Elizabeth could not express openly: the fear that Monsieur would continue to be a burden until death (either his or hers) finally freed her from the legal and financial obligation she had incurred by betrothing herself to him. Unless or until he released her from their marriage contract, Monsieur was her responsibility, someone she'd have to deal with, provide for, and, yes, get "rid" of. Thus, what Elizabeth "dare not" say openly, what she could express only confidentially in conversations with her most trusted counselors and confidants, or privily in the carefully veiled subtext of this most private of manuscript poems, is that she would happily be "rid" of Monsieur if only she could find some "means," some way, "to rid him from my breast."

An outpouring of personal feeling designed for no one's eyes but your own is a very different matter from a poem designed to create the impression of loving sincerity. If Elizabeth wrote "On Monsieur's Departure" for herself, to comprehend and contain her own complicated, tormented thoughts and feelings, it might be tempting to take her expression of "love" at face value. But if the poem was a rhetorical act comprising one side of a private lyric dialogue, Elizabeth could have adopted the role of disconsolate, caring lover to placate Monsieur who was upset with her for postponing and then trying to back out of their betrothal. The poem rests upon the opening claim that "I love, and yet am forced to seem to hate;" interestingly, the only usage of "love" as an intransitive verb is *to give praise, to flatter*, which suggests that the poem was designed to praise and flatter Monsieur so that he would leave the country without demanding even more burdensome reparations for the damage to his honor and reputation.[41] The greatest form of flattery was the claim that she loved him very much and that the reason she was pretending to hate him was her subjects' opposition to the match.

The ambiguous double meanings of stanza 3 summarize the alternatives Elizabeth faced as the optimistic hopes of the betrothal were replaced by the disillusionment that began to set in after she "turned" Monsieur away. Regardless of whether Monsieur actually read the poem, the third stanza comprises a plea for him to see better and behave differently. Here too, the language is susceptible to two distinct, opposing interpretations. Indeed, the line "Let me or float or sink, be high or low" perfectly captures Elizabeth's own conflicting feelings. The absence of a connecting conjunction also makes it possible to read the second half of the line ("be high or low") as an imperative addressed to Monsieur. The vocative voice echoes and strengthens the direct address of the preceding line, suggesting that

Elizabeth will "float or sink" depending on whether Monsieur lives up to his "high" stature, controls his anger, and allows her to enjoy "some gentler passion," or whether he takes the "low" road, follows her trying to extort more financial remuneration the more she tries to flee, and continues to destroy her peace of mind until she becomes a care-worn shadow of her former self. The word "high" urges Monsieur to be high-minded, even as it alludes to and tries to suppress his "high" temper and anger (both literal meanings of the word). If he continues to be base and mean-spirited, Elizabeth almost wishes he would "be more cruel" so that she could end the courtship without being torn apart by guilt and regret.

The strain she was under gives the entire stanza a more disturbing cast, implying that she was so depressed that thoughts of death ("die, and so forget what love e'er meant") had begun to seem like an appealing escape from an impossible situation. Dudley's and Hatton's suggestion that she had put her own life in jeopardy by betrothing herself to Monsieur makes the line all the more disturbing because Dudley had been doing everything in his power to make his threats a reality. As Mendoza reported, "Leicester has not seen Alençon since the matter of the ring, and has incited the London people to rise if the marriage is carried forward, the means adopted being to double the guards who are on duty at night to prevent tumult. By this means they are doubling the number of those who would raise a disturbance."[42] With Dudley and Monsieur, the two men she had most trusted with her affections, ready to turn against her, Elizabeth had good reason to feel anxiety and danger wherever she turned.

In the Woodstock epigram, the ambiguous use of the passive, "much suspected by me," made Elizabeth both the object of other people's suspicions and the author of her own suspicions about them. I think Elizabeth wrote "On Monsieur's Departure" in English rather than French so that she could relegate her deeper reservations and vexations to a subtext that Monsieur would not entirely understand, and that she could either deny or invoke depending on how events progressed. For the moment, she could express her anger and "discontent" without blaming Monsieur directly— much as the psalter posy simultaneously chastises and placates Dudley with the uncertain referent of "an inward, suspicious mind," making it unclear whether the epigram was an apology, a reprimand, or a peace offering. For analogous reasons, the darker subtext of "On Monsieur's Departure" also serves Elizabeth's complicated rhetorical purposes. Should the poem's more consoling surface meaning fail to soothe Monsieur's feelings and convince him to depart, the darker subtext would enable her to deny any obligations Monsieur might claim she had incurred by promising to marry him and by reaffirming her "love" for him in the poem.

Words You Have Written to Me

Before concluding, we need to examine another, even more provocative and mysterious chain of events that adds a further twist to the poem and the courtship. On December 25 Elizabeth told Cecil "that even if it would make her empress of all the world, she would not marry Alençon." The next day she begged Monsieur "to accept her as a friend and sister, without thinking of her as a wife." He responded,

> No, no, madam, you are mine as I can prove by letters and words you have written to me, confirmed by gift of the ring, of which I have sent intelligence to the King my brother, my mother, and the Princes of France, all those who were present at our interviews being ready to bear testimony. If I cannot get you for my wife by fair means and affection I must do so by force, for I will not leave this country without you.[43]

Mendoza reports that Elizabeth "was perturbed at these words," but just how perturbed was she? And what exactly did Monsieur mean by his final threat to "do so by force"? Was he threatening to use military force to take her away with him? Was he threatening to rape Elizabeth if she continued to rebuff his "affection"? Both possibilities are less outrageous than they might seem. After all, he had already engaged in military skirmishes with his own brother. Moreover, words of betrothal uttered by both parties in front of witnesses, technically known as a contract *de praesenti*, comprised a legally binding common law marriage if followed by intercourse.

Whatever he may have meant, Monsieur's threat made Elizabeth face her ultimate vulnerability as a woman, and she did not like the way that made her feel. An argument ensued, and Elizabeth "protested, finally, that she was entirely free from any matrimonial engagements, and, on the contrary, was desirous of remaining in her present state, until she could at all events overcome her natural hatred to marriage."[44] Here, as she had done so often in the past when a marriage prospect turned sour, Elizabeth expressed her personal antipathy to marriage in general; under the circumstances, however, the allusion to her much-vaunted virginity was clearly an attempt to assuage Monsieur's mounting aggression.

In describing the altercation to the Earl of Sussex, Elizabeth ventured one of her most evasive remarks: "she hated the idea of marriage every day more, for reasons she would not divulge to a twin soul, if she had one, much less to a living creature."[45] Here, as in the psalter posy, the generalizing language enables Elizabeth to avoid explicitly incriminating either Monsieur or herself. Yet, she clearly had specific "reasons" in mind, because she said she would not "divulge" them to any "living creature." This raises further questions about how Anjou made his threat to take her by force. What happened that was so shameful she could never tell it to "a living creature"? Did Monsieur enact his threat? Did he rape her, or try to rape her, or pretend to try to rape her?

Although he was shorter than she, Monsieur was a seasoned soldier, and no doubt considerably stronger than she was. But if he tried to take her "by force," wouldn't one of her attendants have heard the ruckus and come running? Not necessarily. Elizabeth might have been too shocked and frightened to call out or fight back. Moreover, there may not have been anyone nearby because, after the betrothal, Elizabeth had taken to dismissing her attendants so that she and Monsieur could be alone in her chamber.[46] Although it seems extremely unlikely that Monsieur actually forced himself upon her, he may have become so angry and violent that he frightened her into believing that he would do so if she continued to refuse his demands.

The threats continued. Monsieur "told friends of his that, although he does not show any dissatisfaction, if the Queen gives him no further security than before for the fulfillment of her promise to marry him, he will let her see before he goes how displeased he is, and in a way that she will be sorry."[47] On January 24 he "saw the Queen would not marry him. This was a great blow to his honor and reputation, about which he must dissemble, until he was in a position to exact satisfaction." What kind of "satisfaction" did he intend to "exact"? A possible explanation emerges a year later when the French ambassador told Elizabeth she needed to marry Monsieur for a reason "of more importance than any, namely, that it was said that he (Alençon) had slept with her." Elizabeth retorted that such gossip should be ignored, to which the ambassador responded, "she might well do so in her own country, but not elsewhere, where it had been publicly stated. She was extremely angry, and retorted that a clear and innocent conscience feared nothing."[48] The report does not specify whether "it had been publicly stated" by Monsieur or someone else, but the gravity and force of the ambassador's warning imply that the source was Monsieur himself, for who else would have had the authority to make such a statement seem serious enough to force a queen into marriage?

The telling parallels between these incidents and the poem suggest Elizabeth may well have written "On Monsieur's Departure" as a response to Monsieur's continually delayed and increasingly problematic departure. To begin with, Elizabeth's enigmatic comment to Sussex that she could never tell a living soul the reasons why she could not marry Monsieur resonates with the poem's initial premise of silence and concealment. By threatening to force himself upon her, moreover, Monsieur quite literally made himself "too familiar," which in turn made Elizabeth "rue it"—made her regret that she ever betrothed herself to him. By alluding to his sexual prowess, perhaps Elizabeth was trying to flatter Monsieur's wounded pride and thus convince him that he did not have to use physical force to prove his manhood in her eyes. Moreover, the poem's most discordant and puzzling line, "Or be more cruel, Love, and so be kind," could have been a reference to Monsieur's explosive anger or a response to his violent threats.

Yet, even if Elizabeth could have summoned the wherewithal to write such a carefully balanced, multifaceted poem under such distressing circumstances, which seems unlikely given how distraught she was, what would the motivation have been? Given how "perturbed" she was, and how erratically Monsieur was behaving, and how "repugnant" the notion of marriage had become, I doubt that she would have risked provoking further aggression by reiterating her love, expressing her vexation, parading her feminine weakness ("For I am soft, and made of melting snow"), and inciting him to "be more cruel."

Yet, even if the poem was not a response to Monsieur's aggression, his threats might have been a response to the poem. If Elizabeth wrote "On Monsieur's Departure" after the betrothal, when he was still being solicitous, promising "as he had often done, and indeed was doing now, to save her from annoyance, by pressing his suit with less ardour at her request,"[49] the declaration of love, the hints of sexual intimacy, the admission that she was "soft and made of melting snow," and the injunction to "be more cruel, love, and so be kind," could all have backfired, inciting Monsieur first to press his suit with more ardour and then, when that failed, to say, "If I cannot get you for my wife by fair means and affection I must do so by force."[50] Of course, that is not the effect Elizabeth "meant" the poem to have, but then again, authors are never fully in control of how their words will be interpreted.

When Monsieur first threatened Elizabeth, he cited "the gift of the ring" and the testimony of witnesses, which, he said, proved Elizabeth was bound to marry him. Moreover, he prefaced his comments by protesting, "No no, Madam, you are mine, as I can prove by letters and words you have written to me."[51] Mendoza's report does not specify what Elizabeth had "written to" Monsieur, but he seems to be alluding to two different kinds of texts: letters and some other kind of "words." In response, Elizabeth told him "that she had never written anything that she could not justify, and she did not care what interpretation people chose to put upon her letters as she knew her own intention better than anyone else could."[52] Her initial reference to "anything" also seems to suggest that she had written something else to him in addition to letters. Regardless of what "interpretation" Monsieur or "anyone else" gave her writing, Elizabeth maintained that she knew what her words meant and could easily refute his claims, presumably by pointing to an alternative interpretation of the words she wrote to him.

Elizabeth's writing comprises five main genres: letters, speeches, prayers, translations, and poems. Monsieur would not have said that a speech, prayer, or translation was "written to me," so he was probably referring to her letters and to a poem. "On Monsieur's Departure" is the obvious choice, since, as we have seen, it supports completely opposing interpretations of what Elizabeth "meant." If Elizabeth wrote the poem before their argument on December 26, and if her "words" were in part responsible for provoking Monsieur "to be more cruel," she would have felt complicit. Furthermore, if she thought the physical intimacy she encouraged by dismissing her attendants and writing the poem, if her "too familiar care" stirred his passions and incited his aggression making him feel all the more betrayed, it is easy to understand why she would not divulge those "reasons" "to a twin soul, if she had one, much less to a living creature."[53]

As we have seen in the previous chapters, blunt, colloquial speech balanced by indirection and ambiguity was the hallmark of Elizabeth's style. The "shadow" that follows Elizabeth flying and flies when she pursues it represents a number of things at once: her affection for Monsieur; her responsibility to her subjects; the anxieties that made her a shadow of her former self. It also represents the various *shades of meaning*, the competing interpretations and concealments (for in addition to its literal meaning, the word "shadow" meant *to screen from view or to conceal*) that make this poem, like the courtship it represented, so difficult to sort out and pin down.

For all these reasons, I believe Elizabeth wrote "On Monsieur's Departure" after tensions started to emerge around December 11 but before things got nasty on December 26. That would account for the feelings of consolation and regret as well as the darker, more disturbing subtext that we have been exploring here. It seems more than likely, therefore, that the words of "On Monsieur's Departure" are the same "words" Anjou cited as "written" evidence of Elizabeth's promise to marry him. Yet even if he was not alluding to the poem, the documents we have examined suggest that the poem was written sometime after November 23—when Elizabeth was still trying to convince Monsieur that she loved him but could not marry him, when his "high" dudgeon and "low" motives were beginning to create vexatious grievances—and before December 26 when his aggressive anger started to spin out of control.

What She Meant

Like so many of the great Elizabethan love poems including Sidney's *Astrophil and Stella*, *Shakespeare's Sonnets* and Donne's *Songs and Sonnets*, "On Monsieur's Departure" discovers its meanings as it unfolds, beginning with a definitive declaration, confronting contradictions and uncertainties, and offering an overarching explanation at the end of stanza 1 and another at the end of stanza 2, each of which yields further complications. Having worked its way through an intricate process of thought and feeling, the poem ends with a series of dualities or alternatives that summarize but do not resolve the tensions and conflicts posed by Monsieur's departure. By refusing to say exactly what she "meant," Elizabeth acknowledges but does not resolve the conflicting pressures that pulled her in so many different directions throughout the poem and throughout the weeks of Anjou's anxiously anticipated and continually delayed departure.

At once an admonition to herself and (I think) a plea to him, "On Monsieur's Departure" explores the difficulties that emerged after Elizabeth was "forced" to retract her betrothal. As the active verbs of the opening stanza imply, she took the initiative in this courtship and pursued Monsieur as she had never pursued a suitor before. Nonetheless, there were limits to her agency and liberty. She could not make her advisors and subjects support her betrothal and proposed marriage any more than she could make Monsieur act the way she wanted him to act or be the person she wanted him to be. Elizabeth's words and actions were deeply attuned to and contingent on the reactions of others, as the poem's remarkable number of reciprocal or interactive images indicates. Moving from the declarative "I love," to the optative "Let," to the vocative "Be more cruel, love," "On Monsieur's Departure" enacts the complex interdependency of self and other, substance and shadow, pursuit and flight, which is the quintessential experience of being both a lover and a manuscript poet whose rhetorical persuasions are always in danger of producing unforeseen interpretations and undesired responses from the person the poem was designed to sway.

The Woodstock epigrams enact and reflect upon the need to guard her words, to be enigmatic and mute, so as to avoid incriminating herself. By the time Elizabeth wrote "On Monsieur's Departure," she had far more power and freedom to act than she did when, as a princess, she was accused of treason and held under house arrest. Yet even after establishing her political authority and gaining the freedom to conduct her own courtships, what Elizabeth could say and do was still constrained by and interpreted according to cultural expectations of how she *should* behave as a monarch and as a woman. Finally, like any mistress addressing an embittered suitor, or any political ruler trying to appease a restive constituency, or any manuscript poet writing for an all "too familiar" private lyric audience, Elizabeth had to admit that her rhetorical persuasions depended on an answering response that she could neither fully anticipate nor control, no matter how loving, commanding, or clever she was.

The fact that there are no extant Elizabethan manuscripts of "On Monsieur's Departure" suggests that Elizabeth did not show it around. If it was always intended for Elizabeth alone, which seems unlikely given the complex layering of meaning the language contains, it nonetheless explores the tormented, contradictory feelings and attitudes generated by the Anjou courtship. If it was provoked by the Protestant writers and courtiers who were trying to construct Elizabeth as the Virgin Queen in order to derail the match, it never made its way into that wider literary/political scene because the courtship became far too messy for Elizabeth to discuss it in public. If Elizabeth thought she could deploy her considerable rhetorical skills to convince Monsieur to cool his demands and depart without making further trouble, her plan backfired, leaving her feeling even more distraught, anxious, vulnerable, and, worse yet, complicit. If subsequent readers still find the poem as compelling as I do, that is because Elizabeth neither denied her "love" and "passion" nor suppressed the "discontent" and "cares" that the betrothal produced.

"On Monsieur's Departure" represents the Anjou courtship as an ongoing, irreconcilable struggle between personal yearning for "some gentler passion" and public "cares," "high" principles and "low" desires or low blows, "inward" turmoil and external constraint, oneself and "another self." The intrinsic dramatic situation and the extrinsic historical situation are so closely intertwined that interpretations of one are inextricably implicated in interpretations of the other. Whether Elizabeth "meant" it when she said, "I do" promise to marry Monsieur, or whether she "meant" it when she said, "and not" so much was widely debated in England and abroad, and it is still the overriding question the Anjou courtship poses for historians today.

The constant state of doubleness, of saying one thing and meaning another, or thinking and feeling one thing while being forced to say and do something different, is the fate of being both a public personage and a private poet, which is why Puttenham attributed the courtly figure *allegoria* to Elizabeth and her court. Yet, as we saw in chapter 2, Puttenham's *Art of English Poesy* presented a duplicitous and ultimately reductive view of rhetorical dissimulation. By comparison, "On Monsieur's Departure" uses the lyric's enigmatic concision to sustain multiple layers of meaning that continue to play themselves out as the complexities of the situation unfold. When Elizabeth told Monsieur "that she had never written anything that she could not justify, and she did not care what interpretation people chose to put upon her letters as she knew her own intention better than anyone else could," she recognized that people would inevitably put different meanings on her words. At the same time, she implied, her own powers of interpretation were sufficient to "justify" her meaning regardless of what "anyone" might think or say. Furthermore, she insisted "that she knew her own intention better than anyone else could." Yet, she did not say what that "intention" was, because she recognized that whatever she said could be interpreted differently than she intended. Thus she left open the possibility that her spoken and written words could mean any number of things. Finally, it is that assumption more than any other that connects Elizabeth's speech and writing to later Elizabethan writers such as Philip and Mary Sidney, Edmund Spenser, William Shakespeare, and John Donne whose poetry and prose we continue to read and admire, and whose meanings we are still discovering and debating today.

Notes

Preface

1. Martin A. S. Hume, ed., *Calendar of Letters and State Papers Simancas* (1892; Nendeln/Liechtenstein: Kraus, 1971), 239; *Queen Elizabeth and Some Foreigners,* ed. Victor von Klarwill (New York: Brentano's, 1928), 241.

2. The most detailed and illuminating account of Elizabeth's marriage negotiations is Susan Doran, *Monarchy and Matrimony: The Courtships of Elizabeth I* (London, New York: Routledge, 1996). Catherine Bates, *The Rhetoric of Courtship in Elizabethan Language and Literature* (Cambridge, New York: Cambridge University Press, 1992), provides the most focused study of the language of Elizabethan courtship. Also apropos is Mortimer Levine, *The Early Elizabethan Succession Question 1558–1568* (Stanford: Stanford University Press, 1966).

3. See Ilona Bell, *Elizabethan Women and the Poetry of Courtship* (Cambridge, New York: Cambridge University Press, 1998).

4. In "'Video et Taceo': Elizabeth I and the Rhetoric of Counsel," *Studies in English Literature* 28 (1988), 2, Mary Crane associates Elizabeth's motto with "the silence thought suitable for a woman in an age when women were relentlessly advised to remain 'chaste, silent, and obedient.' As a whole, the motto displays the delicate balancing act between assertion and abnegation of authority upon which Elizabeth relied." On the connection between silence and female chastity, see Suzanne Hull, *Chaste, Silent, and Obedient: English Books for Women, 1475–1640* (San Marino: Huntington Library, 1982), and *Silent But for the Word: Tudor Women as Patrons, Translators, and Writers of Religious Works,* ed. Margaret Patterson Hannay (Kent, OH: Kent State University Press, 1985).

5. Biographies that incorporate Elizabeth's language but do not analyze it at length include Maria Perry, *The Word of a Prince* (Woodbridge, UK: Boydell, 1995) and *Elizabeth I: Her Life in Letters,* ed. Felix Prior (Berkeley: University of California Press, 2003).

6. Louis Montrose's monumental study of the Elizabethan imaginary, *The Subject of Elizabeth: Authority, Gender, and Representation* (Chicago: University of Chicago Press, 2006), explores many of the same questions. In the introduction, 2, Montrose asserts that "the ways in which masculine subjects of the Elizabethan state negotiated their agency are as interesting to me as the ways in which Elizabeth negotiated hers," but that is an understatement, for the ways in which Elizabeth shaped "[h]erself" through her speech and writing as "a gendered and historical situated subject" are peripheral to the project.

7. For valuable overviews of Elizabeth's writings, see Frances Teague, "Elizabeth I: Queen of England," in *Women Writers of the Renaissance and Reformation*, ed. Katharine M. Wilson (Athens: University of Georgia Press, 1987), 522–47, and Janel Mueller, "Elizabeth I," in *Teaching Tudor and Stuart Women Writers*, ed. Susanne Woods and Margaret P. Hannay (New York: MLA, 2000), 119–26. Mueller concludes, 126, "Queen Elizabeth has yet to receive her full due as a writer of consummate versatility, intellect, subtlety, and erudition."

1   From Princess to Prince—A Brief Life Story

1. Camden, *The historie* (London, 1630), A.3.r.
2. For an insightful and wonderfully readable short history, see Carole Levin, *The Reign of Elizabeth I* (Houndmills, Basingstoke, Hampshire; New York: Palgrave, 2002). For a useful bibliography, see "Studies of the Queen's Life and Reign," compiled by Donald Stump and Susan M. Felch, available on the Queen Elizabeth I Society website: http://research.uvu.edu/Moss/ Life_%26_Reign.html. The bibliography homepage, http://research.uvu. edu/Moss/Bibliography.html, provides a long list of works by and about Elizabeth.
3. For a fascinating account, see Retha M. Warnicke, *The Rise and Fall of Anne Boleyn* (New York: Cambridge University Press, 1989).
4. Charles Beem, *The Lioness Roared: The Problems of Female Rule in English History* (New York: Palgrave Macmillan, 2006), 12–23, provides a helpful survey of the challenges Elizabeth faced as a female monarch. David Starkey, *Elizabeth: The Struggle for the Throne* (London: Perennial, 2000) explores the difficulties of her early years.
5. Victor von Klarwill, ed., *Queen Elizabeth and Some Foreigners* (New York: Brentano's, 1928), 36.
6. Susan Doran, *Monarchy and Matrimony* (London, New York: Routledge, 1996); John N. King, "Queen Elizabeth: Representations of the Virgin Queen," *Renaissance Quarterly* 43 (1990): 30–74, demonstrates that the speech was rewritten by William Camden after Elizabeth's death.
7. *A Midsummer Night's Dream* 1.1.73. Shakespeare's plays are quoted throughout from *The Riverside Shakespeare*, 2nd edition, ed. G. Blakemore Evans et al. (Boston: Houghton Mifflin, 1997).
8. Klarwill 41, 47.
9. Norman Jones, "Elizabeth's First Year: The Conception and Birth of the Elizabethan Political World," in *The Reign of Elizabeth I*, ed. Christopher Haigh (Athens: University of Georgia Press, 1985), 29, writes, "It was assumed that she would marry and provide an heir to the throne; and it was assumed that the man whom she married would in some sense rule her." Two biographies that focus on Elizabeth's courtships are Alison Plowden, *Marriage with my Kingdom: The Courtships of Elizabeth I* (London: Macmillan, 1977) and Josephine Ross, *Suitors to the Queen* (London: Phoenix, 2005).
10. Klarwill 81.
11. G. D. Ramsay, "The Foreign Policy of Elizabeth I," in Haigh, 159, writes, "The marriage negotiations were a personal contribution of the Queen's to the technique and substance of international relations."

12. Martin A. S. Hume, ed., *Calendar of Letters and State Papers Simancas* (1892; Nendeln/Liechtenstein: Kraus, 1971), 1:123.
13. Quoted by Doran 21. "The presence of so many suitors at her court was of great value to the queen," Doran explains incisively, "she took the opportunity whenever she could, of making a public display of these courtships—not necessarily out of vanity, as is so often alleged, but for political advantage."
14. "It was no small part of the scandal," writes Carolly Erickson in *The First Elizabeth* (New York: Summit, 1983), 181, "that she fondled Dudley like a lover in public. Then too she may have taken him as her lover out of sheer exultant rebelliousness. For in the first year of her reign—and beyond—Elizabeth was stridently, aggressively self-willed."
15. Hume 3:229.
16. Hume 1:57, 1:63.
17. *Elizabeth I: Collected Works*, ed. Leah S. Marcus, Janel Mueller, and Mary Beth Rose (Chicago, London: University of Chicago Press, 2000), 304.

2 The Art of Poetry, the Art of Courtship: Elizabeth I and the Elizabethan Writing Culture

1. Patti Smith, *Just Kids* (New York: Harper Collins, 2010), 234–35.
2. This chapter counters the arguments made by Lisa Hopkins in *Writing Renaissance Queens: Texts by and about Elizabeth I and Mary, Queen of Scots* (Newark: University of Delaware Press, 2002), that the dominant image of Elizabeth's writing was one of erasure; that the queen is conspicuously absent from Shakespeare's comedies; and that Elizabeth confidently exercised control over visual images but not through her words.
3. See Mary Hill Cole, *The Portable Queen: Elizabeth I and the Politics of Ceremony* (Amherst: University of Massachusetts Press, 1999), and John Nichols, *The Progresses and Public Processions of Queen Elizabeth*, 3 vols. (1823; rpt. New York: Burt Franklin, 1961).
4. For a range of competing views about the division of power between monarch, Privy Council, and parliament, see: Patrick Collinson, "The Monarchical Republic of Queen Elizabeth I," in *Elizabethan Essays,* ed. Patrick Collinson (1994; London, Rio Grande: Hambledon Press, 2003), 31–57; John F. McDiarmid, *The Monarchical Republic of Early Modern England: Essays in Response to Patrick Collinson* (Burlington, VT: Ashgate, 2007); A.N. McLaren, *Political Culture in the Reign of Elizabeth I: Queen and Commonwealth 1558–1585* (Cambridge, New York: Cambridge University Press, 1999); Natalie Mears, *Queenship and Political Discourse in the Elizabethan Realms* (Cambridge, New York: Cambridge University Press, 2005).
5. Wallace T. MacCaffrey, *Queen Elizabeth and the Making of Policy, 1572–1588* (Princeton: Princeton University Press, 1981) and Paul Johnson, *Elizabeth I, A Study in Power and Intellect* (London: Weidenfeld and Nicolson, 1974), both maintain that Elizabethan policy embodies the queen's views.
6. Quoted from Steven May's wonderful, brief introduction, "Queen Elizabeth, a Writer's Life," in *Queen Elizabeth I: Selected Works,* ed. May (New York: Washington Square Press, 2004), xx. As May observes, xviii, Elizabeth "seems to have written constantly and voluntarily from her

girlhood to shortly before her death." Linda Shenk, *Learned Queen: The Image of Elizabeth I in Politics and Poetry* (Houndmills, Basingstoke, Hampshire; New York: Palgrave, 2009), was in production as this book was being completed.

7. *The Poems of Queen Elizabeth I*, ed. Leicester Bradner (Providence: Brown University Press, 1964), 75–76 FN. Important recent editions of Elizabeth's writing include: *Selections: Elizabeth I, Queen of England, 1533–1603*, ed. Leah S. Marcus, Janel Mueller, and Mary Beth Rose (Chicago: University of Chicago Press, 2000); *Queen Elizabeth I*, ed. Steven W. May; *Elizabeth I and Her Age: Authoritative Texts, Commentary and Criticism*, ed. Donald Stump and Susan M. Felch (New York: W.W. Norton, 2009). For a more complete bibliography, see "Studies of writings by the Queen," at http://research. uvu.edu/Moss/Writings.html.

8. See *Elizabeth I: Autograph Compositions and Foreign Language Originals*, ed. Janel Mueller and Leah S. Marcus (Chicago, London: University of Chicago Press, 2003).

9. For illuminating studies of Elizabeth's poetry, some Jennifer Summit, *Lost Property: The Woman Writer and English Literary History, 1380–1589* (Chicago: University of Chicago Press, 2000), 163–202, and Nona Fienberg, *Elizabeth, Her Poets, and the Creation of the Courtly Manner: A Study of Sir John Harington, Sir Philip Sidney, and John Lyly* (New York: Garland, 1988).

10. Richard A. Lanham offers a terrific account of the rhetorical mindset in *The Motives of Eloquence: Literary Rhetoric In The Renaissance* (New Haven: Yale University Press, 1976).

11. For information on Elizabeth's translations, see *Renaissance Drama by Women*, ed. S. P. Cerasano and Marion Wynne-Davies, 7–8. For an invaluable account of the tradition and its English transformations, see Heather Dubrow, *Echoes of Desire: English Petrarchism and its Counterdiscourses* (Ithaca, NY: Cornell University Press, 1995).

12. *Elizabeth I: Collected Works*, ed. Leah S. Marcus, Janel Mueller, and Mary Beth Rose (Chicago, London: University of Chicago Press, 2000), 182. Hereafter (CW).

13. See B. W. Beckingsale, *Burghley, Tudor Statesman, 1520–1598* (London, Melbourne: Macmillan; New York: St. Martin's Press, 1967); Michael A. R. Graves, *Burghley: William Cecil, Lord Burghley* (London, New York: Longman, 1998); Stephen Alford, *The Early Elizabethan Polity: William Cecil and the British Succession Crisis, 1558–1569* (Cambridge, New York: Cambridge University Press, 1998) and *Burghley: William Cecil at the Court of Elizabeth I* (New Haven, London: Yale University Press, 2008).

14. On the continuing importance of orality and the shift to print, see Martin Elsky, *Authorizing Words: Speech, Writing, and Print in the English Renaissance* (Ithaca, NY: Cornell University Press, 1989); Walter J. Ong, *Rhetoric, Romance, and Technology: Studies in the Interaction of Expression and Culture* (Ithaca, NY: Cornell University Press, 1971); Virginia Cox, *The Renaissance Dialogue: Literary Dialogue in its Social and Political Contexts, Castiglione to Galileo* (Cambridge, New York: Cambridge University Press, 1992).

15. Thomas O. Sloane's fine study, *On the Contrary: The Protocol of Traditional Rhetoric* (Washington, DC: Catholic University of America Press, 1997), 203, cites these quintessential Elizabethan terms. Thomas Wilson, *The Art of Rhetoric*, ed. Peter E. Medine (University Park, PA: Pennsylvania State University Press, 1994), 49. In George Puttenham, *The Art of English*

Poesy: A Critical Edition (Ithaca, NY, London: Cornell University Press, 2007), 44–45, the editors, Frank Whigham and Wayne A. Rebhorn, note Puttenham's emphasis on the ear over the eye.

16. For examples of poems by Shakespeare and Donne that become more boldly unconventional and multilayered when read as part of a private lyric dialogue, see Ilona Bell, "Rethinking Shakespeare's Dark Lady," in *A Companion to Shakespeare's Sonnets*, ed. Michael Schoenfeldt (Malden, MA: Blackwell, 2006), 293–313, and "'What if it be a she?' The Riddle of Donne's 'Curse,'" in *John Donne's "desire of more": The Subject of Anne More Donne in His Poetry*, ed. M. Thomas Hester (Newark: University of Delaware Press, 1996), 106–139.

17. See Steven W. May's introduction to *The Elizabethan Courtier Poets: The Poems and their Contexts* (Columbia: University of Missouri Press, 1991).

18. Puttenham 334–35. Cf. Arthur F. Marotti, *Manuscript, Print, and the English Renaissance Lyric* (Ithaca, NY: Cornell University Press, 1995); Margaret J. M. Ezell, *Social Authorship and the Advent of Print* (Baltimore: Johns Hopkins University Press, 1999); Harold Love, *Scribal Publication in Seventeenth-Century England* (Oxford: Clarendon Press; New York: Oxford University Press, 1993).

19. See Annabel M. Patterson, *Censorship and Interpretation: The Conditions of Writing and Reading In Early Modern England* (Madison: University of Wisconsin Press, 1984); Richard Dutton, *Licensing, Censorship, and Authorship in Early Modern England: Buggeswords* (Houndmills, Basingstoke, Hampshire; New York, 2000).

20. Of the first parliamentary speech, J. E. Neale, *Elizabeth I and Her Parliaments* (London: Alden Press, 1953), 50, writes, "publication was immediate, it suggests a propaganda purpose." Publication of the pre-coronation procession is discussed in chapter 3.

21. "The Court also reflected her intellectual and artistic tastes," Simon Adams observes in "Eliza Enthroned? The Court and its Politics," in *The Reign of Elizabeth I*, ed. Christopher Haigh (Athens: University of Georgia Press, 1985), 72.

22. For a collection of encomiastic poems, see *The Queen's Garland; Verses Made by Her Subjects for Elizabeth I, Queen of England*, ed. M. C. Bradbrook (London, New York: Oxford University Press for the Royal Society of Literature, 1953).

23. See *An Anthology of Elizabethan Dedications and Prefaces*, ed. Clara Gebert (Philadelphia: University of Pennsylvania Press, 1933).

24. Sloane, 205, describes Wilson as "a self-made man in a great age of self-fashioning" who "found his chief instruments—in more ways than one—through logic and rhetoric."

25. The anonymous publication created some uncertainty, but modern editors agree that the author was George Puttenham. Quoted from Steven May, "George Puttenham's Lewd and Illicit Career," *Texas Studies in Literature and Language*, 50 (2008), 143. May's revelatory research raises serious questions about Montrose's influential essay, "Of Gentlemen and Shepherds: The Politics of Elizabethan Pastoral Form," *ELH* 50 (1983), 415–59.

26. Puttenham 133, quoted here and throughout from Whigham and Rebhorn's 2007 Critical Edition.

27. Puttenham 239, 94–95. For an illuminating survey of "the drab age" of English poetry and Elizabeth's place therein, see May, *Courtier Poets*,

1–68. Ironically, Puttenham later advises his courtly readers, 374, that, "in craving their [prince's] bounty or largesse," they should take care "in their commendations, not to be excessive, for that is tedious and always savors of subtlety more than of sincere love."

28. The comment is cited and discussed in the introduction to Gladys Doidge Willcock's and Alice Walker's groundbreaking edition, *The Arte of English Poesie* (Cambridge: Cambridge University Press, 1936), li. Willcock and Walker observe, xliii, "The *Arte* was originally composed, without thought of publication for Elizabeth and a courtly circle and was, therefore, written with ease and intimacy." The premise seems right, though the appearance of "ease and intimacy" is a fabrication, as we shall see shortly. Whigham and Rebhorn comment, 49, "By writing it, as he says over and over, for courtiers and ladies, he seeks to align himself with the social and intellectual elite of early modern England, to establish himself as a leading theorist of poetry, and to exhibit his own accomplishments as a poet."

29. Puttenham 90, 239, 105. This underlying political purpose is supported by the *Partheniades*, a collection of lyrics Puttenham wrote when Elizabeth was considering marriage to the Duke of Alençon. As Willcock and Walker explain, xxxi–xiii, the *Partheniades* were written with the object "of pointing out that [Elizabeth's] duty was to provide her subjects with an heir to the throne." Wayne A. Rebhorn, "'His tail at commandment': George Puttenham and the Carnivalization of Rhetoric," in *A Companion to Rhetoric and Rhetorical Criticism*, ed. Walter Jost and Wendy Olmsted (Oxford: Blackwell, 2004), 101, observes: "the majority of poems Puttenham supplies as examples involve courtly love poems."

30. On Puttenham's strategies of obliquity and concealment, see Daniel Javitch, "Poetry and Court Conduct: Puttenham's *Arte of English Poesie* in the Light of Castiglione's *Cortegiano*," *Modern Language Notes* 87 (1972): 19–37, and Rosemary Kegl, The *Rhetoric of Concealment: Figuring Gender and Class in Renaissance Literature* (Ithaca, NY, London: Cornell University Press, 1994), 11–42. Like so many scholarly accounts of *The Art* written before May's exposé, these otherwise illuminating studies are marred by the mistaken premise that Puttenham was "a singularly favored courtier" (Kegl 41) who exemplified the "good grace" and "decencie" of a courtier. Javitch's remark, 867, 866, about "the mutuality which Elizabethan poets perceived in their style of life and modes of poetry" looks particularly ironic in retrospect.

31. Wilson 46.

32. Puttenham 270–72.

33. For an instructive discussion of Puttenham's library and literary debts, see Whigham and Rebhorn 23–43.

34. Puttenham 378–79. Whigham and Rebhorn, 1–5, provide a fuller analysis of this passage.

35. See Marcy L. North, "Anonymity's Revelations in *The Arte of English Poesie*," *Studies in English Literature* 39 (1999), 3.

36. May's research, based on the Jervoise of Herriard papers at the Hampshire Record Office, appears in "George Puttenham's Lewd and Illicit Career," 143–76. If, as Whigham and Rebhorn suggest, 51, 63, Puttenham's subtext of "sadism" and "hostitlity" directed against Elizabeth "begins to make the queen, a 'quean,' a strumpet who will serve his desires," that says more about him than about her.

37. For a defense of the theory, see Phoebe Sheavyn, *The Literary Profession in the Elizabethan Age*, 2nd edition, rev. J. W. Saunders (Manchester: Manchester University Press, 1967; New York: Barnes and Noble, 1967) and J. W. Saunders, "The Stigma of Print," *Essays in Criticism* 1 (1951): 139–64. For a critique of the theory, see Steven May, "Tudor Aristocrats and the Mythical 'Stigma of Print,'" *Renaissance Papers* 10 (1980): 11–18.

38. Puttenham 95, 379.

39. The argument was first made by Willcock's and Walker's introduction, xliv–liii, and tentatively affirmed by Whigham and Rebhorn, 41–43. All definitions here and throughout are from the *Compact Edition of the Oxford English Dictionary* (Oxford: Oxford University Press, 1971).

40. For additional information about the important role played by the Elizabethan spy network, see Alan Haynes, *Invisible Power: The Elizabethan Secret Services, 1570–1603* (New York: St. Martin's Press, 1992).

41. Although May's "Lewd and Illicit Career" appeared in 2008, Whigham and Rebhorn thank May for sharing his research with them.

42. See for example, the discussions of decorum (3.23), or decency in behavior (3.24), or the relation between art and nature (3.25), where Puttenham's attempt to win Elizabeth's favor and to excuse his own malfeasance continually disrupts and undermines the argument he strives to make.

43. Puttenham 302.

44. Sloane, *On the Contrary*, explores the theory and practice of this central rhetorical principle.

45. In *The Icy Fire: Five Studies in European Petrarchism* (Cambridge: Cambridge University Press, 1969), 147, Leonard Wilson Forster argues, "She saw her advantage and she used it." P. Thomson makes an analogous argument in "Petrarch and the Elizabethans," *English* 10 (1955): 177–78, "The Petrarchan pattern proved perfectly adaptable to the nature of poet-patron relationships. But the circumstance which most strongly favoured the growth of this offshoot from Petrarch was, of course, the presence of a queen on the throne.... clearly she expected to be treated as a Petrarchan heroine." See also Katherine Eggert, *Showing Like a Queen: Female Authority and Literary Experiment in Spenser, Shakespeare, and Milton* (Philadelphia: University of Pennsylvania Press, 2000).

46. Louis Adrian Montrose, "The Elizabethan Subject and the Spenserian Text," in *Literary Theory/Literary Texts*, ed. Patricia Parker and David Quint (Baltimore, London: Johns Hopkins University Press, 1986), 326.

47. Leah S. Marcus, "Shakespeare's Comic Heroines, Elizabeth I, and the Political Uses of Androgyny," in *Women in the Middle Ages and the Renaissance: Literary and Historical Perspectives*, ed. Mary Beth Rose (Syracuse, NY: Syracuse University Press, 1986), 135–53, and Marie Axton, *The Queen's Two Bodies: Drama and the Elizabethan Succession* (London: Royal Historical Society, 1977). Philippa Berry, *Of Chastity and Power: Elizabethan Literature and the Unmarried Queen* (London, New York: Routledge, 1989), 5. The many feminist reassessments of Elizabeth include: Susan Bassnett, *Elizabeth I: A Feminist Perspective* (London, Boston: Allen & Unwin, 1986); Crane, "Video et Taceo"; Susan Frye, *Elizabeth I: The Competition for Representation* (Oxford, New York: Oxford University Press, 1993); Carole Levin, *The Heart and Stomach of a King: Elizabeth I and the Politics of Sex and Power* (Philadelphia: University of Pennsylvania Press, 1994).

48. Harington 1.360.

49. These poems are quoted from May's carefully edited text in *Queen Elizabeth I*, 14–18; the version of Elizabeth's response printed *Collected Works* is missing a line.

50. For further information, see May, *Courtier Poets*, 119–34. Leonard Tennenhouse, "Sir Walter Ralegh and the Literature of Clientage," in *Patronage in the Renaissance*, ed. Guy Fitch Lytle and Stephen Orgel (Princeton: Princeton University Press, 1981), 240, comments, "the poetic fiction presumes that the lover is a victim through the accident of birth or class, and not through some fault or error on his part."

51. Stephen J. Greenblatt, *Sir Walter Ralegh: The Renaissance Man and His Roles* (New Haven, London: Yale University Press, 1973), 58. Elizabeth's poem continues to be ignored. In *The Subject of Elizabeth* (Chicago, London: University of Chicago Press, 2006), 90–91, Louis Montrose discusses Ralegh's courtship of the queen through poetry, but does not analyze Elizabeth's response to Ralegh's lyric.

52. Helen Hackett, "Courtly Writing by Women," in *Women and Literature in Britain, 1500–1700*, ed. Helen Wilcox (Cambridge, New York: Cambridge University Press, 1996), 176, explains: "Ralegh himself was base-born...he thus at once alludes to and defiantly repudiates his dependence on her. Her reply opens with intimacies that are both affectionate and diminishing...She asserts her supremacy over both fortune and him."

53. Adams, 70, notes that Ralegh's "rise was meteoric...due to a concentrated assault on the Queen, but his manner of proceeding was bitterly resented and Ralegh uniformly disliked. He survived...through a mixture of effrontery and ability."

54. May, *Courtier Poets*, 122, comments, "Elizabeth's response, carefully coordinated with Ralegh's lines, develops its own remarkably tender, coaxing tone," though to me Elizabeth's tone sounds more trenchant than "coaxing."

55. The awkward demonstrative pronoun "that" alludes to the key moment in Ralegh's argument, "And only joy that fortune conquers kings," where a syntactical sleight of hand transforms joy from a noun to a verb, undercutting Ralegh's own initial claim that Elizabeth herself is "my life's joy."

56. Harington 1:167.

57. Harington 1:172–73.

58. Harington 1:321.

59. For a more extended treatment of these poems and their relation to the *Amoretti* as a whole, see Ilona Bell, *Elizabethan Women and the Poetry of Courtship*, 152–84.

60. *The Yale Edition of the Shorter Poems of Edmund Spenser*, ed. William A. Oram et al. (New Haven, London: Yale University Press, 1989); Edmund Spenser, *The Faerie Queene*, ed. Thomas P. Roche, Jr. (New Haven, London: Yale University Press, 1981).

61. Marcus, "Shakespeare's Comic Heroines," 145, explores the "underlying correlations" between "the androgynous rhetoric of the Queen and the sexual ambiguity of Shakespeare's comic heroines." Numerous feminist critics followed Marcus's lead by focusing on Shakespeare's cross-dressed heroines.

62. Neale 1:142. Martin A. S. Hume, ed., *Calendar of Letters and State Papers Relating to English Affairs, Preserved Principally in the Archives of Simancas,*

vol. 1. Elizabeth. 1558–1567 (London, 1892; Nendeln/Liechtenstein: Kraus, 1971), 1:123.

63. *The lawes resolutions of womens rights* (London, 1632), 126.

64. See Margaret Ezell, *The Patriarch's Wife: Literary Evidence and the History of the Family* (Chapel Hill: University North Carolina Press, 1987).

65. Teresa de Lauretis, "Feminist Studies/Critical Studies: Issues, Terms, and Contexts," in *Feminist Studies, Critical Studies,* ed. de Lauretis (Bloomington: Indiana University Press, 1986), 10.

66. Andre Hurault De Maisse, *A Journal of All That Was Accomplished by Monsieur de Maisse Ambassador in England… 1597,* ed. and tr. G. B. Harrison (Bloomsbury: Nonesuch, 1931), 61.

67. Panegyric is only the beginning of Elizabeth's complex legacy, as recent studies of her posthumous reputation explain more fully than I can convey here: *Resurrecting Elizabeth I in Seventeenth-Century England,* ed. Elizabeth H. Hageman and Katherine Conway (Madison, Teaneck: Fairleigh Dickinson University Press, 2007); Michael Dobson and Nicola J. Watson, *England's Elizabeth: An Afterlife in Fame and Fantasy* (Oxford: Oxford University Press, 2002); Julia M. Walker, *The Elizabeth Icon, 1603–2003* (Houndmills, Basingstoke, Hampshire; New York: Palgrave Macmillan, 2004); John Watkins, *Representing Elizabeth in Stuart England: Literature, History, Sovereignty* (Cambridge, New York: Cambridge University Press, 2002).

68. *The Collected Works of Mary Sidney Herbert, Countess of Pembroke,* ed. Margaret P. Hannay, Noel J. Kinnamon, and Michael G. Brennan (Oxford, New York: Clarendon Press, 1998), 1:103.

3 The Pre-coronation Procession: So Prince-like a Voice

1. Andre Hurault De Maisse, *A Journal,* ed. and tr. G. B. Harrison (Bloomsbury: Nonesuch, 1931), 82.

2. Charles Wriothesley, *A Chronicle of England during the Reigns of the Tudors, from A.D. 1485 to 1559,* ed. William Douglas Hamilton (Westminster: Camden Society, 1877), 2:143.

3. The date on the title page is 1558, since the New Year began on March 25. Here and throughout the dates have been regularized to conform with the modern practice of beginning the New Year on January 1.

4. The Lord Chamberlain's record describing Elizabeth's apparel is reproduced in Germaine Warkentin, *The Queen Majesty's Passage and Related Documents* (Toronto: Centre for Reformation and Renaissance Studies, 2004), 123. For additional information about Elizabeth's costume, see Janet Arnold, "The 'Coronation Portrait' of Queen Elizabeth I," *Burlington Magazine* 120 (1978): 727–41.

5. On the symbolic importance of the conduits, or watering cisterns, see Hester Lees-Jeffries, "Location as Metaphor in Queen Elizabeth's Coronation Entry (1559): *Vertitas Temporis Filia,*" in *The Progresses, Pageants, and Entertainments of Queen Elizabeth I,* ed. Jayne Elisabeth Archer, Elizabeth Goldring, and Sarah Knight (Oxford, New York: Oxford University Press, 2007), 67–76.

6. Burghley's note is reproduced in *Annals of the Reformation and Establishment of Religion,* ed. John Strype (Oxford: Clarendon Press, 1874), 7.

7. Warkentin, 41, explains: "Pageant-making was a valuable skill in Renaissance Europe, and the task of displaying the prince's grandeur was often assigned to the trained humanists who were the civil servants of the typical Renaissance court."

8. The letter, reproduced by Warkentin, 121–22, was discovered at the Folger Shakespeare Library and printed by David Bergeron in "Elizabeth's Coronation Entry (1559), New Manuscript Evidence," *English Literary Renaissance* 8 (1978), 3–8.

9. In *Elizabeth I: The Competition for Representation* (New York, Oxford: Oxford University Press, 1993), 29, Susan Frye describes "the message at the heart of *The Queen's Majesty's Passage*, that both the new regime and the London elites regarded the sovereign as vulnerable because of her gender."

10. Citing the large number of disgruntled poor and homeless in the crowd, William Leahy, *Elizabethan Triumphal Processions* (Aldershot: Ashgate, 2005), stresses the disunity, ambiguity, and complexity of the occasion.

11. Warkentin 78.

12. In "'He That Saw It Would Not Believe It': Anne Boleyn's Royal Entry into London," in *Civic Ritual and Drama* (Amsterdam; Atlanta, GA: Rodopi, 1997), 70, Gordon Kipling comments: "Anne's only place in the image they created was as the mother of the messianic prince to be. She must be that or she would be nothing."

13. Warkentin 78, 79.

14. Opinions about Elizabeth's role in designing the pageant differ widely. Helen Hackett, *Virgin Mother, Maiden Queen* (New York: St. Martin's Press, 1995), 48, contends that Elizabeth had either been briefed on what to expect or had been involved in the planning. Richard C. McCoy, "Thou Idol Ceremony: Elizabeth I, the Henriad, and the Rites of English Monarchy," in *Urban Life in the Renaissance*, ed. Susan Zimmerman and Ronald F. E. Weissman (Newark: University of Delaware Press; London, Toronto: Associated University Presses, 1989), 243, writes: "The citizens may have written their own speeches, but the queen probably previewed them." Sandra Logan, "Making History: The Rhetorical and Historical Occasion of Elizabeth Tudor's Coronation Entry," *Journal of Medieval and Early Modern Studies* 31 (2001), 244, makes a strong case for my own view that Elizabeth was neither involved nor informed in advance: "The queen's quip about 'time,' her immediate resolution of the problem of receiving a gift from an elevated stage, and her adjustment when she is informed of the method of delivery, all indicate that she is participating spontaneously and 'naturally' in an event which the city has carefully planned and arranged."

15. Warkentin 80.

16. Warkentin 80.

17. John N. King, *Tudor Royal Iconography: Literature and Art in an Age of Religious Crisis* (Princeton: Princeton University Press, 1989), 221.

18. Warkentin 75, 77.

19. Warkentin 79.

20. Warkentin 79.

21. Warkentin 80.

22. The classic statement of this iconic view is by Clifford Geertz, "Centers, Kings, and Charisma: Reflections on the Symbolics of Power," in *Culture and its Creators: Essays in Honor of Edward Shils*, ed. Joseph Ben-David and Terry Nichols Clark (Chicago: University of Chicago Press, 1977), 15–16: "Her whole public life—or, more exactly, the part of her life the public

saw—was transformed into a kind of philosophical masque in which everything stood for some vast idea and nothing took place unburdened with parable... The center of the center, Elizabeth not only accepted its transformation of her into a moral idea, she actively cooperated in it... It was allegory that lent her magic, and allegory repeated that sustained it."

23. Warkentin 76.
24. Warkentin 77. Jean Wilson, *Entertainments for Elizabeth I* (Woodbridge: D.S. Brewer; Totowa, NJ: Rowman & Littlefield, 1980), 6–7, concludes that Elizabeth's behavior was "markedly different from reports of previous royal behavior," especially her "seizing upon the political allusion as an occasion for an important political action, her recognition of the importance of the public entertainment for the purpose of popular propaganda, and her adeptness at theatrical extemporization to serve that purpose."
25. Shakespeare's plays are quoted from Blakemore Evans et al., eds., *The Riverside Shakespeare*, 2nd edition (Boston, New York: Houghton Mifflin, 1997).
26. Surveying the historical precedents, Judith Richards, "Love and a Female Monarch: The Case of Elizabeth Tudor," *The Journal of British Studies* 38 (1999), 133, contends that Elizabeth's love language was not gender specific because it "en-capsulated an intersection of humanist beliefs and Tudor policy, with serious political purposes and significant political implications."
27. Warkentin 75–76.
28. Warkentin 76.
29. Warkentin 86–87.
30. Warkentin 86.
31. See Winfried Schleiner, "*Divina virago*: Queen Elizabeth as an Amazon," *Studies in Philology* 75 (1978): 163–80. Warkentin comments, 33, "Elizabeth evidently grasped very early that no matter what robes she wore, a literal chastity would have to be central to her authority as a queen regnant. Her unmarried state was to become, for the Virgin Queen, what military *virtù* was for her male predecessors, the mysterious sign and source of her power to rule." Since this is not based on anything Elizabeth reportedly said or did during the pageant, Warkentin seems to be importing a premise she thought could be taken for granted—a premise this book calls into question.
32. For an analysis of the mixed accounts of Mary's pre-coronation procession, see Judith M. Richards, "Mary Tudor as 'Sole Quene'?: Gendering Tudor Monarchy," *The Historical Journal* 40 (1997): 899–902.
33. See Richards 139.
34. See Jonathan Goldberg, *James I and The Politics of Literature: Jonson, Shakespeare, Donne, and Their Contemporaries* (Baltimore: Johns Hopkins University Press, 1983). R. Malcolm Smuts, "Public Ceremony and Royal Charisma: The English Royal Entry in London, 1485–1642," in *The First Modern Society: Essays in Honour of Lawrence Stone* (Cambridge, New York: Cambridge University Press, 1989), 68, affirms that "the royal entry declined under the Stuarts, so that by the eve of the Civil War Charles almost never appeared in the streets of his capital."
35. Warkentin 91. For an analysis of Deborah as "the chief biblical precedent for government by a powerful and godly woman," see King, 227–30.
36. Sydney Anglo, *Spectacle, Pageantry, and Early Tudor Policy* (Oxford: Clarendon Press; New York: Oxford University Press, 1997), 357, writes: "there is one

feature of the pageants for Elizabeth which marks them off from their predecessors. This is the degree to which they…give advice on a right course of action. To a certain extent most civic pageantry includes this element, *laudando praecipere*—but rarely in so emphatic a fashion."

37. McCoy, 245, emphasizes "the essentially theatrical nature of these ceremonies." David M. Bergeron, *English Civic Pageantry, 1558–1642* (Columbia: University of South Carolina Press, 1971), 12, argues that Elizabeth's reign saw "a growing consciousness of pageantry as drama."

38. For the court record, dated January 17, 1559, see Warkentin, 124. On the Court of Aldermen, see Ian W. Archer, *The Pursuit of Stability: Social Relations in Elizabethan London* (Cambridge, New York: Cambridge University Press, 1991), chapter 1.

39. Warkentin 125.

40. Smuts, 73, sees Elizabeth's royal entry as "the coming together of two distinct hierarchies, one based on the wealth created by London's crafts, the other anchored in the traditions of the royal court and the kingdom's great feudal families."

41. Warkentin 125.

42. Warkentin 92. According to Frye, 166, FN 76, at least three of the aldermen were active Catholics.

43. As Warkentin explains, 16, the two others were the pageant's "probable scenarist, Richard Grafton," and the bookseller, Richard Tottel.

44. Richard L. DeMolen, "Richard Mulcaster and Elizabethan Pageantry," *Studies in English Literature* 14 (1974), 211.

45. In *The Queens Majesties Passage,* ed. James Osbourne (New Haven: Yale University Press for the Elizabethan Club, 1960), 14–15, J. E. Neale, writes: "In all probability it was no mere journalistic or publisher's venture but propaganda for the new regime…The Queen herself was even more alive to the value of propaganda than Cecil…She would have approved both the idea and its execution." Bergeron, *Civic Pageantry,* 13, also describes Mulcaster's account as "a marvelous piece of propaganda in addition to providing a record of the events." Warkentin, 19, is more skeptical: "Such publications were of course propaganda, not reportage, and cannot be relied on for factual accuracy." Leahy, 72–74, offers a scathing critique of Mulcaster's reliability.

46. Warkentin 125.

47. DeMolen 220.

48. Warkentin 86.

49. In *The Subject of Elizabeth* (Chicago, London: University of Chicago Press, 2006), 39, Louis Montrose writes, "This collection of human interest stories functions to show the new queen engaged in face-to-face interactions with her common subjects." Though Montrose makes an important point, it nonetheless reduces Elizabeth's speeches to "human interest stories."

50. Warkentin 76.

51. Warkentin 97.

52. London, 1604.

4   Early Days: Parliamentary Speech (1559) and the Woodstock Epigrams

1. Andre Hurault De Maisse, *A Journal,* ed. and tr. G. B. Harrison (Bloomsbury: Nonesuch, 1931), 82.

2. Martin A. S. Hume, ed., *Calendar of State Papers Simancas* (1892; Nendeln/ Liechtenstein: Kraus, 1971), 1:3. Wallace MacCaffrey, *Elizabeth I* (London, New York: Arnold, 1993), 70, 75, writes, "It was unthinkable that she should hold the reins of power by herself.... she found the exercise of power exhilarating, and was loathe to yield it to anyone. But for a woman it was a necessary consequence of marriage that a husband would expect to share, even to monopolize power." By contrast, Janel Mueller, "Virtue and Virtuality: Gender in the Self-Representations of Queen Elizabeth I," in *Form and Reform in Renaissance England: Essays in Honor of Barbara Kiefer Lewalski,* ed. Amy Boesky and Mary Thomas Crane (Newark: University of Delaware Press; London: Associated University Presses, 2000), argues, 224, "Elizabeth's successive public self-accountings seek to dispel the assumption that God's will for her obliges her as queen to actualize the roles of wife and mother."

3. In "'Video et Taceo'" *Studies in English Literature* 28 (1988), 4, Mary Crane writes, "Her parliamentary speeches represent just the sort of authoritative, public discourse for which humanist education prepared men and in which women were not supposed to participate."

4. R. A. Roberts, ed., *Calendar of the Manuscripts of the Most Honorable, the Marquis of Salisbury...Preserved at Hatfield House* (London, 1883–1976), 1:158.

5. T.E. Hartley, ed., *Proceedings in the Parliaments of Elizabeth I* (Wilmington: Michael Glazier, 1981), 1:16–17.

6. John Knox, *The first blast of the trumpet against the monstruous regiment of women* (Geneva: 1558), 21–23, makes an impassioned argument that woman should not rule over man who was appointed by God as her head.

7. Hume *1:*37, 1:52, 1:55, 1:66.

8. Hume 1:68–69. A. N. McLaren, *Political Culture in the Reign of Elizabeth* (Cambridge, New York: Cambridge University Press, 1999), writes, 23, that the new title, Supreme Governor, "resulted from contemporary anxieties over female rule. [Elizabeth's] gender therefore informed, as it shaped, public debate over issues pertaining to the common weal."

9. Hume *1:*69. Anne McLaren, "The Quest for a King: Gender, Marriage, and Succession in Elizabethan England,"*Journal of British Studies* 41 (2002), 266, describes "how tenuous, how provisional, was Elizabeth's hold on the crown, because of her sex, and how she and her councillors both used and altered dynastic terms of reference in order to forward their asymmetric goals: hers to retain unchallenged possession of the English crown during her lifetime; theirs to preserve Protestanism and English imperial authority."

10. Hartley 1:40–41; Hartley 1:34; Hartley 1:40–41.

11. Hartley 1:34–38.

12. Hartley 1:35.

13. Robert Filmer, *Patriarcha, or, the natural power of Kings* (London: 1680), 23–24.

14. Knox 26, 28.

15. Quoted from Leah S. Marcus, Janel Mueller, and Mary Beth Rose, eds., *Elizabeth I: Collected Works* (Chicago, London: University of Chicago Press, 2000), 57; hereafter, cited parenthetically as (CW).

16. In *Queenship and Political Discourse* (Cambridge, New York: University of Cambridge Press, 2005), 51, Natalie Mears argues, "the central

characteristic of the structure of Elizabethan policy-making" was the "active role" Elizabeth played. Mears concludes, 71, "Ultimately, Elizabethan court politics cannot be defined in institutional terms. Elizabeth sought and received counsel from a personally selected group of counselors, with whom she had a close personal relationship."

17. Shakespeare's plays are quoted from Blakemore Evans et al., eds., *The Riverside Shakespeare*, 2nd edition (Boston, New York: Houghton Mifflin, 1997).

18. J. R. Tanner, *Tudor Constitutional Documents, A. D. 1485–1603* (Cambridge: Cambridge University Press, 1922), 123, 124.

19. See Alan Macfarlane and Gerry Martin, *Glass: A World History* (Chicago: University of Chicago Press, 2002).

20. For information about Woodstock Castle, see Simon Thurley, *The Royal Palaces of Tudor England: Architecture and Court Life, 1460–1547* (New Haven: Yale University Press, 1993) and Ian Dunlop, *Palaces and Progresses of Elizabeth I* (London: Jonathan Cape, 1962).

21. Visitors began to make pilgrimages to the site during Elizabeth's reign. "Right into the eighteenth century, sightseers could remember this room...retaining the name of 'Queen Elizabeth's Chamber'" (Dunlop 15).

22. Maria Perry, *The Word of a Prince* (Woodbridge, Suffolk: Boydell, 1990), 11, comments, "she could be magnificently devious, complex and prevaricating, but she saw herself as straightforward, plain-dealing and bound by an invisible power, higher than hers, never to go back on her word—'the word of a Prince.'"

23. Alexander Ross, *Arcana microcosmi: or, The hid secrets of man's body discovered* (London, 1652), 9.

24. The version of the second epigram printed in *Collected Works* includes the first epigram as a single line postscript; the word "Finis," which precedes the signature of the longer epigram, suggests that the copyist added the line from a separate poem. I have therefore followed Steven W. May, *Selected Works* (New York, London: Washington Square Press, 2004), in treating the poems as two separate compositions. The second poem is alluded to in the lyric dialogue between Sir Walter Ralegh and Elizabeth discussed in chapter 2.

25. Some recent fertility research and treatments also "sho[w] women are slightly more likely to orgasm during periods of fertility and that sperm uptake is increased during orgasm," see "Female orgasm is 'down to genes'" (http://news.bbc.co.uk/1/hi/health/4616899.stm), and Kris Turner, "Fertility Boosting Tactics: Why the Female Orgasm is your best friend" (http://ezinearticles.com/?Fertility-Boosting-Tactics—Why-The-Female-Orgasm-Is-Your-Best-Friend&id=918086). For the counterargument, see Amanda Schaffer, "The Study of O: The female orgasm as evolution's happy accident" (http://www.slate.com/id/2119551/).

26. Mears argues that parliament did not meet regularly enough to play a significant role in Elizabethan governance. McLaren, 3–4, argues for a mixed monarchy or "corporate body politic," which "conjoined the three estates—now, queen, lords, and commons, or queen-in-parliament," and which sought to limit Elizabeth's power and thus to soothe male anxieties about female rule. My point is that Elizabeth defended her authority so forcefully precisely because parliament sought to undermine it.

27. For an analysis of the various texts of the speech, see John N. King, "Queen Elizabeth: Representations of the Virgin Queen," *Renaissance Quarterly* 43 (1990), 38, FN 23, and Neale 1:50, FN 1. Frances Teague, "Queen Elizabeth in her Speeches," in *Gloriana's Face*, ed. S. P. Cerasano and Marion Wynne-Davies (Detroit: Wayne State University Press, 1992), 74, concludes, as I do, that the Elizabethan version "is the more effective piece of political rhetoric precisely because Elizabeth does not state her position forthrightly."

28. William Camden, *The historie of the life and reigne of the most renowmed [sic] and victorious Princesse Elizabeth* (London, 1630), 1:26–27. In *Elizabeth I: The Shrewdness of Virtue* (New York: Viking, 1988), 82, Jasper Ridley draws on this line to conclude: "In her reply, Elizabeth stated that she had no intention of ever marrying."

29. Camden 26.

5   Diplomacy and Correspondency: Elizabeth's Reported Speech

1. Cf. John Watkins' compelling claim in "Marriage à la Mode, 1559: Elisabeth de Valois, Elizabeth I, and the Changing Practice of Dynastic Marriage," in *Queens and Power in Medieval and Early Modern England* (Lincoln, London: University of Nebraska Press, 2009), 76–97, that "Elizabeth's decision to decline Philip's proposal of marriage, and her persistence in saying no to other suitors for the next forty years, was a remarkable achievement" with enormous "significance for the history of diplomacy."

2. Martin A. S. Hume, ed., *Calendar of Letters and State Papers Simancas* (1892; Nendeln/Liechenstein: Krauss, 1971), 1:xiv. In his introduction, 1:xxii, Hume describes Feria's "interviews with the Queen" as "wordy combats in which Elizabeth's nimbleness and womanly wit usually outmatched his hot-headed arrogance."

3. Hume 1:35.

4. Hume 1:37, 1:35.

5. Hume 1:49.

6. Hume 1:8.

7. Hume 1:12.

8. Victor von Klarwill, ed., *Queen Elizabeth and Some Foreigners* (New York: Brentano's, 1928), 63.

9. Hume 1:58.

10. Hume 1:69.

11. Klarwill 35, 37.

12. Klarwill 148.

13. Susan Doran, *Monarchy and Matrimony* (London, New York: Routledge, 1996) is one of the few historians assiduous enough to cite the Spanish text: *Colección de Documentos Inéditos para la Historia de España*, ed. M. F. Navarete et al. (Madrid, 1842–95).

14. Hume 1:69–70, 1:82.

15. Klarwill 64.

16. Elizabeth's letters to the Emperor appear in Klarwill 25–26, 74–77. The second letter is cosigned by Roger Ascham and Robert Cecil. References to Elizabeth's speaking knowledge of Latin can be found in Klarwill, 59 and 187.

17. This chapter cites the printed English translations of the Latin, German, and Spanish letters for the following reasons: (1) the ambassador's accounts of Elizabeth's words were themselves translations; (2) the printed English texts are the versions used (and misused) by other scholars; (3) the English texts are readily available to anyone interested in exploring Elizabethan diplomacy further at British History Online: http://www.british-history.ac.uk/period.aspx?period=6&gid=138.
18. Klarwill 41, 70.
19. Klarwill 100, 68, 98.
20. Hume 1:71.
21. Hume 1:72.
22. Hume 1:72.
23. Hume 1:72
24. Hume 1:75.
25. Hume 1:73.
26. Klarwill 165.
27. On Ferdinand's morganatic wife, see Doran 27. Hume 1:72.
28. Hume 1:72–73.
29. Hume 1:70.
30. Hume 1:70.
31. Hume 1:73.
32. Klarwill 81.
33. Quoted from *A Midsummer Night's Dream* 1.1.78–82.
34. Hume 1:74.
35. Klarwill 78.
36. Klarwill 79.
37. Klarwill 96.
38. Hume 1:75.
39. Hume 1:77.
40. Klarwill 99. In December Breuner reported that he "made most diligent inquiries into the calumnies that are current about the Queen not only abroad but also here in England; but have not been able to learn anything definite" (Klarwill 113).
41. Klarwill 113.
42. Klarwill 114.
43. Hume 1:70.
44. Klarwill 107.
45. Hume 1:73.
46. Breuner supported the plan enthusiastically: "it was in my opinion better if His Highness came here incognito; that if he then found favour in her eyes, Your Imperial Majesty might let him stay here, and then at a favourable opportunity proclaim him to be her consort" (Klarwill 148). When the emperor rejected the plan, Breuner found it difficult to explain why he had "often written before, beseeching His Imperial Majesty not to make any difficulties, but to send the Archduke here in all secrecy as this would be done with the Queen's consent" (Klarwill 156).
47. Hume 1:100.
48. Hume 1:99.
49. Hume 1:99, 1:107.
50. Hume 1:100, 1:103.
51. Hume 1:98–99.

52. Hume 1:101.
53. Hume 1:100–01.
54. Hume 1:104.
55. Hume 1:102.
56. Klarwill 133, 149, 163.
57. Hume 1:102, 89.
58. Hume 1:108.
59. Breuner reported, Hume I:157, that Elizabeth was "puffed up with pride, and imagines that she…may therefore marry whomever she pleases. But herein she errs, for if she marry the said Mylord Robert, she will incur so much enmity that she may one evening lay herself down as Queen of England and rise the next morning as plain Mistress Elizabeth."
60. On the men's club of Messina, see Harry Berger, Jr.'s excellent essay, "Against the Sink-A-Pace: Sexual and Family Politics in *Much Ado about Nothing*," *Shakespeare Quarterly* 33 (1982): 302–13.
61. Hume 1:106.
62. Klarwill 150.
63. Hume 1:112. Carole Levin, *Heart and Stomach* (Philadelphia: University of Pennsylvania Press, 1994), 66–90, offers a fascinating account of the rumors of Elizabeth's sexuality, which she sees as evidence of anxiety about a female ruler.
64. Quoted in *Calendar of State Papers, Domestic series, of the reigns of Elizabeth and James I*, ed. Mary Anne Everett Green (London: Longmans, 1872), 12:13.
65. F. G. Emmison, *Elizabethan Life: Disorder* (Chelmsford: Essex County Council, 1970), 42.
66. Hume 1:123.
67. Hume 1:123.
68. Hume 1:122.
69. Klarwill 153.
70. Klarwill 97.
71. Hume 1:103.
72. Hume 1:89.
73. Hume 1:91.
74. Klarwill 152, 153, 162, 171.
75. See M. M. Bakhtin, *The Dialogic Imagination: Four Essays*, ed. Michael Holquist, trans. Mikhail Mikhailovich (Austin: University of Texas Press, 1981).
76. Hume 1:74.
77. Hume 1:73, 1:75.
78. *Keats Poetry and Prose*, ed. Jeffrey N. Cox (New York, London: W. W. Norton, 2009), 109.
79. Klarwill 41.
80. Hume 1:123.

6 Parliamentary Speeches (1563, 1566) and the Psalter Posy

1. This popular ballad from 1565–66 is quoted in *Black-Letter Ballads*, ed. J. P. Collier (London, 1868), 151.
2. Quoted from Leah S. Marcus, Janel Mueller, and Mary Beth Rose, eds., *Elizabeth I: Collected Works* (Chicago, London: University of Chicago Press, 2000), 73; cited parenthetically throughout as (CW).

3. J. E. Neale, *Elizabeth I and Her Parliaments, 1559–1581* (London: Alden Press 1953), 88, writes, the main "emphasis had shifted abruptly to the succession"; however, as Susan Doran points out in *Monarchy and Matrimony* (London, New York: Routledge, 1996), this is a misreading of the situation. As the quoted passage illustrates, parliament's petitions placed considerably more emphasis on marriage and giving birth to an heir.

4. As Mary Douglas writes in *Natural Symbols: Explorations in Cosmology* (London; New York: Pantheon, 1996), 74, "Interest in [the body's] apertures depends on the preoccupation with social exits and entrances, escape routes and invasions. If there is no concern to preserve social boundaries, I would not expect to find concern with bodily boundaries."

5. See Allison Heisch, "Queen Elizabeth I: Parliamentary Rhetoric and the Exercise of Power," *Signs* 1 (1975), 34–35. For a compelling counter-argument, see Mary Thomas Crane, "'Video et Taceo,'" *Studies in English Literature* 28 (1988), 10.

6. Knox 12, 17–18.

7. Citing this remark, Allison Heisch, "Queen Elizabeth I and the Persistence of Patrimony," *Feminist Review* 4 (1980), 52, criticizes Elizabeth for acquiring her power at the expense of other women: "In the *de facto* weakness of her sex lies the evidence of her special strength. And, as if to make a demonstration of her powers...Elizabeth sets herself apart from other women."

8. Cf. Elizabeth's confidence in her own acuity and her scorn for those subjects who lacked wit in "The doubt of future foes": "For falsehood now doth flow / And subjects' faith doth ebb, / Which should not be if reason ruled / Or wisdom weaved the web" (CW 133).

9. For a survey of anti-feminist stereotypes, see Katherine Usher Henderson and Barbara F. McManus, *Half Humankind: Contexts and Texts of the Controversy about Women in England 1540–1640* (Urbana: University of Illinois Press, 1985), 47–71.

10. *Tudor Constitutional Documents*, ed. J. R. Tanner (Cambridge: Cambridge University Press, 1922), 411.

11. *Hardwicke Papers—Miscellaneous State Papers from 1501–1726* (London, 1778), 1:123.

12. Martin A. S. Hume, ed., *Calendar of State Papers Simancas* (1892; Nendeln/ Liechtenstein: Kraus, 1971), 1:263.

13. Susan Doran makes a compelling case for this interpretation in *Monarchy and Matrimony*, 64.

14. Hume 1:313.

15. Doran thinks Elizabeth was serious about the proposal, although the Scottish ambassador dismissed it immediately, and other historians have been skeptical. MacCaffrey, *Elizabeth I* (London, New York: Arnold, 1993), 85, writes, "For the historian it is hard to regard Elizabeth's proposal as anything but preposterous."

16. At this juncture, the contention made by Natalie Mears, *Queenship and Political Discourse* (Cambridge, New York: University of Cambridge Press, 2005), that Elizabeth made important political decisions in consultation with a few carefully chosen advisors rather than in parliament seems apropos.

17. Simonds D'Ewes, *The Journals of all the Parliaments* (London, 1682), 81.

18. Hartley 1:35.

19. J. L. Austin, *How To Do Things With Words* (Cambridge: Harvard University Press, 1975), 12.

20. Citing this line, Susan Doran, *Queen Elizabeth I* (New York: New York University Press, 2003), 77, interprets this very differently: "As Elizabeth was thinking to marry 'as a prince' and not for private pleasure, she decided to choose a man of royal blood from abroad as her consort."

21. Printed in *Elizabeth I: Autograph Compositions and Foreign Language Originals*, ed. Janel Mueller and Leah S. Marcus (Chicago, London: University of Chicago Press, 2003), 34–35.

22. The term, "political unconscious," comes from Fredric Jameson, *The Political Unconscious: Narrative as a Socially Symbolic Act* (Ithaca, NY: Cornell University Press, 1981). The gender unconscious is my own adaptation of Jameson's term. MacCaffrey, 91, notes that Elizabeth's speech contains "a vague reference to the proposed Dudley match with Mary," but does not specify what the reference is.

23. *Collected Works*, 132, mistakenly prints the signature as Elizabeth R.

24. George Puttenham, *The Arte of English Poesie* (1589; Kent, OH: Kent State University Press, 1970), 68, explains that posies, or short epigrams, were extremely fashionable—"made as it were upon a table, or in a windowe, or upon the wall or mantell of a chimney in some place of common resort, where it was allowed every man might come," but also "put in paper and in bookes, and used as ordinarie missives."

25. *A Collection of State Papers Relating to Affairs in the Reign of Elizabeth from the Year 1571 to 1596*, ed. William Murdin (William Bowyer, 1759), 2:760. Marcus, Mueller, Rose, and Doran all believe the epigram was written during the first part of Elizabeth's reign. Steven W. May, *Elizabeth I: Selected Works* (New York: Washington Square Press, 2004), thinks the poem was written while Elizabeth was still a princess because the signature ends with a knot similar to the one her father used in his signature. May points out that there are no extant examples of this signature after Elizabeth became queen, when she began signing her letters "Elizabeth R." Though the point is well taken, we cannot know for certain that Elizabeth stopped using the knotted signature entirely because, as Susan Doran commented in response to my query, virtually all the extant autograph letters written while she was queen are official correspondence. Most of her more intimate letters to Leicester have disappeared; the ones printed in *Collected Works* are copies and thus lack a signature. As Carol Levin suggested to me at the Elizabeth I Conference where I first presented my reading of this poem, Elizabeth may have chosen the more intimate signature on this particular occasion, using a knot instead of an R for Regina, to strike a more reassuring and less regal tone.

26. Janel Mueller, "Elizabeth I," in *Teaching Tudor and Stuart Women Writers*, ed. Susanne Woods and Margaret P. Hannay (New York: Modern Language Association, 2000), 120, writes: "Again and again in her writings, Elizabeth is found assessing a situation, action, or emotion in terms of the Bible verse or the classical maxim or the proverbial saying that it exemplifies; if there is no such encapsulation at hand, she just as directly proceeds to fashion the new sententia that the present occasion requires."

27. The possibility that Elizabeth gave Dudley (or whomever the poem was addressed to) the psalter is strengthened by the fact that the book did not

remain at Windsor Castle, although it was re-acquisitioned and resides there in the Royal Library today.

28. Murdin 2:760.

29. See *Elizabeth: The Exhibition at the National Maritime Museum,* ed. David Starkey and Susan Doran (Greenwich, London: Chatto & Windus with National Maritime Museum, 2003), 201. The commentary suggests that Elizabeth may have written the poem "to Robert Cecil who was a hunchback"; however, the poem itself suggests the addressee had a suspicious mind not a deformed body.

30. This is Cecil's first journal entry for August, and atypically, the day is not noted. The second entry is dated August 10. De Silva reports that the queen arrived at Windsor from Richmond on August 8. If Cecil wrote his journal entries singly, in sequence, that would mean Elizabeth wrote the obscure sentence on August 9; however, Cecil may have omitted the date because he did not know exactly when Elizabeth wrote the obscure sentence. De Silva first mentions the rift between Elizabeth and Dudley on August 27. On September 2 he writes again, having discovered "[t]he real ground for the dispute between Lord Robert and Heneage" (Hume 1:472). It could easily have taken two to three weeks for the story to reach de Silva.

31. Hume 1: 456.

32. Hume 1:445.

33. Victor von Klarwill, ed., *Queen Elizabeth and Some Foreigners* (New York: Brentano, 1928), 238–41.

34. Hume 1:72.

35. Hume 1:448.

36. Hume 1:468.

37. Hume 1:454.

38. Hume 1:472.

39. Hume 1:472.

40. Given the verbal similarities and the knotted signature, it is tempting to think that this epigram was also written when Elizabeth was at Woodstock; however, the only psalter she had was in Latin (Manning 161), and she was not allowed to communicate with anyone whom she would have addressed as "Your loving mistress."

41. Hume 1:472.

42. D'Ewes 125.

43. Neale 1:142.

44. Neale 1:142.

45. Neale 1:142.

46. A petticoat was either a skirt detached from the bodice worn externally or an underskirt, usually made of flannel or calico. Both meanings emphasize Elizabeth's femininity. Since the distinction between the two is not easy to make, the more intimate meaning is always lurking, evoking the symbolic disrobing described in this chapter. Marcus, 56, gives a more qualified reading of the 1566 speech.

47. Mary Russo, "Female Grotesques: Carnival and Theory," in *Feminist Studies, Critical Studies,* ed. Teresa de Lauretis (Bloomington: Indiana University Press, 1986), 224.

48. Knox 6.

49. Knox 28.

50. In "The Comedy of Female Authority in *The Faerie Queene*," *English Literary Renaissance* 17 (1987): 170, Maureen Quilligan comments, "A female head to a male body politic poses the problem of monstrosity Knox trumpeted so impoliticly months before Elizabeth ascended the throne, and she was continually forced to remind her Parliaments, in exactly those terms, of her authority."

51. Barbara Babcock, ed., *The Reversible World: Symbolic Inversion in Art and Society: Forms of Symbolic Inversion Symposium* (Toronto, Ithaca, NY: Cornell University Press, 1978), 14.

52. Peter Stallybrass and Allon White, *The Politics and Poetics of Transgression* (Ithaca, NY: Cornell University Press, 1986), 23.

53. Jasper Ridley, *Elizabeth I: The Shrewdness of Virtue* (New York: Viking, 1988), 148.

54. Victor von Klarwill, ed., *Queen Elizabeth and Some Foreigners* (New York: Brentano's, 1928), 241.

55. Klarwill 239.

56. Neale 1:142.

7 Popular Debate and Courtly Dialogue: Always Her Own Free Woman

1. Camden, *The historie* (London, 1630), A.3.r.

2. Martin A. S. Hume, ed., *Calendar of Letters and State* Papers *Simancas* (1892; Nendeln/Liechtenstein: Krauss, 1971), 1:7.

3. *A brief and pleasant discourse* was printed twice in 1568 and again in 1571, 1577, 1587. I have retained the y in the maydens' name, although the i's and y's are regularized throughout this book.

4. For a more extensive discussion of Whitney's letter and admonition, see Ilona Bell, *Elizabethan Women and the Poetry of Courtship* (Cambridge, New York: Cambridge University Press, 1998), 113–25.

5. Citations to Whitney refer to the first edition (London, 1567). Here A.2.r, A.2.v, A.2.r, A.4.r.

6. Whitney A.3.v, A.6.v.

7. Whitney A.5.v. See Martin Ingram, *Church Courts, Sex, and Marriage in England, 1570–1640* (Cambridge, New York: Cambridge University Press, 1987).

8. Whitney A.5.v.

9. The letter is reprinted in, and cited here from R. J. Fehrenbach, "A Letter Sent by the Maydens of London (1567)," *English Literary Renaissance* 14 (1984): 285–304.

10. In *A Transcript of the Registers of the Company of Stationers of London; 1554–1640* (London, 1875), 161–66, "A mery metynge of the maydes in London" is number 12 and "a letter sente by the maydes of London to the vertuous matrons and mistres[ses] of the same" is number 37 out of 110 entries for the period July 22, 1567 to July 22, 1568, which suggests that the two books were printed within a few months of each other, probably in the second half of 1567.

11. For a refutation of Fehrenbach's argument that the author was most likely a man because the text includes legal terminology and women could not study law, see Ilona Bell, "*A Letter sent by the Maydens of London*—In Defense of their Lawful Liberty," in *Women, Writing, and the Reproduction*

of Culture in Tudor and Stuart Britain (Syracuse, NY: Syracuse University Press, 2000), 177–92.

12. Fehrenbach 301.
13. Fehrenbach 297–98.
14. Fehrenbach 295.
15. Neale 1:156, 1:142, Fehrenbach 296–97.
16. Fehrenbach 300, Hume 1:123.
17. Fehrenbach 301, 300.
18. Fehrenbach 294.
19. Fehrenbach 295.
20. Fehrenbach 295.
21. Knox, *The first blast of the trumpet* (Geneva: 1558), 26–27.
22. Fehrenbach 294.
23. Rita Felski, *Beyond Feminist Aesthetics: Feminist Literature and Social Change* (Cambridge: Harvard University Press, 1989), 166; Fehrenbach 297.
24. Tilney 100. W. R. Streitberger, *Edmond Tyllney: Master of the Revels and Censor of Plays* (New York: AMS Press, 1996), 5.
25. Tilney 99.
26. Wayne 45.
27. Tilney 99.
28. Tilney 99, my emphasis. T. E. Hartley, ed., *Proceedings in the Parliaments* (Wilmington: Michael Glazier, 1981), 1:94.
29. The word "discourse" meant: *an onward course or succession of time and events; a tale or narrative; a spoken or written treatment of a subject; the act of understanding or the faculty of reasoning; conversation, or mutual intercourse of language.*
30. Tilney 101–2.
31. For a study of Elizabeth's love of flower gardens and the gardens her courtier's built to please her, see Trea Martyn, *Elizabeth in the Garden: A Story of Love, Rivalry, and Spectacular Design* (London: Faber and Faber, 2008).
32. Roy Strong, *The Cult of Elizabeth* (London: Thames and Hudson, 1977), 71. Strong's preoccupation with Elizabeth's virginity makes it difficult for him to explain the Elizabethan love poems he cites that associate passion with a "sweet-smelling arbour" of eglantine, or Spenser's Bower of Bliss where eglantine mingles with "wanton ivie" and red roses, the symbol of passion—another example of the ways in which the presumption of virginity has led scholars to slant the evidence.
33. Klarwill 231; Tilney 99.
34. Klarwill 237.
35. For a more complete account of the negotiations between England and Austria, see Doran, *Monarchy and Matrimony* (London, New York: Routledge, 1996), 73–98.
36. Klarwill 239.
37. Tilney 106, 107–8.
38. Tilney 99. For additional information about Tilney's borrowings from Luxan's 1550 *Coloquios matrimoniales,* see Wayne, 34 ff., and Ernest J. Moncada, "The Spanish Source of Edmund Tilney's 'Flower of Friendshippe'," *Modern Language Review* 65 (1970), 242: "Of forty-five sources which Tilney cites, thirty-five are to be found in Luján. Excepting the speakers, of the forty-six personages historical and fictional mentioned in Tilney's text proper, thirty-eight are from Luján."
39. Tilney 105. Quoted by Doran 80.

40. Tilney 108.
41. Tilney 109.
42. Sloane, *On the Contrary* (Washington, DC: Catholic University of America, 1997), 314–20.
43. Hartley 1:91. Wayne, 146, notes the allusion, and suggests that the views attributed to Isabella were actually uttered by Elizabeth. Citing Camden's version of the 1558 parliamentary speech, Wayne (like so many other scholars) assumes Elizabeth represented herself as the Virgin Queen from the outset of her reign.
44. Tilney 109.
45. Tilney 110, Fehrenbach 301, Hume 1:123.
46. Tilney 107, 112.
47. Tilney 119.
48. Tilney 120–21, 106.
49. Doran comments, 80, "The pro-Hapsburg lobby also pointed to Charles's age, dignity and descent as compatible with those of the queen. ... Though not a king himself, Charles was the son of an emperor and, they claimed, he might one day reach an even higher status and be elected Holy Roman Emperor."
50. Klarwill 241.
51. Tilney 117, Klarwill 241.
52. Tilney 112. As Heather Dubrow explains in *A Happier Eden: The Politics of Marriage in the Stuart Epithalamium* (Ithaca, NY: Cornell University Press, 1990), 24–25, the law gave husbands and wives equal right to payment of "the marriage debt"; this "egalitarianism involves a recognition of female sexual desire."
53. *Certain Sermons or Homilies Appointed to Be Read in Churches, in the Time of Queen Elizabeth* I (Gainesville, FL: Scholars' Facsimiles & Reprints, 1968), 470; Tilney 112.
54. Tilney 118.
55. Tilney 112. Wayne's introduction cites Catherine Belsey's claim that love subordinates the woman to the man, and thus assures the culture's suppression of female subjectivity. Wayne reiterates the point in "Advice for Women from Mothers and Patriarchs," in *Women and Literature in Britain, 1500–1700*, ed. Helen Wilcox (Cambridge, New York: Cambridge University Press, 1996), 68: "the effect of love's reign in the wife is an erasure of her desires and will. The husband therefore remains the only subject in the union. The wife loses not only her 'appetite' or sexual desire, but her 'private will,' the volition by which she remains a separate person." Knox, 15, explains the conventional patriarchal position.
56. Knox 13, Castiglione 275.
57. As Ben Saunders explains in *Desiring Donne: Poetry, Sexuality, Interpretation* (Cambridge: Harvard University Press, 2006), the word "sex" acquired its modern meaning during this period, when sexual pleasure was beginning to be discussed more openly.
58. See Katherine Park, "The Rediscovery of the Clitoris: French Medicine and the Tribade, 1570–1620," in *The Body in Parts: Fantasies of Corporeality in Early Modern Europe*, ed. David Hillman and Carla Mazzio (New York, London: Routledge, 1997), 171–94.
59. Castiglione 274.
60. Tilney 133, Castiglione 222.

61. Knox 21, 25, 26.
62. Aemilia Lanyer, *Salve Deus Rex Judaeorum* (London, 1611), 73.
63. Knox 26.
64. Tilney 134. Thomas Smith, *De Republica Anglorum*, ed. Mary Dewar (London, New York: Cambridge University Press, 1982). The treatise was not published until after his death, presumably because it displeased the queen. As the editor remarks tersely, 8, in the years after he wrote it, Smith "was not in Elizabeth's favour."
65. Tilney 134.
66. Catherine Bates, *The Rhetoric of Courtship* (Cambridge, New York: Cambridge University Press, 1992), chapter 4, analyzes a number of other, similarly open-ended debates about courtship, marriage, and sexuality. Wayne Rebhorn, *Courtly Performances: Masking and Festivity in Castiglione's Book of the Courtier* (Detroit: Wayne State University Press, 1978), 125–31 and 146–47, discusses "the institutionalized tension between men and women" in *The Courtier*.
67. Thomas Smith 88. For a modern discussion of this theory of parliament, see A. N. McLaren, *Political Culture in the Reign of Elizabeth I* (Cambridge, New York: Cambridge University Press, 1999).
68. Tilney 122, 113.
69. Drawing upon Raymond Williams, *Marxism and Literature* (Oxford: Oxford University Press, 1977), Wayne, 42–48, describes Isabella's remarks as emergent discourse. I would argue that her views were more prevalent than that term suggests. Instead, I suggest, Gualter's views should be seen as "residual" discourse, as remnants of previous ideologies no longer considered appropriate at Elizabeth's court.
70. Klarwill 239.
71. George Puttenham, *The Art of English Poesy*, ed. Frank Whigham and Wayne A. Rebhorn (Ithaca, NY, London: Cornell University Press, 2007), 379. Tilney 102.
72. Moncada 247.
73. The Elizabethans habitually blurred the line between fictional and historical characters, as Judith H. Anderson explains in *Biographical Truth: The Representation of Historical Persons in Tudor-Stuart Writing* (New Haven: Yale University Press, 1984).
74. Tilney 101–2.
75. For a fuller account of the early publishing history, see Wayne's introduction, 5. *A brief and pleasant discourse* is the 69th out of 110 listings in the Stationers Company listings for the period July 1567 to July 1568 which means that it was probably submitted for publication at the beginning of 1568, shortly after the negotiations with Archduke Charles came to an end in December 1567.
76. Gosson, *The schoole of abuse* (London, 1579), 19, 10, 10.
77. Thomas Nash, *The anatomie of absurditie* (London, 1589), B.2.r.
78. Nash A.1.r.
79. Nash B.4.r.
80. Nash B.1.v, B.1.r, A.2.r, B.2.r, B.3.r, A.3.v, B.2.
81. Nash iii.v, A.1.r.
82. Arber's transcript of the Stationery's Company records does not list licenses for individual books in 1589, so it is not evident whether Anger's or Nash's book appeared first.

83. Anger B.1.r, A.2.r, B.1.v.
84. Nash B.1.r, Anger C.3.r-v, B.3.r.
85. Anger B.2.v, B.1.v, B.2.v, B.1.r.
86. Stockwood 16–17, 45–46.
87. John Lane, *Tell-Trothes New Yeares Gift*, ed. Frederick J. Furnivall (London, 1876).
88. Nash C.3.r, Stubbes A.4.r.

8 The Queen of Enigma and Monsieur's Departure

1. *Elizabeth I: Collected Works*, ed. Leah S. Marcus, Janel Mueller and Mary Beth Rose (Chicago, London: University of Chicago Press, 2000), 302–3.
2. T. S. Eliot, *The Complete Poems and Plays 1909–1950* (New York: Harcourt Brace: 1951).
3. In *Elizabeth I: A Feminist Perspective* (1968; New York: St. Martin's Press, 1969), Susan Bassnett writes: "Her poem is couched in conventional expressions of sentiment, but the first verse has a note of honesty I feel points to the deep frustrations that she must have felt had come to a head in her life." Helen Hackett, "Courtly Writing by Women," in *Women and Literature in Britain, 1500–1700*, ed. Helen Wilcox (Cambridge, New York: Cambridge University Press, 1996), writes: "While in 'On Monsieur's Departure' Elizabeth speaks as a Petrarchan Lover, in other poems she speaks as the self-conscious object of reams of courtly love poetry."
4. Helen Hackett, "Courtly Writing by Women," in *Women and Literature in Britain 1500–1700* (Cambridge, New York: Cambridge University Press, 1996), ed. Helen Wilcox, 175, argues, "their marriage had effectively ceased to be a realistic prospect in November, 1579, when widespread popular objection was joined by the decision of the Privy Council not to oppose the match but not to support it either... the poem probably served an equally political purpose, soothing any feelings on the French side that they had been toyed with, and announcing to England's enemies in Spain that France was still regarded as England's ally."
5. The introduction to G. B. Harrison, *The Letters of Queen Elizabeth I* (1935; rpt. Westport, CT: Greenwood, 1968), 96–97, mistakenly states that Monsieur came for a brief two-day visit in June 1579; he never crossed the channel because storms forced his ship back to shore.
6. William Camden, *The History... of Princess Elizabeth* (London, 1688), 227.
7. Doran 157.
8. *A Collection of State Papers... from 1571 to 1596*, ed. William Murdin (William Bowyer, 1759), 2:320–21.
9. Murdin 3:334. Martin A. S. Hume, ed., *Calendar of Letters and State Papers Simancas* (1892; Nendeln/Liechtenstein: Krauss, 1971), 2:693.
10. Hume 2:693.
11. See *John Stubbs' Gaping Gulf with Letters and other Relevant Documents*, ed. Lloyd E. Berry (Charlottesville: University Press of Virginia for the Folger Shakespeare Library, 1968), xxvi. The books were confiscated, and the Privy Council wrote to the Lord Mayor to suppress its circulation.
12. Berry 69.
13. Mack P. Holt, *The Duke of Anjou and the Politique Struggle during the Wars of Religion* (Cambridge: Cambridge University Press, 1986), 122.

14. Doran, 167, comments: "It is a measure of the Queen's rage and resolution to marry Anjou that she meted out such severe punishments to men who had such powerful friends on the Council." See Wallace MacCaffrey, "The Anjou Match and the Making of English Foreign Policy" in *The English Commonwealth, 1547–1640: Essays in Politics and Society*, ed. Peter Clark, Alan G. T. Smith, and Nicholas Tyack (New York: Barnes and Noble, 1979), 59–75.

15. *Calendar of State Papers, Foreign Series, of the Reign of Elizabeth*, ed. John Butler (London: Her Majesty's Stationery Office, 1863) 15:274.

16. *Calendar of the Manuscripts of…The Marquis of Salisbury* (London: Her Majesty's Stationery Office, 1888), 2:406.

17. William Camden, *The History of…Princess Elizabeth* (Chicago: University of Chicago Press, 1970), 135.

18. Hume 2:226.

19. Hume 1:72.

20. Holt, 162, writes that "Elizabeth's display on the 22nd was clearly just a ruse, in all probability designed to pressure Henry III into the treaty she had so long desired." Doran, 188, disagrees for reasons I find compelling: "It is difficult to see, however, how these antics could have either pressurised or lured Henry into a treaty; after all Elizabeth retracted her promise within a day. If she had been merely play-acting, why did she not warn her councilors in advance and so avoid a political storm and why was she so angry with Norton that he ended up in the tower? All in all, it seems most likely that Elizabeth meant the exchange of rings before witnesses to stand for an espousal but had to withdraw because of renewed opposition at court."

21. Hume 3:227.

22. Camden, *The History of Princess Elizabeth* (1970), 135.

23. Hume 3:229. A year later Hatton told a friend "he had never had any fear of the marriage but once, when the Queen had given Alençon the ring; but even then, after he had spoken to the Queen, he said, he was reassured" (Hume 409).

24. Hume 3:233.

25. Hume 3:230 FN.

26. Hume 3:230. Two days before the betrothal, Mendoza reported: "The ambassador accompanied him until recently when he went to see the Queen, but Alençon has told him not to do so unless he is ordered" (Hume 3:222). Conyers Read, *Mr. Secretary Walsingham*, 2:90, quotes a contemporary letter: "there goes much babbling in so much as there is no talk of weighty matter of the realm, and the Queen doth not attend unto other matters but only to be together with the Duke in one chamber from morning to noon and afterwards till ii or iii hours after sunset. I cannot tell what a devil they do." For more gossip, see Martin Hume, *The Courtships of Queen Elizabeth; a History of the Various Negotiations for Her Marriage* (New York: Brentano's, 1926), 265.

27. Murdin 330.

28. In her letters to Monsieur, Elizabeth repeatedly refers either to her own or to Monsieur's "content" or "contentment" (*Harrison* 136, 138, 147). In May 1582 she writes, "desiring nothing more than the continuation of our contentments, and cursing (my charity in such a case being very cold) all who overset your designs" (Harrison 153).

29. Murdin 334.
30. Cf. her May 1581 letter to Anjou: "in the name of God, I am resolved to end my days with the sole desire, that you think of me always as I plan to be, drawing no other aim but to be pleasing to you" (Harrison 147).
31. Quoted from *The Poems of Sir Philip Sidney*, ed. William A. Ringer (Oxford: Clarendon Press, 1962), *Astrophil and Stella* 6:4.
32. See Berry xlvi–lvi and Doran 168–72.
33. If she showed it to Cecil, he did not keep a copy along with all the other voluminous documents pertaining to the marriage negotiations preserved at Hatfield House.
34. Josephine Ross, *Suitors to the Queen* (London: Phoenix, 2005), 147, is one of the few scholars to comment on the poem, but she assumes it expresses the nostalgia Elizabeth felt after Alençon left England.
35. Elizabeth and Alençon corresponded in French, but he probably understood some English. Holt, 120, claims (but does not provide any evidence) that Monsieur could not speak English.
36. Hume 3:227. This had been a theme of Elizabeth's letters to Monsieur since his first visit. For example, a year earlier she wrote, 135, "You are not ignorant, my dearest, that the greatest impediments lie in making our people rejoice and applaud."
37. Read, 2:1, writes: "The situation was as bewildering as it was dangerous. A half-hundred threads of policy were so knotted and joined that the pulling of any one meant the displacement of all the rest. What Spain would do in Ireland depended largely upon what Elizabeth would do with the Catholics at home, with the Dutch rebels across the Channel, with the Portuguese pretender. What the Guises would do in the north depended upon the Queen's behavior toward her Scottish partisans and her treatment of the French King's brother. Everything reacted upon everything else."
38. Hume 3:233. Elizabeth expressed a similar feeling before Monsieur's first visit, when she wrote to Sir Amyas Paulet that the French conditions "giveth us just cause to suspect that the mark that is shot at, is our fortune and not our person" (Harrison 133).
39. Hume 3:233.
40. Hume 3:244.
41. Speaking with a heavy note of irony, Elizabeth told Simier, "You may see how Alençon loves me by a very good thing I will tell you in strict secrecy. On the 22nd, he asked me at least to let him have some money to maintain the war in Flanders, which he said he had begun for my sake, and that I should thus recompense him for the affront of my refusing to marry him. As I saw no other convenient way to get rid of him, I offered him a considerable sum every month" (Hume 3:244).
42. Hume 3:230.
43. Hume 3:243.
44. Hume 3:243.
45. Hume 3:252.
46. Hume 3:230.
47. Hume 3:276.
48. Hume 3:348.
49. Hume 3: 233.
50. Hume 3:243.

51. Hume 3:243.
52. Hume 3:243. Mendoza would surely have mentioned "On Monsieur's Departure" if he had read it, or even heard of its existence; his failure to mention it provides further evidence that the manuscript did not circulate at court.
53. Hume 3:252.

INDEX